The Approachable Argument

Michael G. Leigh

Orange Coast College

KENDALL/HUNT PUBLISHING COMPANY
4050 Westmark Drive   Dubuque, Iowa 52002

With Special Thanks to:

Norm Fricker

Craig Grossman
my mentor, Dick Strong
and
my loving and supportive wife, Diane

Contents

Introduction: The Approachable Argument

When students hear the terms "argument" or "critical thinking" some may be intimidated.

Arguments, to the average Jack and Jill, are unpleasant interpersonal conflicts involving emotional pain. They just seem to happen, like some force of nature outside our control. The notion of constructing an argument intentionally may seem foreign or abstract. The word "critical" may suggest something destructive.

Indeed, an argument may mean a ***quarrel,*** which we'd like to avoid, but it can also mean a reliable and approachable form for the creation of intelligent opinion. The word as we will use it refers to an argument as ***an individual artifact,*** especially as described by British logician, Stephen Toulmin. Argument may also mean ***a process of reasonable exchange,*** like a discussion or debate, in which several individual arguments are passed back and forth.

The difference between a quarrel and an argument, in the two senses we intend to emphasize, is that quarrels often consist of dirty fighting, attacks addressed to people rather than ideas. If we learn how to fight fairly, one of our goals, we may find that our interpersonal relations improve along with our ability to discuss public issues.[1]

Critical thinking is the attempt to achieve more than merely impulsive, conditioned or unconsidered opinion making. It is the constructive process of discovering the most accurate and wise opinions available by examining ***multiple points of view*** on an issue. It's the effort to take an empathic look at opinions we don't hold ourselves. We're not concerned here with searching for truth in some ultimate or absolute sense. Critical thinking is an attempt to arrive at reliable ideas and practical actions, with regard to everyday personal and social issues.

People who learn to think critically and make arguments tend to be more assertive, independent thinkers with higher credibility and greater likelihood of job success.[2]

This text focuses on ***simple approaches to argument form.*** Our effort is to make arguments approachable. Lots of practical examples are provided along the way to secure understanding, rather than emphasis on a lot of theory.

This is not to say that there is no ***new vocabulary.*** We just try to ground vocabulary in ***real world illustrations.*** To this end, we use a lot of newspaper articles or editorials about current events. These may provide frameworks for class discussion, as well as topics for written and spoken assignments. Illustrations and other **evidence** are important as a model for student behavior.

At this point, a student may be saying, "Well, I'm not really 'into' the news." That's fine . . . except **the news IS into you.** That is, our lives are being shaped daily by other arguers and persuaders who have an advantage on us, if we don't know about these things. Had trouble getting your classes? What do you know about the economics of your state and the budgeting process? Not concerned about foreign military operations? How will you respond when you find a friend has died in Iraq, or some other battleground, and you want to know why?

Opinions about controversial subjects are often reactive. That is, the first thing we've been conditioned to say pops out of our mouths and passes through our pens, without necessarily visiting our minds. Sometimes we merely repeat what we've heard often enough to make an impression, accurate or not. Sheer force of repetition, as our advertisers well know, is persuasive though not necessarily accurate or responsible.

For instance, we experiment in class about name brand recognition and repetition. We ask students to name the toothpaste that they use. The vast majority, often as many as 75%, mention the numbers one and two advertisers, but they can offer no evidence whatsoever for the superiority of the product. That's harmless enough. Yet the same kind of decision making occurs with much more important matters, like choices on serious policy issues and in elections.

We want to inspire you to encounter many such issues, along with new techniques with which to respond, hopefully, leading you to more **responsible social decision making and action.**

Since students do sometimes think of criticism as destructive, they may develop defensive or aggressive approaches that alienate audiences, as well as those who may agree with you. Aggressive attitudes are different than argumentative ones, since they tend to focus on personal attacks, and we attack when we ourselves feel stressed and attacked.[3]

We'll try to deemphasize winning and losing arguments, but it's difficult because people get attached to their opinions. Even very bright people sometimes argue badly, but when this is pointed out to us by an argumentative opponent, it's as though we ourselves have been attacked.

"You tore **me** apart," a student may say, if someone takes their argument to task.

We'll try to learn to look at arguments apart from ourselves, because **we are not our arguments.** Critical thinkers come to look at arguments as tools we use to achieve better understanding, perhaps even toys we can game with. (Don't play too rough now. Remember to wear proper "head gear.")

Other attitudes to be attained are a sense of **detachment** and a willingness to suspend one's own opinion long enough to respect the viewpoints of others and to get the facts on both sides.

Tolerance of ambiguity is a good characteristic for an arguer to have. That is, in the face of uncertainty, lack of information, or the incoherence of the available information, we have to suspend premature judgment and search further for the truth. Since there are very few clearly right or wrong opinions when dealing with practical public affairs, this is important. This quality in itself is attributed to management ability. Even scientists working toward an understanding of the neutrino write openly about the need for this trait in pushing at the frontiers of knowledge.[4]

Be patient, like a good fisherman. Don't jump to conclusions. Let the conclusions come to you through the research process.

This text also tries to emphasize that appreciation and understanding should precede criticism. **Empathy or perspective taking** are important goals, both for interpersonal reasons and to assist our persuasive purposes by building a sense of common ground among participants.

Indeed, **disagreement may be mutually illuminating** to those who disagree. The flint and steel of opposing positions may strike the spark by which we better see our own positions and how to improve their defense. We may even change our views in the face of superior arguments and evidence from another.

If one can see another's point of view and express appreciation for it, disagreements may be less harsh and involve less interpersonal resentment. Students, as a matter of form, need to learn to **paraphrase** the arguments they are refuting before they counter them, anyway, simply as a matter of clarity. Arguments work better when everyone is clear what we're arguing about. They're certainly easier for an audience to follow.

We concern ourselves with audience opinion, because argument has a **rhetorical dimension,** as well. That is, we try to persuade others once we've arrived at a reliable approximate truth about a controversy. Rhetoric attempts to adjust to audiences. Rhetoric is adapting messages to particular people, at particular times and places.

After all, it may matter little if you form an argument that is only persuasive to those who already agree with you. The real challenge is to encourage people to consider the reasonability of positions with which they disagree.

This leads to a final point. There is **something transformational** about the process of argumentation. One measure of human intelligence is the willingness to change and grow. In a very real sense, personal transformation is a wonderful by-product, if not a goal, of critical thinking.

If we do not change our opinions on social issues, we may very well change our opinion of ourselves. As our argumentative abilities increase, we may find that our confidence, integrity and self respect will, too.

We may begin to feel better qualified to participate in elections and other community responsibilities. Even arguments in the more mundane sense of personal quarrel may become manageable, given our new knowledge and self regard.

We hope much such change will visit you as you work with this text and with each other as students.

At least, we think, you'll find argument a slightly less intimidating issue.

Sources

1) Gottman, J.M. (1979). Marital Interaction: Experimental Investigations. New York: Academic Press, Inc.

2) Colbert, K.E. (1993). The Effects of Debate Participation on Argumentativeness and Verbal Aggression. Communication Education 42, 206–214.

Infante, D.A. (1981). Trait Argumentativeness as a Predictor of Communicative Behavior in Situations Requiring Argument. Central States Speech Journal 32, 265–272.

Infante, D.A. (1982). Argumentativeness: It's Effect in Group Decision Making and It's Role in Leadership Perception.

Infante, D.A. (1987). Aggressiveness. In J.C. McCroskey and J.A. Daly (Eds.) Personality and Interpersonal Communication, (pp. 157–192). Newbury Park, Calif: Sage Publications, Inc.

Shutz, B. (1982). Argumentativeness: It's Effect In Group Decision-Making and It's Role in Leadership Perception. Communication Quarterly 30, 368–375.

3) Festinger, L. (1957). A Theory of Cognitive Dissonance. Stanford, Calif: Stanford University Press.

Stamp, G.H., A.L. Vangelisti and J.A. Daly (1992). The Creation of Defensiveness in Social Interaction. Communication Quarterly 40, 177–190.

4) Sherrill, W.W. (2001). Tolerance of Ambiguity Among MD/MBA Students: Implications for Management Potential. Journal of Continuing Education for Health Professions, Spring 21 (2), 117–122.

Stoycheva, K., D. Stetinski, and K. Popova (2003). Tolerance for Ambiguity. Bulgarian Academy of Sciences. Website: http://mail.ipsyh.bas.bg//ipsych/projengkop.htm.

I
A First Look at Arguments

When we use the word "argument," it has at least three connotations. Our most common sense of the word is an ***interpersonal quarrel,*** a conflict between two or more persons in intimate relationships, involving differing goals and disagreements about values, appropriate interaction, or unmet personal needs.

Often, because people lack skills in conflict resolution, quarrels include emotional excess, irrational behavior, screaming, and name calling. We'll focus specifically on that sense of the word in the last chapter of this text. In the meantime, we'll try to avoid the excess emotion, screaming, and name calling .

There are two other connotations for "argument" that we'll be interested in here. First, we look at argumentation as ***a process,*** the natural give and take of discussion, dialectic, or debate. Second, we will be concerned with the building of ***individual, formal arguments,*** several of which would be passed back and forth in a debate.

It is our belief that learning something about these aspects of formal argumentation can help improve, even elevate, interpersonal quarrels, as well as help us to relate more easily to universal discussion of issues facing the human community.

The field of studying arguments is called ***rhetoric.*** The name comes from "The Rhetoric," Greek philosopher Aristotle's study of argument, the first comprehensive attempt in modern history. He called rhetoric, "the faculty of observing in any given case the best available means of persuasion."[1]

Great. But what do we mean by ***persuasion?*** Persuasion is the motivational aspect of argumentation, trying to get others to agree with a well-examined idea or social action. Aristotle saw persuasion as imbedded in the character of the speaker (ethos), appeals to emotion (pathos), and appeals to logic (logos). Aristotle emphasized communal connections, or ***common ground,*** between the speaker and the audience as an important aspect of persuasion.

Rhetoric is also ***instrumental communication,*** a tool used to achieve social change, rather than merely expressing self. Rhetoric is based in community goals, and there are certain basic community standards that should be observed, as will be discussed below under the term ethos, or ***"credibility,"*** the quality of a speaker who can be trusted, liked, and believed. We'll focus more on that and the other appeals in Chapter III.

Finally, *we are arguing in terms of probabilities, rather than certainties.* That's so because rhetoric deals with difficult and subjectively perceived social issues. This also means that rhetoric is *primarily involved in inductive rather deductive reason,* although that too may come into play. We'll discuss kinds of reasoning in Chapter IV.

For our present purposes, think of rhetoric as a process of adapting your arguments to particular audiences, at particular times, in particular places. Think of persuasion as your attempts to convince and motivate.

Argument Format

Formal arguments will be discussed through a modified version of *a model designed by Stephen Toulmin,* a British logician.[2] Understanding and using Toulmin effectively will take a bit of time. So, start now. The most basic parts are:

CLAIM

WARRANTS

GROUNDS

We claim something is true. We can only make *one such claim at a time.* We explain reasons for believing the claim in warrants, and we use pieces of evidence to support the argument in grounds. Here's a simple example in everyday conversation:

Claim: I want to go see movie A, instead of movie B.

Why?

Warrant 1: Two reasons. It's a late enough starting time that we can get something to eat first.

Yeah. I'm hungry, too.

Warrant 2: Also, the actors are better in movie A.

Who says?

Grounds: Well, two have been nominated for academy awards, and a National Critics Association picked them for best ensemble acting.

O.K. Cool. Let's munch down.

Yeah, and since we're going to movie A, that puts us near restaurant C, so. . . .

Here we go again!

Obviously, our first fictional speaker is using rhetoric to his own advantage.

A claim unsupported by warrants or grounds is called ***an assertion.*** A process of merely exchanging assertions can be frustrating. People who operate this way have an idea that "my opinion is just as good as anybody's," but how do you know? You know by examining arguments and discovering which ideas have the ***preponderance of evidence*** behind them, not just the most, but also with the most reliable qualities.

The truth is, you may already be using a format something like Toulmin's. Yet you may be doing so unconsciously. By better understanding parts of argument, you can become more self-aware, artful, and persuasive in the way that you declare yourself.

Start thinking about this format for an individual argument and remind yourself to be clear about what you're arguing, understand and express your own reasoning, and ***don't make a claim if you can't offer evidence for it.*** You won't understand this all at once. Yet it's worth the trouble, as this form of argument has been directly linked to improvement in critical thinking, as well as basic skills like reading and writing.[3]

Critical Thinking

The critical thinking movement gained widespread interest among educators during the 1990s. It's an attempt to get beyond simple rote learning, in which someone lectures, then you memorize and regurgitate on tests. Critical thinking study urges you to think for yourselves, to search out information, and understand and analyze it sensibly. According to California Educational Code, some of the goals of critical thinking are:

To identify hidden presumptions, ideas that we assume to be true without really knowing how we came to them or why we believe them. Often these are deeply held cultural assumptions that have simply been repeated to us by family, friends, and authority figures. We will try to "sunshine" our hidden presumptions, make them explicit in our discussion, and examine them carefully for errors in reason. In a court of law, they call hidden presumptions "assuming facts not in evidence."

To apply sound logic to problem solving in daily situations. This includes recognizing common patterns of reason, parallel reasoning, generalization, reasoning from cause to effect, and avoiding common fallacies.

To learn to structure arguments. The individual arguments we will build will follow Toulmin's basic three-part form: claim, the individual point you're trying to prove, grounds, some evidence for your point, and warrant, a statement about your reasoning that the grounds support the claim. The order of these parts may change according to circumstance and format, but Toulmin expressed them in this order. Generally, in speech making, it's useful to go from claims to warrants to grounds, for the sake of easier audience comprehension.

To recognize and understand the language of argument in everyday text and speech. We'll examine that language, both by reviewing the vocabulary in italics throughout this text and analyzing argumentative texts, editorials, essays, and speeches.

To build issue-oriented texts, papers or speeches dealing with modern social problems.

And to develop and practice ***an appropriate ethic & attitude*** for applying these skills.[4]

R.H. Ennis focused on instrumental functions, defining critical thinking as, "reasonable reflection that is focused on what to believe or do." He suggests the following actions:

1. Judge the credibility of sources.

2. Identify conclusions, reasons, and assumptions.

3. Judge the quality of an argument, including the acceptability of its reasons, assumptions, and evidence.

4. Develop and defend a position on an issue.

5. Ask appropriate and clarifying questions.

6. Plan experiments and judge experimental design.

7. Define terms in a way appropriate for the context.

8. Be open-minded.

9. Try to be well informed.

10. Draw conclusions when warranted, but with caution.[5]

Another way of saying this last goal is that critical thinking is a process, and that the quality of the journey is more important than jumping to conclusions along the way.

Attitudes

There is such a thing as ***pre-critical thinking.*** We may have attitudes that prevent us from allowing new information and ideas from affecting our opinions.[6]

We may have reactive attitudes. ***Primary certitude*** is an immediate, strongly held feeling, "I know the truth about that!" You may notice that when certain topics come up, some people will thrust their hands up to answer before they've quite heard the question, because they've already made up their minds about that topic.

They may have automatic arguments, even rehearsed monologues, on certain deeply held opinions. Some reactions are automatically negative. ***Reaction formation*** is just such an immediately strong, negative reaction against something. They may not even consider it a possibility that they could have anything in common with someone who thinks that way.

These reactive attitudes may reveal a strong **resistance to change,** refusing to alter deeply held notions, even when they're proven to be inadequate.

Open mindedness is an important attitude for argument, not to say that you should allow yourself to be pushed around by others. Keep some sense of integrity among your ideas. We simply want to observe that one aspect of intelligence is the ability to be persuaded by new knowledge.

It's difficult to be open-minded, due to our **cultural conditioning.** Values and principles are formed by input from others, by the times and places in which we were raised.

Personal experience, race, and nation are aspects of such conditioning. There are such things as **egocentric, ethnocentric, and socio-centric attitudes,** respectively, a sense that our ideas, our race, or our nation are automatically more normal or right somehow.[7]

President Bush, in a statement he later repented, called the war against terrorism "The New Crusades." The question became, in world circles of opinion, whether the war was against terrorists or people of the Muslim faith. The old crusades, you see, were wars between Christians and Muslims.

Consider this somewhat ethnocentric view of Afghans from an anonymous U.S. intelligence officer:

> These guys are savages. I can't call them human. They have no respect for anything, not for each other or for themselves, let alone people who are trying to help them. Their language is babble. They strike out at us and at each other. They beat their women and force their children into fights with other children to defend family pride. Savages. Roaming packs of sub-human beasts. They should just kill each other off.

Anger is understandable. It's a very different way of life. My own speech professor wanted to "nuke 'em all," but it's irrational to view other people as less than human, and it twists us toward aggressive, possibly even violent response.

After 9/11, there were acts of aggression against American Muslim citizens. One Sikh gas station near Phoenix, a man who had nothing to do with Al Queda but was wearing a turban, was murdered on sight. In fact, in Orange County, California:

> (A)ccording to a Human Relations Commission report released Thursday, sixty-nine people said they were targets of some form of anti-Arab bigotry, compared to eight a year earlier. The cases ranged from a woman who said she received a harassing phone call, to a man who was severely beaten outside a bar.[8]

That becomes especially persuasive for me, not only because I live in this county, but because I had a private experience that supported the generalization. I've seen members of the Muslim Student Union on our campus harassed and their tires slashed.

If this is the sort of intelligence the world sees from us, how can we ourselves be regarded as civilized in any global sense? Yet that is precisely the point of this kind of ethnocentric speech: it's a way of focusing and expressing fear and frustration with the world. We should, however, see that this is a limited form of expression, as well as make a distinction between our ideas and the dangerous acts that may flow from them.

Arguing vs. Aggressive Behavior

We're not likely to do away with emotional utterance, or crazy letters to the editor, as it has a cathartic purpose. However, emotional utterance can lead to violence. Ask any policeman who has to answer domestic disturbance calls, or who knows that most murders occur within the family who involve alcohol with arguing. So, making choices in favor of argumentative rather than aggressive behavior is a very important attitude goal.[9]

Argumentative people are open-minded, assertive, and capable of putting their ideas and feelings into reasonably inoffensive language. They listen carefully. They try to paraphrase what people say, before they argue back. They believe that appreciation should precede criticism. The point for them is not just winning, but understanding the relative strengths and weaknesses among the arguments themselves, so that we can arrive at the best approximate truths about difficult social controversies.

Aggressive people argue against people, rather than to the point. They use personal attacks, are prone to belligerence, lack objectivity, and tend to be emotionally reactive. They have "knee jerk" responses to certain topics and tend not to hear other people out before they judge them.

Aggressive behavior has nonverbal dimensions, as well. While argumentative people maintain relaxed and positive manner while discussing ideas, aggressive people may roll their eyes, look away, and shake their heads. They may ball up their fists in anger. They tend to interrupt. Their volume may get loud. Their tone may become sarcastic. They are defensive about their ideas and highly resistant to change.

In sum, aggressive behavior, both verbal and nonverbal, tends to escalate personal conflict and create an artificial distance among social opinions. That is, ***discussions become polarized*** into "your either for it or against it" kinds of oversimplifications.

The pro-life vs. pro-choice debate is one of our most polarized discussions. Yet it is unlikely that a person believing in the right to abortion would say, "Yes, I'm anti-life. I just wish everyone would die." It is equally unlikely that an anti-abortionist would say, "Oh, yes. I hate human choice. I want us all to be robots." What needs to be appreciated is that there are many possible opinions along a range of belief between "for" and "against."

Disagreeing with someone shouldn't necessarily create enemies. If you get past alienation and defensiveness, you may find that your **thesis** and their **antithesis** can find someplace in the middle, call it **synthesis,** that is stronger than either of your original points of view.

Attitude and Language

Our normal desire to keep conversation lively, as well as our need to be perceived positively, may lead us to **exaggerations and stereotypes.** We say things are bigger in quantity than we really know to be true, and we assert wildly that it's "true most of the time," even "ninety percent of the time," though we have no particular statistics about the matter. We use **language like "always" and "never."**

We make **sweeping generalizations** about classes of people who are different than we are, usually more out of frustration than actual knowledge, or even actual belief on the part of the speaker. We may use **ethnic slurs** against other drivers in the privacy of our car that we would never think to utter in a personal encounter.

The point is that **language sometimes emphasizes and reinforces poor attitudes** against critical thinking.

Even **euphemisms,** literally "words of good omen," can interfere with a realistic perception of issues. A euphemism is a nice word used to conceal a less savory reality. They can be harmless, like calling a garbage man "a sewage engineer," or a stewardess the less sexually biased term "flight attendant," or simply telling somebody in the wrong dress, "You look very nice tonight."

At this least offensive level, a euphemism may even be considered a normal matter of courtesy. It's not always necessary for others to know our opinions.

However, euphemisms at the level of national politics may be weighted with more significance. Some attempts to whitewash unsavory national policy include:

> "The Final Solution" in Germany was what they called the ovens.
>
> In America, "separate but equal" meant "segregated schools."
>
> The first U.S. troops in Vietnam were called "advisors."
>
> That war was first called "a police action," then "intervention," not a war.
>
> Later, Vietnam was a "war of attrition." This was a nice way of noting that the land goals shifted so much in a guerilla war, that the only way we could measure our effectiveness was to count bodies.

When we began to withdraw troops, we didn't call it a retreat. It was called the "Vietnamization" of the war.

Laying off people became "downsizing."

In more recent conflicts, "collateral damage" has meant accidental civilian deaths.

Military interventions have been called "reconnaissance in force."

Most recently, in Iraq, The White House has endorsed "preemptive strike," as a new approach to foreign policy. If we put that in plain language, it's saying we may attack others before we've been attacked, much as we ourselves were attacked at Pearl Harbor in WWII. The Japanese also had a suspicion that the U.S. would enter the war against them, so they issued a "preemptive strike." Ironically, few events have been more emotionally devastating to modern Americans, besides Pearl Harbor, the assassination of President Kennedy, and the crash of the space shuttle, than 9/11.

It's certainly uncomfortable to look at such parallels, isn't it? We want to believe that we're more righteous in performing the same acts that we've condemned in others. That's how ethnocentrism tends to work.

Repeated often, these ideas can take deep root among our social assumptions, numbing our awareness of harsh realities. So, when euphemisms are used with regard to important public issues, we should look carefully at what such words may conceal.

Repeated often enough, even ridiculous rumors and stories can gain the momentum of truth. **Urban legends,** or simple rumors, can create a false view of things. There is a website devoted to such tales at *www.snopes2.com*. One example of an urban legend that potentially may have impacted social views goes like this:

> I heard from a friend of mine about this guy. He went dancing over at this club and met a girl. So, they got real cozy and wound up going to his house, and . . . you know. So, he gets up the next morning, and the girl is gone, but written on his bathroom mirror in lipstick were these words, "Welcome to the wonderful world of AIDS.

We've heard this story now, with slight variations, in a half a dozen different cities, but they usually start "I heard this from a friend of mine." Boy, this friend really gets around! It's like the "patient zero" myth, the airline steward who single-handedly spread AIDS all over the world.

These stories and other folklore also serve a social function, just like venting our emotions in letters to the editor. They're often cautionary notes reinforcing local mores. For instance, what is the theme of the above story, if not "don't have sex with strangers," or maybe even "don't have sex at all?"

Unfortunately, these tales can also create misunderstanding and prejudice. You may each have been the victim of rumors. You know the effect.

Propaganda

Sometimes we use language and images to attack others and to unfairly manipulate public opinion about them. We call this kind of persuasion *"propaganda,"* the use of intentional deceptions in speech and image to unfairly manipulate audiences into belief and compliant action.

One form of propaganda is *"demonization,"* reducing opponents to stereotyped and unfairly negative images. In Nazi poster propaganda, Jews were shown with Frankenstein green skin, never normal flesh color, usually clutching at money.[10]

In the first Gulf War, three major news magazines, "Time," "Newsweek," and "U.S. News and World Report," featured Saddam Hussein's face on the cover, painted green. It's the same technique Nazis used, but most people would never make the connection. They would tend to join with most in sensing a subjective repulsion. Afterwards, the American public was highly supportive of the invasion.

There was also the use of a lot of video showing how our missiles could do precise strikes, supposedly without harming the civilian population, though that was later disproved in documentaries by Bill Moyers with film of injured civilians.

I've mentioned these points about Hussein, not because he's a wonderful guy and I want you to introduce him to your friends and family. Just know that there's much manipulation in such communication, and it works both ways. There are still rumors among Arabs abroad that Zionists were behind the 9/11 attacks, presumably to involve the United States against Arabs. There are rumors that 4000 Jewish workers stayed home from work near the Twin Towers on 9/11, and that Israeli spies videotaped the towers collapsing. Others in the bazaars of Pakistan believed that the U.S. attacked itself for an excuse to come after oil.

In international politics, starting rumors about opponents and enemies is another form of propaganda called *"disinformation."* Saddam Hussein's name was somewhat suddenly, after his invasion of Kuwait, pronounced "Sodom," with all its Biblical implications. Stories circulated in the media that he was a cross-dresser who liked little boys. There was no actual evidence to this idea. It simply served, in wartime, to make the enemy even more unsavory than he was. Nobody wanted to be reminded that we had actually helped Hussein into office as a buffer against extremists in Iran. Nor has Osama Bin Laden been spared the rumor machine:

> By now, you probably know that the photo of the man on the World Trade Center observation deck with one jet pointed at the towers is a hoax. But

did you hear that Osama Bin Laden penned a memo to his cave mates, warning them to lay off his "Cheez-It" stash? Or that a New Yorker found bodies, still strapped in their airplane seats, inside a lower Manhatten apartment.[11]

The Bin Laden story has a purpose. It is a form of instrumental communication other than argument. At an obvious level, it has a humorous effect for the troops searching for him. It demystifies a larger than life figure. It also makes a slightly more subtle point of propaganda: even these rigid Muslim fundamentalists secretly like things American. At an international level, disinformation leverages the self-interests of nations, even ours. At a national level, disinformation is used to distract a public from other truths propagandists wish you wouldn't notice.

Glittering generalities are also a typical propaganda technique. They are words that are so universally acknowledged that simply saying them sounds good in the name of God, patriotism, heroism—even when they are used to cover despicable acts on the part of the propagandist.

Ethics

When it comes to ethics in argument, we each have ***certain rights and responsibilities:***

The first thing most would probably think of is their ***right to free speech,*** their first amendment rights. Yet that also bears with it certain ethical responsibilities.

You can't use free speech to yell "fire" for fun in a crowded theatre, nor incite a riot, nor abuse it to the ends of libel or slander.

Rieke and Sillars mentioned some ***specific practical responsibilities*** appropriate for argument in a classroom setting. Among them are:

- Participants must not try to silence each other to prevent the exchange of arguments and criticism.

- If you make a claim, you must be willing to provide support if it is requested.

- When you criticize someone's argument, you should be sure you are talking about what was really said.

- You should defend your claims with arguments relevant to them.

- You should not claim that others have presumed something they have not, and you should be willing to admit your own presumptions.

- You should not say your claim has been established unless you've provided proper argumentative support.

- You should stick to arguments that are logically valid or can be made valid.

- If you fail to establish your claims, admit it; if others establish their claims, admit it.

- Avoid unnecessary ambiguity, and try to interpret other's arguments as clearly as possible.[12]

We should also be concerned about **academic ethics,** not only whatever **honor codes** exist in your school regarding cheating, but also about **plagiarism,** claiming other people's ideas or language as your own.

As a sign of how Americans feel about it, recall that Senator Joseph Biden's Presidential bid was ended when he stole lines for his stump speech from Irish statesman Neal Kinnock, without properly crediting him. Even John F. Kennedy's famous phrase, "Ask not what your country can do for you, ask what you can do for your country," was from another important rhetorician, Cicero.

In fact, we tend to value honesty highly in this country. Nixon was less reviled for Watergate itself, an offense of little more importance than dirty tricks among frat boys, than the fact that he covered it up. Ronald Reagan did not admit direct knowledge of the Contra-gate scandal, a much more serious issue than Watergate, since the war making powers of Congress were circumvented. Yet he admitted, "It happened on my watch, so I'm responsible," and the American public forgave him. Bill Clinton's offense of infidelity was less important, in some respects, but the fact that he lied about it brought on an impeachment proceeding.

In a year after major corporate crime was an everyday feature in the news, arbiter of taste Martha Stewart was sentenced to spend time in jail, not because she used insider knowledge to dump stock, but because she lied to federal officers about the details.

Honesty includes practical matters like appropriate source citation, which we'll cover in more detail in the next chapter. Properly crediting sources includes using **quotation marks,** so we can distinguish between your words and those of experts.

Implicitly, we have a **responsibility to research.** We don't pass rumor, use hearsay stories from "a friend of a friend," and we don't repeat rumor and gossip.

Remember to preserve some **tolerance of ambiguity** as you research. One should be aware that social problems don't show up as black or white. Debate involves the observation of many shades of gray, and our private vision of things may not bear up under scrutiny. Some problems seem never to have solutions. Be open-minded. Some things remain a mystery.

The last idea we'll mention is that writing text in a **timely manner** is necessary, and if you're reading text orally to an audience you have an obligation to have rehearsed your presentation. Apart from this being a minimum courtesy to audience members who have allowed you time to address an issue, you represent not only yourself at such moments, but you represent the whole community of those who share that opinion with you. That's a position of some responsibility.

* * * * *

In sum, we should watch ourselves for the various ways in which our culturally-conditioned attitudes emerge through our language, as well as the language and images used by others to persuade us. **We should examine our own prejudices, avoid hasty moral judgment, and try to empathize with multiple points of view** about the issue at hand. Walk a mile in the other guy's moccasins, suspend judgment, and consider that your own opinions may become better forged by incorporating the ideas and experience of others.

Vocabulary

Argumentative vs.
    Aggressive
Aristotle
Argument (three senses of
    the word)
Assertion
Common Ground
Demonization
Disinformation
Empathy

Euphemism
Exaggeration
Glittering Generalities
Hidden Presumption
Instrumental
    Communication
Multiple Points of View
Persuasion
Plagiarism
Primary Certitude

Probability vs. Certainty
Propaganda
Polarized Discussion
Reaction Formation
Resistance to Change
Rhetoric
Stephan Toulmin
Stereotype
Tolerance of Ambiguity
Urban Folklore

Exercises: Go to Interactive Disc to Complete

1) You may do this either in groups or with the class as a whole. Tell each other about personal beliefs you consider to be culturally reinforced. Ask yourself honestly, if any of these beliefs may be prejudicial or irrational. Try to avoid judging each other. Hear each other out. Create an atmosphere in which people feel safe to speak.

2) You may also simply take your own inventory of prejudices and irrationalities. Write a one-page paper defending a deeply held belief. Discuss prejudices, exaggerations, and hidden presumptions, which may not be obvious to you, with your instructor.

3) Can you think of any publicly endorsed euphemisms from your culture. Which are harmless? Which cover up serious social issues?

4) What are some of the latest rumors or urban legends, local or national, which are circulating and what do you think about them? Would you repeat them?

5) What propaganda are you aware of, in our country and the world? If you are near election time, observe political ads and note glittering generalities, ad hominems, and other signs of propaganda.

6) Read the following passages. Notice your own emotional reaction to the subjects. Consider how emotions or cultural prejudices might get in the way of objective judgment.

> It is legal to be stoned to death for having sex outside of marriage. This is the fate of 30-year old Amina Lawai in northern Nigeria, whose appeal to an Islamic court was rejected Monday. As Lawai clutched her baby to her chest, the Islamic court ruled that the execution will occur after the baby's breastfeeding days are past (CNN, August 21, 2002).

> Gee, I thought I lived in a United States based on laws. Now, the Mexican Consulate is organizing a protest against our Border Patrol enforcing the immigration laws of our country. What's next? Junkies organizing to protest drug laws? Felons protesting assault, robbery, and murder laws? What ever happened to the concept of law and order? Why would we want to harbor people who are criminals from their very entry into the country? Doesn't anyone take the terrorist threat seriously?

> When the Episcopal Church decided to appoint an openly gay bishop, I didn't expect more than a slight reaction. I thought we were normalizing the reality that being gay is not a chosen activity. Significant portions of our population—politicians, teachers, indeed, people in every field—are coming out and being accepted as respected members of society. "Queer Eye for the Straight Guy" is standard TV fare. Even Disneyland had a float in the gay pride parade. I can't see why we are still having conversations about the "immorality of gay marriage." How could anyone who just wants to get married be immoral? Isn't marriage supposed to be a socially accepted means to combat promiscuity and other immoralities?

Sources

1) Solmsen, F. (1954). The Rhetoric and Poetics of Aristotle. New York: Random House. Chapter II.

2) Toulmin, S. (1958). "The Uses of Argument." London: Cambridge Press.

   Toulmin, S., Rieke, R., & Janik, A. (1984). "An Introduction to Reasoning." New York: Macmillan.

3) Write Away! (February 1996) Volume 1, No. 2.

The Problem of Writing Knowledge. http://wac.colostate.edu/books/Bazerman_shaping.

TeachingBlog. "Reading and Toulmin." http://www.ndsu.nodak.edu/ndsu/kbrooks/blog/.

4) Calif. Ed. Code.

5) Ennis, R.H. (1987). "A Taxonomy of Critical Thinking Dispositions and Abilities." In J.Baron & R. Steinberg (Eds.) "Teaching Thinking Skills: Theory and Practice," pp.9-26. New York: W.H. Freeman.

6) Kytle, R. (1987). "Clear Thinking for Composition." Boston: McGraw-Hill.

Martin, J.G. (1972). "The Tolerant Personality." Detroit: Wayne State University Press.

7) Sumner, W.G. (1971). Sumner Today: Selected Essays of William Graham Sumner. West Newport, Conn.: Greenwood Press. Sumner, a professor of anthropology at Yale, coined the term "ethnocentrism."

8) "O.C. Reports of Anti-Arab Bigotry Soared After 9/11," LA, Times, April 10, 2002.

9) Colbert, K.E. (1993). The Effects of Debate Participation on Argumentativeness and Verbal Aggression. Communication Education, 42, 206–214.

Infante, D.A. (1981). Trait Argumentativeness as a Predictor of Communicative Behavior in Situations Requiring Argument. Central States Speech Journal, 32, 265–272.

Infante, D.A. (1982). Argumentativeness: It's Effect in Group Decision Making and It's Role in Leadership Perception. Communication Education 31, 141–148.

Infante, D.A. (1987). Aggressiveness. In J.C. McCroskey and J.A. Daly (Eds.) Personality and Interpersonal Communication. Newbury Park, Calif.: Sage Publications, Inc., pp. 157–192.

Shutz, B. (1982). Argumentativeness: It's Effect In Group Decision-Making and It's Role in Leadership Perception. Communication Quarterly, 30, 368–375.

10) Gallo, M. (2000) "The Poster in History." New York: W.W. Norton & Co.

11) "Have You Heard The One About Osama's Cheez-It-Stash?" LA Times, March 24, 2002.

12) Rieke, R.D. & Sillars, M.O. (2001) "Argumentation and Critical Decision Making." New York: Longman.

Brockriede, W. (1972) "Arguers as Lovers." In Philosophy & Rhetoric 5, pp. 1–11.

II
Subject, Form, and Rule

What shall we argue about? What issues of the day are worth the attention that this process requires? In the context of a critical thinking class, the general subject is usually social or political issues. *An issue* is a question to be answered about a subject. Usually the subjects are found in non-fiction essays, journalism, editorials, and speeches, but also potentially in a wide variety of forms and endeavors. One can make arguments about literature, science, or any area of study, though the form of the argument may vary from field to field.[1]

General Subject Matter

General subject matter for the twenty-first century might include:
> Bio-ethical issues,
> Economic issues,
> Educational issues,
> Environmental issues,
> Immigration policy,
> Issues of human rights,
> The effectiveness of scientific discoveries, and medical cures,
> The effectiveness of our foreign and domestic policies,
> And, in some years, who should be elected to office.

Look at the above list now. You may already have ideas. Ask specific questions about any of these, and you'll have an issue to discuss.

Begin a broad subject matter search to consider what specific topic questions you may wish to focus on for this class. Right away. By the next class, you should be prepared to brainstorm about subjects worth discussing, then suggest the issues to be answered.

Gamesmanship

There is a kind of game-like quality about argumentation and debate. As students, we spar with real world arguments to test our opinions and our skills against each other. One should approach this game with a congenial spirit and an open mind. Real world settings, like a presidential election, will intensify argumentation. Yet the confidence one gains in sparring freely with fellow students will help prepare you for the most difficult of argumentative settings.

As with any game, however, ***rules*** are required. How did we determine who speaks first, for instance? Did we draw lots from a hat? Are there any advantages to having one side or the other in a debate, as there is for a chess player moving white pieces first? How do you determine who wins? Here are some rules of the game.

Argument Form

It matters that you understand the form for building arguments about social issues. A form is a kind of rule. Once you understand forms, they can become a model for the future generation and understanding of arguments.

Why do we bother to talk about public issues? We do so because there is some kind of ***rhetorical demand,*** an impending necessity in the human community that calls for us to speak. An election is coming up. There has been a catastrophic event or an on-going problem that requires special action. There is some pervasive injustice.

Ground zero is discussion. Controversy begins with ***discussion.*** During discussion it's possible to find a reasonable middle ground between various positions. One basic format for discussion would involve three parts: ***Thesis, Antithesis,*** and ***Synthesis.*** Someone argues for an idea, someone argues against an idea, then someone tries to put together a balanced middle view, taking into account the best points of either side. This would be a perfectly reasonable format for classroom discussion.

When there is no reasonable middle ground and opposite viewpoints clash without resolution, we begin the process of ***debate.*** At least we move into a more formal threshold of argumentation and speech building.

The first form, the basic particle of argument, is ***the proposition.***[2] A proposition is simply ***a complete sentence*** that declares your opinion on the issue. It's language should be clearly expressed and defined from the beginning of the text. Answer a specific question, an issue raised in the topic list on the previous page, and you'll have made a proposition.

Propositions should be expressed in sufficiently ***neutral terms*** that each side can hold reasonably equal ***argumentative ground.*** For example, the proposition: "Child molesters should be kept away from children," doesn't leave the opponent much ground. What would negatives argue? "They should be encouraged to baby sit?" What is debatable is a more specific topic about ways to treat and/or punish such people.

The proposition ***limits the scope,*** or the relevance, of the arguments that can be made. It helps maintain one of the most important basic norms of communication, sticking to the subject. In what sense do propositions limit the scope of debate? A proposition of the broad kind above is a good starting place, but it raises more questions than it answers. We need to define the terms of the proposition clearly.

We can use a military analogy to explain. Let's use a somewhat obvious yet difficult topic, that of abortion, one of the most volatile and divisive issues in America today.

Let's say we use the illustration of a fort to designate the argumentative ground, that which you choose to defend (Figure 1).

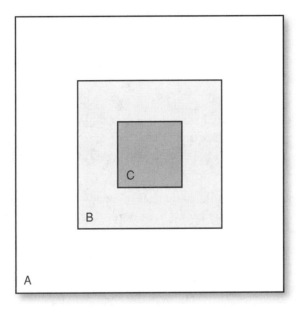

Figure 1

Let's say position A is the most inclusive approach, occupying the largest argumentative ground. The proposition representing that territory is:

"All abortion should be illegal."

Now, empathize with the position and its opposite. Yes, empathize, because one of the best ways of fine tuning and adjusting your proposition is to imagine what both an advocate and an opponent would argue on each side. One might call this kind of thinking ***an interior dialectic.*** It could also be thought of as empathy or perspective taking. For the moment, though, just think of it as ***sparring with your imaginary opponent.***

So, we would think, what are some common arguments an opponent against proposition A might make, or even what they might ask:

"What about cases of rape or incest?"

"Would you force a perhaps underage mother to bear the child of someone who assaulted her?"

An absolutist on the issue might fire back that it should make no difference. It's always wrong. On the other hand, an advocate might think that these were not unreasonable questions and modify, or **qualify the position** to B in Figure 1:

"Abortion, except in cases of rape or incest, should be illegal."

You would have then tightened **the argumentative ground** and preempted one of your opponent's major arguments. Or, to use our metaphor, you would have built a slightly smaller but more defensible fort, a fort you should never be drawn away from, or you're on your opponent's ground where he or she has advantages.

"Yes, but what about cases of endangering a mother's life? Say, you have a single mom with two other kids, and a doctor says she is risking her life having this baby. Would you force her, by law, to possibly, even probably, give up her life and orphan two children for yet a third orphan?"

That's a loaded question, but people do raise loaded questions. How do you bring your perspective to an audience that may not perceive you to be sympathetic? Maybe you argue back that everybody is owed an equal chance at life, or death. Right now, it's an unfair advantage for the mother. Maybe you think that's a fair question, too, and you modify the position to one more reduction of argumentative ground. You move to proposition C:

"All abortion, except for very specific exceptions, should be illegal."

Then, at the beginning of your speech or paper, you can define "exceptions" as cases of incest, abortion, or risk to the mother's life.

Once the advocate has defined the argumentative ground, his fort, in clear language, then the proposition **specifies a direction of change** from a current belief, attitude, or social action. We need "more security," "less restriction," "greater funding for," as opposed to the baseline for discussion, the status quo, the present ways of doing and thinking . . . and spending.

One of you will argue for the present ways of approaching issues, maybe with some minor improvements within that direction, and the other of you will argue for change. Once you've determined direction of change, then the proposition also **determines sides** in the debate.

The proposition also **determines speaker order.** The person who argues for **change speaks first.** If there isn't a voice for change, then there's no impending need for the status quo to defend itself. It has what we call "presumption," which we'll explain later.

The person suggesting something new becomes the ***affirmative*** side in a debate and is called the ***advocate,*** while the person supporting the predominant present point of view is the ***negative*** and is called the ***opponent.*** It may be a little confusing that the person defending the present is called "the negative," but that's the norm. (In truth, the negative may agree that there is something wrong with the present view, but not to the extent that the affirmative proposes. Sometimes negatives offer what are called ***repairs*** to the present view, a slightly lesser change.

If this seems like a somewhat polarized arrangement, you're right, but it's set up that way. One major purpose of argument is to pit alternative positions against each other, to see which is strongest. It requires what might be called ***"artificial clarity"*** to avoid a muddled or confused discussion. In other words, we may take slightly more rigid positions in debate than you might in a regular conversation.

Real World Applications

Let's take just one issue to illustrate propositions. Look at the effectiveness of our foreign policy, specifically with regard to Iraq.

At this writing, United States forces are spread throughout Iraq and Afghanistan, and Saddam Hussein has been ousted and captured. Osama bin Laden, blamed for the destruction of the World Trade Center on 9/11, is still at large, though many Al Queda soldiers have been killed. Our ally Spain had a 9/11 type of an event, ten bombs in one day, 3/11/04, attacking their train system. They have withdrawn their troops from Iraq.

After many American and Iraqi deaths in civil conflict and a powerful controversy over torture of Iraqi detainees, as well as radical beheadings of several noncombatant members of the occupation, the U.S. has turned the country over to a new civil authority, though our armed forces still occupy the land.

Also, at home, there have been high unemployment rates, a growing deficit, which may have been worsened by the war, as well as Congressional 9/11 Committee to consider errors in intelligence. Several questions could constitute issues for discussion or debate:

> "Did the Iraq war hurt the U.S. economy?"

If you answer "Yes, the Iraq war hurt the U.S. economy," then you'd have of ***three basic kinds of propositions, fact.*** Propositions of fact deal with what does or does not exist, what has or has not happened, and what may or may not occur in the future. It also focuses particularly on issues of cause. Here's a significant phenomena. What is the cause of it?

Another issue of fact is currently being investigated by a congressional committee.

"Did the Bush administration receive distorted information about Iraq's weapons of mass destruction from intelligence sources?"

If you answer "yes," that would mean that you would defend this as a proposition of fact: "The Bush administration received distorted information about Iraq's weapons of mass destruction."

This would be the normal give-and-take of a debate, or what philosophers would call a dialectic. For every action in argument, there is an equal and opposite reaction. Most matters are arguable, not just for the sake of argument, but for the sake of illuminating and better understanding everyday social problems.

Now, here's a **proposition of value.** Value issues deal with questions of what's right and wrong, ethical or unethical, moral or immoral, and good or evil. Concerns over human rights, for instance, may typically be expressed as propositions of value.

"Denying equal rights to gays is wrong."

Most importantly, value propositions also **suggest a sense of priority** among our many values. For instance, we have a Bill of Rights, which can and should be read in full in several places on the Web, but those rights often come into conflict. That's one reason we need the Supreme Court, to determine if one right is more important than another in a given circumstance.

Like the Supreme Court, which uses a large body of legal precedent and the constitution itself, we must reason from **a clear, objective standard** to arrange our priorities:

"We are emphasizing foreign military action too much over domestic needs."

One might take "the survival of the Republic" as the standard for deciding. Which goal better serves the survival of the country in the long run?

Or, with regard to the next gubernatorial or presidential election:

"The Republican platform is superior to the Democratic one."

A person defending the Republican platform would speak second, because the standing president is Republican. That is the status quo, as of this writing. If the standing president or governor were a Democrat, that order would be reversed.

Finally, there are propositions of **policy,** which deal with what we should or should not do as a matter of practical social action. We discuss a social problem and come up with a practical solution. That solution would be your policy.

The above order of the types of issues and propositions is somewhat progressive. We discover what circumstances exist, an issue of fact. Then we look at our values about that issue in terms of it being right or wrong, better or worse, than an alternative set of values. Ultimately, we look at policy, what should we do, given the facts and values we've affirmed in examining the issue. Policy discussion includes both issues of fact and value, and so constitutes the most complete discussion.

Propositions of policy, for instance, could include:

> "We should increase medical care coverage for Americans."
>
> "We should reduce (or increase) military spending."
>
> "We should restructure U.S. intelligence services."

* * * * *

Now, let's check to see if these policy propositions meet the criteria, the standards, for a good proposition mentioned above. So, let's apply each criterion.

Is each a complete sentence?

Yes, notice they have nouns and active verbs. They are also in the preferred form of simple declarative sentences. The longer the proposition, the more terms to define, and the more difficult it is to avoid confusion and equivocation. Remember to keep your proposition short and "punchy." A recently retired colleague of mine, Professor Rod Hansen, said that any proposition more than nine words in length is too long for a proposition. I'll give you ten in an emergency. Just avoid too much flowery language. **Be clear first, clever later.**

Is each expressed in neutral terms?

Yes. There are no inflammatory adjectives. There are certainly fairly equal grounds for each side of the debate. Nobody has to fight from a corner.

Does each specify direction of change?

Yes, in each case. There is a particular judgment about changing the status quo: increasing, reducing, or restructuring.

Does each determine sides and, thus, speaker order?

Yes. Republicans are placed against Democrats, hawks against doves, and people who think intelligence is inadequate against those who think the CIA has gotten a bum rap from the 9/11 commission. Speaker order simply follows from whether your side is the current view or a new idea.

Does each limit the scope of discussion?

No, not really. Who are the "we" mentioned in each? "We" the members of the live audience, "we" the members of a particular political party, "we the people" in abstract sum? What kind of medical coverage? Hospitalization? Long-term care? And for which Americans? Everybody, kids and adults alike, the whole forty million who have no coverage of any kind? Reduce military spending by how much? In what sectors of defense? Restructure intelligence how? Shrink it? Unify the agencies? Diversify them? We need more specific tools to limit debate.

Qualifiers

Apart from being specific to avoid confusion in discussion, we are concerned about recognizing argument as a rhetorical activity. Since rhetoric is a process of interacting skillfully with audience attitudes, we may find it useful to moderate or qualify our positions, to avoid alienating our audience. **Word choice matters in persuasion.** Even more importantly, in rhetoric, qualifiers matter because we are not trying to speak in terms of absolute truth. **We speak in terms of probability, rather than certainty.** So, we have to use qualifiers to relate our propositions to the degree of probability with which we speak.

There is a secondary triad in Toulmin's argument form, besides the primary one of claim, warrant, and grounds, but we'll only use one additional element as it helps focus word choice, the qualifier.

Qualifiers describe how much change should occur. Sometimes it's an adjective like "significant" to generalize the extent of change. Other more specific words can be used to limit the extent of change.

For instance, there's this simple declension of **adjectives** down from "in all cases," to "most," to "many," to "some." There is also the phrase "a few specific cases," to account for the usual exceptions.

Toulmin himself mentions **"modal qualifiers,"** which are phrases that show what kind and degree of reliance is to be placed on propositions.[3] They are adverbs, adverbial phrases, or prepositional phrases that modify the action of the verb:

Sometimes
Perhaps
Maybe
Presumably
Necessarily
Certainly
In certain cases
In all probability
With the exception of

We should also mention the word "possibly," which would limit the degree of probability with which we hold the proposition to be true. Of course, more specific statistical thresholds would be appropriate, too, as in, "We should spend another million on this project," or "increase funds by 10%," rather than "we should spend significantly more money."

Qualifiers do help limit the argumentative ground one has to defend in order to win one's position. The broader the position, the more ground you have to defend, the broader the avenues of counter-attack. So, sharpening your proposition not only focuses discussion, it helps one anticipate defenses by considering what attacks may be made against a broader proposition.

We used similar limiting language earlier when describing how to focus our territory or argument, or to ***limit our "fort"*** on the subject of abortion. Like the Spartans at Thermopylae, who wedged themselves in a narrow canyon to limit avenues of attack by a vastly superior Persian force, we may find it is advantageous to limit access by our opponents.

Another modal qualifier is "at this point in time." We sometimes need to ***qualify propositions in time, place, and circumstances.*** If a social problem is imminent, we may need to offer a deadline in the proposition, to achieve something by a given date or year, like our government's "by June 30, 2004," deadline to return Iraq to sovereignty.

We may also ***limit a proposition geographically,*** to a specific city, county, state, region, or the nation. We may propose international . . . or, theoretically, interplanetary change, depending on the planet from which you've come.

The ***limits of specific circumstances*** under which a proposition may apply can be seen among legal criteria. For example, murder in the first degree happens when there is forethought about the act and the slayer lays in wait for the victim. Murder in the second degree includes acts of aggression in the moment, or "crimes of passion." The third degree of murder, or manslaughter, occurs through negligent or irresponsible acts without any particular intent. These are the criteria to determine the various thresholds of murder.

Definitions

The person who is challenging the present system should be offering a specific change, about perceptions (facts), ideas (values), and acts (policies), to audience perspective. The degree to which you propose change can, in the case of policy, be determined in the solution that you offer, but it can also be imbedded in the way you define your terms.[4]

We've said that propositions should be phrased clearly and succinctly and should be qualified to be as specific as possible. We can also use additional phrases, even full sentences to further define the language of the proposition and clarify our intent.

There are several ways to define your terms in a succinct manner, but we must first *decide which terms require definition.*

Reconsider our abortion proposition C:

"All abortions, except in very specific circumstances, should be illegal."

Three terms would be important, as they are either vague or controversial enough to require clarification. They are "abortion," "specific exceptions," and "illegal."

The simplest approach would be to use *definitions from dictionaries.* For instance, *Webster's New World Dictionary* defines abortion as, "Premature expulsion of a fetus so that it does not live, especially if induced on purpose." This would exclude miscarriages which may also fall appropriately under the word "abort."

Often definitions from general dictionaries are too broad to be useful in clarifying the terms of disagreement. For instance, a better definition might be found in a *field-specific dictionary,* like *Dorland's Illustrated Medical Dictionary. Black's Law Dictionary* may be even more useful, since abortion is a legal issue. Black's definition includes the key elements of Roe v. Wade, the Supreme Court decision that forms a legal barrier to banning abortion:

> Prior to approximately the end of the first trimester of pregnancy the attending physician in consultation with his patient is free to determine, without regulation by state, that in his medical judgment the patient's pregnancy should be terminated, and if this decision is reached such judgment may be effectuated by an abortion without interference by the state.[5]

So, making abortion illegal would necessarily include reversal of Roe vs. Wade. So, this is a more specifically useful definition. Understanding the present threshold of the law will become especially important when we get to building policy positions.

You may also define terms with *quotations from experts* in the field, which may turn up in your research.

You may give definitions that are *inclusive or exclusive.* In other words, you may define by listing what your issue focus does and does not include. In proposition C about abortion, our definition of "exceptions" could be done this way.

> "Exceptions" *include* abortions involving rape, incest, or severe risk to health of the mother. That definition excludes financial or emotional reasons for exemption. Under no conditions does it include third trimester abortions.

This brings up one more approach, *operational definitions,* descriptions of the actual operations or actions your proposition intends. Just specify what you intend to do. For instance, you could specify how you intend to determine health risk to mothers:

> . . . health of the mother, such risk to be determined by a state licensed doctor.

Or consider an operational definition for "illegal":

> "Illegal" means that we should reverse Roe vs. Wade at the federal level, pass a national law banning abortion on demand, and support states in authorizing selected clinics to authorize exceptions.

Those are operations one would perform to enact the word "illegal."

The clearer and more concise your proposition and definitions are, the less confusing discussion and debate will be, even within an appropriately qualified definition.

A Legal Analogy

We can use a couple of legal analogies to answer and explain some other important rules of the game.

The first key concept is **presumption.** We're commonly aware of the idea in courts that "**the accused is innocent until proven guilty.**" Similarly, the status quo, the present way of perceiving and doing things, is innocent until proven guilty.

That constitutes a distinct **advantage for the negative side** in the debate, since the opponent defends the status quo.

The advocate on the **affirmative gets a balancing advantage,** as he gets to speak first, laying out the grounds upon which the debate proceeds, the argumentative territory.

This concept of presumption also helps us to understand why the affirmative goes first. In a court, the prosecutor speaks first, as he is advocating against presumption of innocence enjoyed by the defense. Since the status quo, the currently held idea or policy, is already presumed to be okay, the opponent has nothing to speak to until challenged somehow by an advocate. There is no reason to speak, unless there is **confusion, controversy, or conflict.** So, the opponent speaks second, like a defense attorney, but only once there is something to defend against.

While the opponent and advocate each have some advantages, the advocate has some additional burdens. **Advocates have the burden of proof** like the prosecuting attorney, who must support his case with sufficient proof that a reasonable audience member (member of the jury) would find cause to doubt the innocence of the status quo.

That is, there should be sufficient evidence to temporarily suspend the presumption enjoyed by the status quo. Without sufficient cause for suspicion, the judge (your instructor, maybe) throws our case out of court.

This is not to say that the opponent doesn't have to have any evidence. It just means that the affirmative must support his case decisively, or the negative wins by virtue of presumption. A tie in the debate will go to the negative.

Typically, we'd also discuss the notion of a ***prima facie case,*** but it's a little early for that. We'll discuss the structure of prima facie cases and something we call ***stock issues*** in chapters about how to argue each type of proposition. For the time being, think of a prima facie case as one sufficient to meet one's burden of proof.

A Common Mistake

A very common mistake in phrasing propositions is the "I'm talking about X" approach, in which one simply mentions a topic, but doesn't specify a particular area of the announced topic, nor specify a direction of change. This doesn't even make clear what kind of proposition it is.

In fact, initially, you may have some trouble distinguishing among the three. You'll propose something is fact, because you feel deeply about it, but it's really a value. You'll propose what you think is an absolutely moral position, a strongly held value, but you can't help arguing what we ought to do, a policy.

Here are a few somewhat reliable ***"key word clues."***

Propositions of ***fact*** often involve some form of the verb "is," "does," "has," or "will," as you argue here the nature of what is or does exist, and what has or will happen. You may also be arguing about the quantity of something, so words like "more," "less," "increasing," or "decreasing" may also be common as adjectives.

Propositions of ***value*** are essentially comparisons of things along a scale, so we find phrases like "more important than," "more valuable than," "is the higher or highest priority."

Value also involves abstract terms that need to be carefully defined to avoid being glittering generalities, like "loyalty," "freedom," "democracy," and the like.

Propositions of ***policy*** are perhaps the easiest to recognize, as they almost always, as a matter of formality, use the verbs like "should," "must," or "ought to" to describe a sense of the imperative nature of the problem to be solved.

There will be many exceptions, as the lines between these proposition types are not rigidly drawn. Consider this little recognized value:

> "We should pay respect to education."

Just because the word "should" appears doesn't make this necessarily a policy, except to the degree that you're encouraging an audience to act personally upon a principle that you're defending, more an issue of value. Similarly:

> "Honesty is the most important value."

Though it employs the word "is," this proposition offers a sense of priority for one abstract term amongst many. Thus, it is value.

Assignment

As we mull over these concepts, begin to **brainstorm propositions** and research them. Remember that you need three topics for the semester, **one of each type** of proposition.

Then learn to distinguish the three types of propositions from each other and analyze which topic is best for each type.

The sooner you choose them, the sooner your knowledge of each subject can grow, the greater your credibility will be, not only in your presentation, but in open conversation, as well.

Vocabulary

Advocate/Affirmative
Be Clear, Not Clever
Burden of Proof
Confusion, Controversy
    & Conflict
Definitions
Direction of Change
Imaginary Opponent

Inclusive/Exclusive
    Definition
Issue
Kinds of Propositions:
    Fact, Value, Policy
Operational Definition
Opponent/Negative
Presumption

Proposition
Qualifiers
Rhetorical Demand
Sense of Priority through
    Standards and Criteria
Thesis/Antithesis/Synthesis

Exercises: Go to Interactive Disc to Complete

1) Look at this list of propositions and determine which are fact, which are value, and which are policy:

   a) Billy stole five dollars from my wallet.

   b) We should revise the three strikes law, so we don't put people away for life based on minor crimes.

   c) We must strengthen our immigration laws, because our social systems are being strained.

   d) The three strikes law has put a strain on the prison system.

   e) Discretion is the better part of valor.

   f) Neither a borrower nor a lender be.

g) Capital punishment deters murder.

h) Affirmative Action has failed to meet its purposes.

i) This problem requires that we impeach the city counsel.

j) Love of country is more important than international cooperation.

2) Now go over these ten propositions again, but underline the terms to be defined.

3) Choose one of the propositions and actually define the terms. Use several methods of definition for each term (dictionary, field specific dictionary, inclusive/exclusive, and operational).

4) Offer three propositions of your own that you might be interested in writing about, one of each type (fact, value and policy).

5) Decide on a proposition of fact for your first assignment. Remember, you'll be discussing what does or does not exist, what has or has not happened, or what will or will not probably occur. Look in particular for significant phenomena, what causes it and what results from it. Define the terms by the best available method. Be prepared to adjust those definitions according to the research you begin. Look at the appendix of sample speeches for ideas.

Sources

1) "Creativity & Critical Thinking Skills." http://www.au.af.mil/au/awc/awcgate/awc-thkg.htm

"Critical Thinking Across the Curriculum." http://www.nwrel.org/scpd/sirs/3/snapll.html

"Critical Thinking and Pedagogy: CT in Chemical Engineering." http://www.cdtl.nus.edu.sg/ctp/chemengg.htm

"Critical Thinking: The Scientific Method." http://sdb.bio.purdue.edu/SDBEduca/dany_adams/. . .

"Critical Thinking in Social Studies." http://www.ericfacility.net/databases/ERIC_Digests/. . .

"Overcoming Obstacles to Critical Thinking in Your Organization." http://www.phptr.com/articles/. . .

"Teaching CT: Some Lessons from Cognitive Science." http://www.philosoph.unimelb.edu.au/reason/papers/. . .

2) Browne, M. Neil, and Stuart M. Keeley (1990). "Asking the Right Questions: A Guide to Critical Thinking." Englewood Cliffs, N.J.: Prentice.

Church, Russell T., and Charles Wilbanks (1986). "Values and Policies in Controversies: An Introduction to Argumentation & Debate." Scottsdale, AZ: Gorusich-Scarisbrick.

Ehninger, Douglas, and Wayne Brockriede (1967). "Decision by Debate." New York: Dodd Mead.

Freeley, Austin J. (1990). "Argumentation and Debate: Critical Thinking For Reasoned Decision Making." Belmont, CA: Wadsworth.

3) Toulmin, et al (1984), p. 85.

III
Finding and Using Evidence

You've invented some propositions, probably discovering that there's an element of creativity in the process. Rhetoricians call this process *invention,* the act of creating unique points of view and arguments of your own. In particular, you should have found a proposition of fact that you can defend for your first assignment.

One could start with a proposition of value or policy. Indeed, most of the topics you're discussing will suggest issues of value and policy, as well as issues of fact. You could write propositions of all three types about many topics. In fact, while forming your propositions you may have made propositions other than the type you'd intended. It's O.K. Everyone does at first.

There is a certain reasonable, *natural order to the proposition types:*

> We discover what is true and untrue (fact);

> We then assess those facts in terms of our beliefs and priorities (value);

Finally, we choose how to behave, individually and as a society (policy), in terms of those facts and priorities.

Also, this order is *progressively more complex.* Propositions of fact deal with facts that are controversial and disputable. Research for them is fairly straight forward, up to the threshold of what we don't know, or haven't yet discovered. Discussion of values will include issues of fact. Policy is the most complete kind of argument. It includes both issues of fact and issues of value.

Toulmin Arguments

Now, it's time to support your propositions with reason and evidence. We'll do so in a particular form, a slight modified version of British logician Stephen Toulmin's argument model, mentioned in the first chapter, and to be discussed in detail as we go. It involves making claims, warrants, and grounds, as well as qualifiers.

For the time being, understand that our discussion about propositions in the last chapter bears upon "claims." *Claims are propositions.* You'll have, as in most texts, an overarching proposition which is your *thesis,* then several arguments—each with a proposition that is a claim supporting that thesis—will emerge in answer to certain issues.

Look at the sample speeches appendix at the back of the book and notice the following structure in each, in which "CWG" stands for claim, warrant, grounds. Arguments will look much like this:

THESIS (PROPOSITION) — Qualifiers

> Claim (proposition) — Qualifiers
> W
> G
>
> Claim (proposition) — Qualifiers
> W
> G
>
> Claim (proposition) — Qualifiers
> W
> G

Each of these four part arguments should support the main proposition. There is no particular magic number in terms of how many arguments. Each topic will raise different issues, and you'll need at least one argument to answer each.

Notice that we're suggesting *a certain order to the Toulmin parts.* Qualifiers would occur along with the claims as a matter of necessity. Toulmin himself ordered the parts from claim to grounds to warrants (CGW). Warrants, our reasoning, proceed on the basis of evidence, so Toulmin's order seems like a natural mental process. We'll also see that it's a good order for the research process.

However, with apologies to Toulmin, in offering the argument for oral presentations, a slight re-ordering makes Toulmin arguments easier for audiences to follow.

You offer a claim, you give your reasons why you think it is true, then you offer the weight of evidence that supports that thinking. If you give your evidence second, as Toulmin has designed his model, then use your reasoning at the bottom, this presents some problems for oral text. Listening, even reading comprehension, is better served by beginning with a claim, so we know what the issue is, previewing your reasoning, then offering the proof. This then sunlights your reasoning, so that readers or audience members can fairly measure each piece of proof against your thinking.

Often you need multiple warrants to prove a claim, reasons you believe your claim to be true. Yet you'll find that you almost always need multiple pieces of proof to establish a proposition about real world social problems. If you have several grounds, your audience or your reader may well misunderstand what you're trying to prove with your evidence along the way. Grounds may be quite long. After getting through all the evidence, they may also have forgotten what it is you're trying to prove. Thus, CWG.

There are also some suggestions with regard to the ***order of research and argument building.***

While it's normal to have a belief, something we can express as a proposition, we often assume that more is true than can be demonstrated. This is so, in part, due to our cultural conditioning. An idea seems true to us because that's what we've always heard, so we repeat it, then take it for granted as a certainty. Recall that we are dealing in probabilities, not certainties, and probability is discovered by a preponderance of evidence.

Realize that you should ***offer some evidence for any proposition you offer.*** When you do not support your propositions, and you just throw them out there, like they're gospel truth just because you say so, then you are making ***assertions,*** unsupported and un-collaborated personal opinions.

Scientists speak in terms of ***an hypothesis,*** a temporary thesis about the subject matter, which they then set up for testing. Try to think about your own thesis in that manner, then test it against the evidence that you find. Researching toward a particular, rigid view of an issue is very difficult. To understand, think in terms of an analogy in architecture, the pyramid (Figure 2):

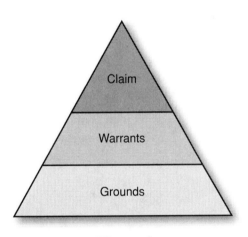

Figure 2

How do go about building something? You start with a vision, a plan about what the building will look like. Then you build a foundation from which the structure rises.

The same with successful argument building. Your foundation is the grounds, the evidence that you find about that issue. Like a pyramid, the reason and the conclusion you draw from it, begins with the evidence. Another word for "claim" is "conclusion."

The most productive process in practical argument building is that one starts with hard proof, then reasons from it to a conclusion, which then becomes your claim. In other words, ***you should build your arguments from the "grounds" up.*** Thus, you should go into the evidence study with as open a mind as possible.

By all means, do have an hypothesis—a temporary claim you're considering—but suspend judgment about it, then let the evidence itself tell you what to claim.

You probably don't quite understand warrants fully. That's fine, we'll get a better understanding of them in the next chapter. For the time being, concentrate on grounds and finding some evidence for your propositions.

Basic Kinds of Evidence

What constitutes convincing evidence? On one hand, since argument is a rhetorical activity, we could say that evidence is what an audience finds to be convincing. Recall that rhetoric is the process of adapting particular arguments to particular audiences, at particular times and places.

However, there are certain basic types of supporting material that you can use to get started. We can divide these materials into two categories, evidence of fact and evidence of opinion.[1]

Evidence of fact consists primarily of three types of material: artifacts, examples, and figures or statistics.

Artifacts are objects used to demonstrate a point. In a court, for instance, lipstick prints on a glass, fingerprints at a crime scene, traces of fiber from clothing, tire tracks, even traces of DNA can be used to prove a point.

For an archeologist, the skull of Piltdown man is an artifact, as would be aging pottery or other art objects depicting the characteristics of another time and place.

In a sense, for a public speech, a model used to illustrate the nature of something could be considered evidence as artifact. For instance, a student explaining the break up of the space shuttle Columbia might use a model to defend a proposition of fact about how it broke up.

Even a visual aid like a map, or a chart, could be considered a kind of artifact. These objects make the subject matter tangible and easier to visualize in an oral presentation.

Examples are stories relevant to the proposition. They usually consist of specific cases in that general subject area, short narratives that are literally true. Sometimes, though, they may be extended ***hypothetical illustrations,*** sometimes a compilation of details from real cases, which are representative of the situation you're discussing. "Let's join Officer Everyman on a typical day on the beat."

Real, documented cases are preferable, especially cases that put a human face on the subject. Individuals that we can ***identify*** with affected by a social issue can be quite compelling.

Aristotle wrote of audiences feeling "pity for one like ourselves" in "The Poetics" in which he discussed plays. Yet the idea applies equally well with rhetoric and choosing the most effective evidence for a given audience.[2]

For instance, if a news agency simply declares "six men died in an avalanche today," we might have particular interest if we were climbers, or we knew people who were in the mountains on that day. However, it would have a lot more impact, if we knew the story in detail, with fuller depictions of the individual characters involved. If we knew names and faces, their hobbies, their professions, their family relations, we might feel more for the lost personnel.[3] Hence, the information may be more persuasive.

However, a few dramatic examples do not answer everything. They can show us how a social problem might affect us, since we've been shown cases of people who may be like us. Yet examples can't answer the questions of how much, how long, how many people does this affect? Or is this the unique case, colorful but not representative of the whole?

We can see the quality of a social problem by looking at examples, but to deal with issues of quantity, we need the use of numbers. ***Figures and statistics "quantify" social phenomena.***[4]

Figures are derived from simple counting, as with the U.S. Census, during which each household is counted to determine population and other demographic details. As a result, we can offer an absolute number as a figure. Statistics are a good deal trickier, because we take figures, as well as estimates of figures, then apply them across a population to achieve a percentage.

To contrast the two uses of numbers, consider a statement from a figure:

> "There are X numbers of AIDS patients in the U.S. today."

Depending on the number, which is certainly too high in this claim or any other, an audience might be quite impressed and shaken.

On the other hand, a statistical impression might sound like this illustration:

> "One in every twenty Americans knows someone who will die of AIDS."

By distributing a figure across a population, we can make statements that may have a clearer illustrative impact on an audience. As opposed to thinking of AIDS patients as "anybody" somewhere out there, statistics can help us envision a localized version of a "somebody" close to their lives.

There are ***two functions*** of statistics. Some are meant ***to describe.*** As an example, we break down the figures of a census to say what percentage of the population is white, black, Asian or Hispanic. There are also statistics ***to infer.*** That is, we observe a specific part of the population, then generalize the characteristics of that sample to the population as a whole.

As a cautionary note, Mark Twain once wrote that, "There are three kinds of lies, white lies, damn lies, and statistics." In a sense, figures are more "factual" than statistics, as there is no abstraction or inference involved. Statistics can be manipulated and are only as reliable as the methods used to gather and interpret them. We'll discuss more specific cautions when we look at tests of evidence below.

Evidence of Opinion

Evidence of opinion consists of quotations from various sources. We sometimes call it *source based evidence.*

If the source is an everyday person, without particular expertise on the subject matter, we call it *personal testimony.* It's really much like an example spoken in first person, in terms of its persuasive impact. You simply share the experience of common people through their quotations. You're probably familiar with these testimonials in product or service advertising.

> "I used 'Bupgoo' tooth paste and had fewer cavities." (Smile for camera.)

> Less facetiously: "I've had cancer for three years. This is what it's like."

If the person has credentials of expertise on the subject matter, then it's considered *expert testimony,* which would generally be more objective and credible, though not necessarily more persuasive than personal testimony. It matters the audience's sense of the speaker, as well as their own predispositions on the topic.

Such testimony can be important in helping you to interpret and understand the area of study. If a qualified someone has had more time with a topic, they may be able to summarize a quick sense of the issues that you yourself cannot. It also may add to your audience impression, your credibility, to associate your opinions with those of the best and brightest.

Tests of Evidence

Sometimes a debate may come down to a comparison of the strength of each side's grounds. This is not just a matter of having more evidence, but of having better quality evidence. So, we'll need to examine tests that will allow us to compare the quality of competing evidence. This will help you, both in choosing which evidence to use now in building arguments, and in using the tests later as a source of counter-argument.[5]

A) **Accuracy.** Begin, first, by directly quoting evidence, rather than paraphrasing it in any subjective sense.

B)   ***Relevancy*** is the most obvious test. You want to make sure the evidence clearly relates to the claim to which it's being applied. For instance, if your topic focus is within American borders, then introducing evidence about Europe wouldn't necessarily work for you. If your topic is confined by state borders, then nationwide statistics would not necessarily be relevant.

In practical terms, ***make sure your grounds directly support your claim.*** This is as much a part of your properly phrasing the claim as it is finding the right evidence. If you are accurately summarizing what the evidence actually says, rather than what you wish it would say, your grounds and claims will relate.

C)   ***Sufficiency*** is another of the most important tests for building arguments. Is the evidence sufficient to prove the claim that you're trying to make? Does it meet your burden of proof? One of the most common novice errors in argumentation is to exaggerate the impact of the available evidence. ***Your claim should say no more than you can prove.***

For instance, let's say that your claim is: "Most Americans oppose gay marriage."

This is an issue of fact, but you use a quotation to support it, which says: "Nobody I know supports gay marriage."

Maybe even it's a famous person saying this, but would that prove the point? No. The point you're making has a qualifier that calls for quantifiable evidence, "most." So, we should try then to use a figure or statistic as support.

"According to a February, 2004, CNN news survey, 62% of Americans oppose gay marriage, though some of those support civil unions for gays."

We could question the methods used, as other surveys yield different numbers. For instance, other sources state similar conclusions more positively: "A majority of Americans favor civil unions," which are not marriages.

Yet CNN directly services the point. In fact, it may be perceived by an audience predisposed to believe CNN as sufficient to meet the burden of proof for this claim.

However, the next issue would become: is the majority always right on such issues? If the majority had had their way, we would not have had civil rights legislation making segregation illegal in the 60's. There's a fallacy called bandwagon argument, discussed in a later chapter, which reminds us that majorities can be mistaken. Ask Copernicus and Galileo about the popularity of their heliocentric theory of the universe.

D)   ***Verifiability*** follows close upon the heels of sufficiency. Can you confirm your findings with more than one source? Does the field of opinion show some coherent point of view, or are you basing your claim on an exceptional case or a single eccentric perspective?

The best way to verify is to read a wide variety of individual sources on the subject. By "individual sources," we mean ten to twelve different authors spread across various kinds of publication. Look at periodicals, magazines, newspapers, along with searches on the internet. If you find exceptions, or convincing contradictory material, you may have to qualify your claim to be accurate.

There's no specific number to how many sources is enough. The depth of research will vary with the complexity of the topic. As a beginner's rule of thumb, though, try to look at one source for every minute of speaking you do. Yet realize that not every source you look through will be equally useful.

E)   ***Recency*** is relatively important, depending upon how immediate the topic at issue. If we're dealing with a subject like elections coming up this fall, it's probably not appropriate to rely on evidence from last year's preliminary campaign.

For instance, the news has just reported that presidential candidate Senator John Kerry has chosen former competitor Senator Edwards to be his vice-presidential candidate. That will have changed the whole complexion of the campaign by the time you've read this.

The speed with which a particular issue unfolds may vary. Some scientific and medical research, for instance, changes very rapidly. Something not possible last week may suddenly become plausible, even likely, with the announcement of new discovery.

Other data, established and still useful theory—such as some of the rhetorical traditions expressed here, as well as historical examples or quotations from famous figures of the past—may still be useful regardless of recency.

Ultimately, ***if new knowledge is available on your topic, you'd best know what it is,*** or your opponent may demonstrate your viewpoint to be obsolete. Even very old events may be made new by the most current instruments of discovery.

These first three tests would be a required consideration for evidence of any kind, of fact or of opinion. Specific types of evidence have other evidence tests.

F)   Statistics are subject to all of the above tests and some others.

1)   Statistics are based upon figures. ***Are the original figures accurate?*** We recall a piece of evidence from our high school debate days, a statistic that was defeating our case. A team member wrote the publication that

had provided our opponent's evidence and asked it how the staff had gathered the statistics. We were told by letter that the original figure upon which the statistic based itself was "a rough estimate." In fact, it was an estimate of an estimate. There was no real number at all to verify. We then were able to find other figures that conflicted with that estimate and were verifiable. Of course, we took the publisher's letter with us to our next encounter with these opponents, waiting hungrily for the evidence in question to be offered.

2) When the statistics are inferences ***are the statistics representative?*** What were the characteristics of the sample population? Who did they sample? Where? Under what conditions? Was the number sampled sufficient, or were too few people included? If you're combining or comparing different statistics, are they working with similar definitions of the field of study? If comparisons are made by statistic, are the units compared really alike?

For instance, consider exit polls at an election. They may be conducted with random samples of people exiting the polls after voting. We know not to rely too much on this kind of quick survey, though. In a given county, we may have both very liberal neighborhoods and very conservative neighborhoods. Focusing on an unbalanced sample of neighborhoods could easily (and unfairly) distort the results. Consider the errors committed by network news in prematurely predicting a presidential victory in the Bush/Gore election of 2000.

3) We also have to look at ***the question of methods.*** Is the method of gathering the statistics reliable in itself, is it in line with what is typical of the field, or eccentric somehow? Even apparently reliable statistics upon which we base important decisions may eventually be discovered to be incorrect.

> Pollution levels in coastal waters fluctuate so wildly that current monitoring efforts are largely futile, according to a study released by a team of Southern California researchers. Intensive testing of waters . . . showed that hot spots of contamination tended to disappear within 100 minutes. But because of the lag time in getting water-sample test results, a beach would be posted as off-limits. 24 hours later, long after the pollutants were gone. Yet the posting couldn't be lifted until another sample tested clean—which takes another 24 hours because of the limits of testing methods.[6]

So, during the next 24 hours of checking tests, the beach could be contaminated again and nobody would know it. In other words, the opening and closing of the beaches is based upon information that is both potentially obsolete and premature for the actual safety of swimmers.

One humorous example involved a UCLA Medical School study. It alarmed male marijuana smokers in the late seventies. Its conclusion was that marijuana caused men to grow breasts. Across America, young men scuttled home to peek inside their T-shirts. Even young women got big ideas.

A closer examination of the study's methodology yielded some odd methods. Human subjects were not used. Rats were. That brings up an interesting question: How do you get a rat to smoke "a joint?" Can you just see it? Men in white lab coats putting a joint in a rat's maw and pumping its lungs with their rubber gloved hands. Answer: You don't. You inject the rat with pure THC, a concentrated version of the active ingredient in marijuana. They were also rather large dosages, representing many joints a day, skewing the results from the effects likely for a moderate marijuana user.

Here is an example of what might be considered good statistical evidence, because it ***makes the method explicit:***

> The authors evaluated 400 models and determined "green scores" by using each vehicle's fuel estimates from the Environmental Protection Agency, average annual fuel costs and California or federal emissions ratings, along with an industry average for manufacturing pollutants and public health costs. On a 100-point scale, the best score was the Insight at 56. A natural gas powered Honda Civic model was second with 53.[7]

G) The following tests are ***especially important when it comes to source-based evidence,*** like expert testimony, though they may apply to other evidence, too:

1) Obviously, we have to ask for ***the qualifications of the person offering testimony.*** What is their connection with the issue? Do they have educational degrees or some other credentials relevant to the issue? Does their professional history or personal experience qualify them in some particular way?

A PhD, "doctor" or other title in front of your name, may not be sufficient qualification unless the accreditation is directly relevant. A general practitioner is not a specialist on hearts, kidneys or any other particular organ. Any scrupulous medical generalist would send you on to a person of more specific qualifications.

Even ***you may have some expertise*** on a given subject. If so, you might find a way to drop that fact into your introductory or concluding comments, but that would not replace your obligation to support yourself with other authorities.

2) This leads us to **bias.** Are the authors of the evidence being objective? Are there reasons to believe that they have a skewed perspective? Are they influenced, perhaps by some self-interest they can gain from your acceptance of the claim. Also, they may be invested in it emotionally, because it's their idea.

One example would be the use of expert witnesses in trials. While they are experts, they are also paid. In fact, for some, that is a primary means for their income. The opposing attorney would typically point this out as a factor to consider when looking at their evidence. Are they simply "guns for hire" with a predisposition to favor those who pay them?

Also, realize that **publications and news agencies also have bias.** There are liberal publications and conservative ones. There are magazines designed to inform, but many of them are designed to entertain. The influence on the publication may be a matter of financial necessity. Even magazines and newspapers have powerful contributors and sponsors in the corporate world that can influence the view of editorialists and reporters.

Bias is important in all matters of source-based proof. In fact, we've devoted a later chapter on the matter of "spin" by news sources (see chapter XI). Even scientific study should be observed carefully for bias. A researcher working with a grant might exaggerate his results to preserve the financing that the grant offers. Recall the great "cold fusion" boondoggle. Utah researchers claimed to have harnessed fusion power in a water glass. There was lots of buzz about the glass, but no nuclear "fizz" in it.[8]

3) One might ask if the evidence is the result of **firsthand observation?** How close was the source of a story to the actual event? Is it a news writer from the Chicago Tribune who downloaded a story from the AP wire and is merely repeating what he is told? Or is it a reporter in the field who was actually present for the event?

The farther one is from the primary source, the more subjective filters there are to the information. The more error-prone technology and bias-ridden bureaucracy the information passes through, the less pristine the information may be. In a court of law, for example, we don't allow hearsay testimony, only eyewitness testimony that is a first hand account. You may have experienced rumors that were passed around about you and seen them grow and get distorted by people who didn't even know you. Same thing here.

After several beheadings of civilians in the 2004 Iraq war, a marine turned up missing and was reported to be a prisoner of the beheading radicals. Subsequent reports said he had been beheaded. He then turned up in a

Lebanese village where he had family and is being informally investigated to see if he was merely AWOL. Nobody actually saw the beheading. It was a matter of rumors based upon other rumors.

4) **Consistency,** both external and internal, is also important. **External consistency** involves finding out if the source's claims are in line with other sources commenting on the subject matter. Are you quoting the eccentric individual, the lone wolf on a given subject?

By **internal consistency,** we mean that the arguments within their text are not contradictory.

By the way, self-consistency is an issue for you, as well. As you build your first assignment, remember that it is a common novice error to grab a piece of evidence that makes one point, without considering its impact on the sum of the points made. It's possible to prove two individual points that yet disprove each other. If one contradicts oneself, one doesn't get to choose which point you really want. You simply lose both, along with the trust of the audience.

Research

Now that you know a few of the basic types of evidence and ways to explore the quality of said evidence, let's explore how to find the evidence. The primary goal of research is **to find the best approximate truth** about the issue studied. It's not to prove a preconceived point of belief at the expense of the truth.

We don't speak often in rhetoric about "truth" in some absolute or ultimate sense. We generally leave that to philosophers, although some value propositions may lead to philosophical discussion. When we say "truth," remember that we mean it in a relative rather than absolute way. We seek the best available sense of the truth about difficult social subjects. We seek truth in the sense of probability, rather than certainty.

The best way to achieve this is to **explore the topic from multiple points of view.** Otherwise you might be tempted to gather only information that supports your idea, without exploring the other side through the eyes of an imaginary opponent.

To explore multiple points of view about the topic, **use a wide variety of sources,** both from the internet and from periodicals, magazines, journals, newspapers.

Books may more rarely be used, as they take longer to absorb and editing useful information is more difficult. They also tend to be less recent, as it takes awhile to build a book and get it published, let alone get to your library.

Journalistic sources are more convenient, as they contain more condensed information, and it's easier to keep recency from being a problem. Scanning newspaper files can be time consuming, but on local topics not covered by national magazines they may be your best available source. Newspapers, for a fee, may also recopy recent articles for you.

Books in the sense of **reference sources** are useful: dictionaries, encyclopedias, and statistical abstracts. "The Statistical Abstracts of the United States," for instance, includes annual figures from the U.S. Government Printing Office, about everything from how much oil we imported to how much corn we grew. A "Who's Who" can be a way of finding the qualifications of experts you might quote.

If all of this is new to you, arrange a conversation with your local librarian, about what reference sources are available to you, including internet search services like Lexus/Nexus. Your instructor may include a library tour as an aspect of the course.

A word about the net. WWW could easily stand for "the wild, wild west." It's thriving, interesting, but largely unregulated, except to the degree that we regulate ourselves with the highest possible standards.

You can find excellent sources there, and exploring a topic search can either broaden or focus your brainstorming. Just remember anybody with the resources to put up a website can say just about anything they want. There are a lot of undocumented assertions out there, as well as many self-proclaimed experts. Apply the same tests of evidence here that you would for any source of evidence.

There should be some information about the source and the last date at which the website was updated on the cited page. Otherwise, you'd best find another source.

It is a good idea to reinforce your knowledge from the net with a variety of periodicals in your library. If you are unfamiliar with libraries and hard copy research, you may feel helpless in pursuing your study in the face of power outages. Computers are one source, but certainly not the only one.

Documentation

Whatever materials you use, it's important that you document them with a source citation. That is, your audience should know enough about where you got your material to replicate your research and examine the sources themselves. It's certainly not enough to report that you "got it in the library," or "a magazine," or "a book."

What information do you need to refer to in your texts? The minimum requirement, for source citation, both to be credible to your audience and fair to your opponents, would be:

> The source's name;
> His or her qualifications;
> The title of the publication;
> The date of publication cited.

This information is required to make inquiry into the quality of sources anyway, so you ought to have it. Consider it good practice for keeping records for your future IRS audits.

Proper documentation is a matter of ***following a process from the start.*** Develop a careful note-taking habit when you examine research materials. If you're going to copy information as you find it in the library, enter it directly on your laptop computer. If you don't have one, consider the use of index cards described below in the four step system.

The problem with ***handwriting evidence in a notebook*** as you find it, as students sometimes seem to do, is that it comes out on the page of your notebook in random order, the order by which you stumbled upon it. It seems like you're saving time at first. However, you then have to copy the information over.

You look at the stuff on page one. There's an item that goes with something on page four, but the rest of page four goes with something on page two, also page eight, and . . . Confusing. So, you decide to recopy all the stuff that goes together, maybe a page for each topic. It can be very time-consuming. You often have to type material again within topics to get it into some reasonable order for analysis.

Of course, you can recopy it once into the computer at home, rearrange and edit it there, building the speech a "brick" of information at a time. You can also, though, use ***a simple four step system*** that takes less total time than the notebook method.

1) It's worth the coins to xerox the original sources you intend to use. Look up your references, either in an Index to Periodicals which your librarian can show you, or on the library computer search system. Retrieve the articles. Skim them to see which are most useful. Xerox them. Two copies of each is useful. Simply print net materials. Take them home.

2) Read the materials more thoroughly. Pen in brackets around the best examples, numbers, and quotations, or highlight them with a yellow highlighter. Pen in a topic note in the margin. Apply tests of evidence to determine quality.

3) Either transpose the individual items onto your computer by topic or issue, or use some index cards. Cut each individual item of evidence out and glue stick it to an index card. This is where two copies come in handy, one to clip, one to keep. Rather than recopy the source information for every card, make a bibliography, number the sources, then write the source number on each card. Page numbers are useful, too. (This is only for those few who do not have a computer to use at home or at school.)

4) A computer makes it easy to arrange the information into sub-groups. Arrange the evidence into common themes. You can do the same thing with index cards. Just lay them out on a table in topical piles. You can or-

der and re-order them without rewriting. Analyze the sub-groups of evidence. Then brainstorm the propositions that best represent the truth about what you've found in particular groups of proof.

* * * * *

It's hard to be objective in this process. You'll keep wanting to edit the information in a way that's most favorable for your originally intended position. It's OK to edit for focus and brevity, but not to exclude qualifiers or what Toulmin called "rebuttals," significant exceptions and contradictions. Just try to let the evidence speak to you and inform you of the best approximate truths.

A student once told me that she wanted to write a speech against welfare fraud. I sent her to the library. Then the student came back and said, "I found some testimony, but only estimates for statistics." I sent her back again, and she returned a week later.

"The only example I can find is a woman who traded some of her food stamps for haircuts for her children. In fact, I'm finding a lot more information for the other side."

I smiled, shrugged my shoulders, and replied, "Those pesky facts. They just keep getting in the way of your ideas."

It's hard, once we've become invested in an opinion, to admit the possibility that we've been mistaken. Yet one's ability to be persuaded by new information is one sign of an intelligent and well-informed individual.

Evidence and Persuasion

So, all this research seems like a lot of trouble. Why do we bother? It's because its use has certain positive effects on our desire to convince others. According to the rhetorician John C. Reinhard in his review of fifty years of research on the effects of evidence, these are among the positive effects:[9]

1) Testimony seems to be consistently persuasive, as long as the source of the testimony is documented.

2) Factual information such as reports of events or examples seem to be persuasive, but more specific facts are more effective than general ones.

3) In spite of the almost reverent attitude many people have toward statistical evidence, such evidence is not as persuasive as other factual evidence. However, when powerful, involving and vivid examples are backed up by statistics that show the examples to be typical, the examples become more powerful.

4) Presenting audiences with evidence seems to "inoculate" or protect audiences against subsequent counter-persuasion.

5) Novel evidence is more persuasive than evidence the audience already knows.

6) Evidence is most effective with highly intelligent people who are concerned about getting the facts.

7) Evidence that reinforces the audience's beliefs is more persuasive than evidence that challenges it.

8) Good delivery enhances the effectiveness of evidence.

9) Evidence consistently increases speaker credibility.

10) A source's credibility has persuasive effects—that is, credible sources are more persuasive than less credible ones. This is one of the most consistent patterns identified by Reinhard.

Similar results were found by Rodney Reynolds and Michael Burgoon in 1983. They also mention the importance of source citation in persuasiveness. The clarity of evidence citations increases evaluations of the evidence and the advocate. That is, clear citation involves the audience more directly in the process of judgment.

The last two points by Reinhard emphasize the term "credibility," but what does that really mean?

Credibility

Some sources, speakers and writers, are more persuasive than others. We say that certain communicators have "charisma," some personal quality that makes us want to believe and follow. In rhetoric, we call that credibility, and we can identify some ***personal qualities*** that are usually associated with the term :[10]

> ***Attractiveness,*** in the sense of clothing, personality and personal features
> ***Believability,*** appearing to be sincere
> ***Competence,*** the ability to perform tasks well
> ***Consistency,*** some sense of integrity among the person's messages
> ***Dynamism,*** the ability to excite and activate
> ***Good Will,*** having a sense of what's best for the people and a wish to give it
> ***Honesty,*** which is not the same thing as the appearance of same
> ***Knowledge,*** both in the sense of study and experience
> ***Moral Character,*** however one may judge it
> ***Wisdom,*** which is the ability of someone to use knowledge well

This first item, ***attractiveness,*** may be somewhat irritating, but it cannot be denied as a persuasive factor. Many studies have demonstrated that the same text read by differently attractive people yields different results. Across the board, people judged to be more attractive are generally evaluated as more persuasive, as well.

The classic real world example is the presidential election between John F. Kennedy and Richard Nixon in 1960. Their televised debate was well spoken, respectful by current standards, and well informed. Yet there was a distinct difference in the way Kennedy, a handsome fellow, was perceived on camera. Nixon, who was a debater for Whittier College, was judged by many in the live setting to have won, but when it came time for his close-up, he was regarded less well by people watching at home. He had a heavy 5 o'clock shadow and was less easy with the camera than Kennedy. This debate changed the face of politics forever. From that time forward, image, advertising, and focus groups became key to electoral success.

Yet, even if you're no Sleeping Beauty or Prince Charming, you might at least be well-groomed and dressed appropriately when speaking or giving reports.

Let's look at some **examples of public figures,** seeing if we can discover the above qualities of good credibility. The first is a positive example:

> Though he is frail and bent by age, he sent a shudder through the dark heart of Big Tobacco the second he took the oath. Doll, an epidemiologist, spoke elegantly and with great modesty of the work for which he'd been knighted by the queen of England. Prodded by an attorney for a Newport Beach woman who is dying of lung cancer and has sued Philip Morris, he told a medical detective story that began in 1949. . . . Doll who had smoked for 20 years immediately quit and implored his wife to do the same. He also stepped up his research, and published a groundbreaking 1950 report contending that "smoking is a factor, and an important factor, in the production of lung cancer."[11]

This is a picture of a generally agreed credible witness. He has both a sympathetic image in his frailty, a contrast with his eloquence. He has **competence** as a scientist. He's consistent in that his quitting smoking matches his words. His message is one that reveals a concern for people, a sense of his **good will.** He has demonstrable **knowledge,** and his age confers a sense of **wisdom** upon him. He's an actual knight, for heaven's sake, jousting with the tobacco dragon. Their very fear of him enhances his credibility.

Consider an example in which our sense of credibility may be mixed:

> Radiologist examining mammogram X-rays gave false positives up to 15.9% of the time, with the youngest and most recently trained doctors having 2 to 4 times the false positive rate of older radiologists, a study finds.[12]

On one hand, we have an organization with a generally **spotless record,** very high credibility. Yet that very fact may make claims against them more surprising, as well as potentially more disturbing. When the entities that we rely on falter, it may contribute to feelings of insecurity. **Who can you trust when the trustworthy have issues of competence?** How would you like to be told you have cancer when you don't? Would you go back to that doctor?

It also should be said that the **method** used could be a contributing factor to error. There are further indications that **experience** is a factor in the false positives, since younger radiologists get two to four times more false positives than older, more experienced radiologists.

> Last week cardiologists at a prominent Arizona clinic began advising patients to try a new, untested dietary supplement that has never before been used to treat heart disease. It's not just any supplement, the clinic says: it's a proprietary formula designed by doctors. . . . But there's a catch. The Arizona Heart Institute has struck a deal with the supplement's maker, Vital Living, that gives the clinic a share of profits from sales of the supplement, as well as 1 million shares of stock options.[13]

For this example, there may not be any issue of competency, or experience, and since we know nothing about the product itself we can't say if it works or not. This, though, is a classic example of **conflict of interest,** or bias. The endorsing agency is making a profit from what it endorses, so we might think twice about both. There may even be some legal recourse, especially if the patient is harmed somehow. Reasonably, at least, we could **question their good will.**

This next example illustrates two issues of credibility:

> An internal police probe has concluded that a former officer, whose fatal shooting of an unarmed black man sparked three days of rioting last year (in Cincinnati), mishandled his revolver and gave conflicting statements to investigators. . . . According to the report, Roach told homicide investigators that he believed Thomas to be a threat. Three days later, Roach said the shooting was an accident.[14]

The officer apparently mishandled his weapon, which brings up concerns about **competence.** Also, it's difficult to believe the officer as he's told two conflicting stories about the incident, a failure in **consistency.**

Consider next how **moral character** can affect credibility:

> The United Nations Iraq weapons inspection team includes a 53-year-old Virginia man with no specialized science degree and a leadership role in sadomasochistic sex clubs. The U.N. acknowledged that it did not conduct a background check on Harvey John "Jack" McGeorge of Woodbridge, VA., who was in New York waiting to be sent to Iraq as a munitions analyst. . . . A U.N. spokesman said McGeorge was part of a group recommended by the State Department, which in turn said it was merely forwarding names for consideration.[15]

Clearly, we don't know "Jack." He certainly doesn't project the forthright image that such an important inspection team ought to possess. **Knowledge and experience** are also in question, since he has no particular citations or degrees as a munitions analyst. A final example, however, is less clear-cut:

> Few things define Southern California's Vietnamese-American community more than its passionate brand of anti-communism, on display in heated discussions along the sidewalk cafes of Little Saigon and in frequent demonstrations. That's what makes the case of Van Duc Ho different. His activities went beyond words to action, making him a folk hero to many in Little Saigon and a wanted terrorist in Vietnam. Vo . . is being held in a Los Angeles jail, accused by the U.S. Attorney's Office of trying to blow up the Vietnamese Embassy in Bangkok.[16]

It has to be acknowledged again, that ***credibility is a rhetorical process.*** Our individual senses of credibility may be in great conflict with each other. For the most volatile anti-communists, Van Duc Ho has heroic qualities. For more moderate Asian-Americans, he represents the lunatic fringe. Thus, while the qualities of credibility illustrated above are a beginning, the issue of ***"credible to whom"*** will often come up as a practical matter of persuasion.

Appeals and Evidence Selection

The above supporting materials are not the only way to convince an audience. There are also what we call appeals, ways of motivating an audience to feel a particular way about the subject matter. Sometimes, if our evidence search doesn't cover a vital topic, an appeal may be all you have to sway your public.

Aristotle, the fifth century Greek philosopher and father of study for both rhetoric and poetics, observed that there were three ways to appeal to an audience:

LOGOS, appealing to an audience's sense of logic and reason

PATHOS, appealing to an audience's sense of emotion, as in the case of the word "pathetic"

ETHOS, appealing to ethics, an audience's sense of right and wrong

These qualities may simply occur as a matter of ***persuasive language.*** In other words, appeals are often imbedded in claims and warrants, as well as in introductions, transitions, and conclusions.

As sensible people, we reject the illogical point made by my opponent.

Can't we feel some pity for these children abandoned by the system?

Come on, folks, we must know that this is just wrong on the face of it.

Yet the appeals may also be ***imbedded in evidence.*** While it's possible that a single piece of evidence might evoke all three qualities, here are some tips about evoking these qualities with the grounds that you choose.

For **Logos.** the most obvious choice would be to use statistics and figures. Logos is also available, however, in descriptions of scientific process, manufacturing or medical process, describing how something is discovered or made. As we know, though, statistics are stronger if accompanied by examples. Good organization is an aspect of logos.

If you're trying to inject a little **pathos,** consider using some examples of people affected by the issues, people we can relate to. As Aristotle said in **"The Poetics,"** a tract about Greek drama and how it exerts influence on an audience, "We feel pity and fear for one who is like ourselves." In other words, we relate to, we identify with people in stories. An example of somebody affected by the issue might be a good place to imbed pathos.

If you're looking for **ethos,** you might consider using testimony from people your audience is likely to find upright and credible. Boost your credibility by associating yourself with the best and the brightest. That's important, because there are really two senses of the word "ethos": appealing in an argument to an audience sense of right and wrong, but there's also what Aristotle called **"ethos of the person."** In more modern terms, this refers to what we call credibility.

It's wise to **balance** your evidence and your use of appeals, perhaps as described above. If you balance your types of evidence, your appeals may be more likely to balance as well. You wouldn't want a text that was all examples, as your audience would have no sense if these moving stories were really typical, or an exception to the rules. If we pair examples with statistics, though, we'll have a good sense of perspective on the issue at hand.

Think of evidence selection like directing a movie. What would you think of a film with nothing but close-ups? That's what a speech with all examples would be like. You'd have no sense of place or the social dynamics behind the characters. Adding statistics would be like pulling back for a wide shot, a look at the big picture.

Imagine a speech of all statistics, nothing but wide shots, with no close-ups, no sense of individuality among the characters.

Sometimes, when statistics are not available for the point, you can use expert testimony to back up your examples with a sense of perspective. In sum, try for complementary pairs of evidence. If you don't have examples, put some personal testimony with statistics for a similar 1-2 combination punch. Yes. That's right. You can also think of evidence selection like combination punching.

Though this is no guarantee, there is a good chance of imbedding ethos in quotations, pathos in examples, and logos in figures and statistics.

Think of it loosely as selecting something for the mind, something for the heart, and something for the spirit, respectively, with the use of logos, pathos, and ethos.

* * * * *

Go directly to the library and begin research NOW. Do not pass "go," do not collect $200. Just go! If possible, start research on all three of the topics you've chosen for your fact, value and policy texts. Focus on your library time early in the process, so you can read the material through carefully. You should at least have a clear sense of what your proposition for your fact speech is, by this time. If you do not, get one today.

By next class, you should have samples of the various types of evidence, all relevant to your proposition of fact.

Vocabulary

Appeals: Ethos, Pathos, Logos
Artifacts
Assertions
Attractiveness
Believability
Citation
Claim/Warrant/Grounds
Competence
Consistency
Credibility
Dynamism

Examples
Expert Testimony
Figures & Statistics
Firsthand Observation
Good Will
Honesty
Inference
Knowledge
Moral Character
Multiple Viewpoints
Qualifications
Quantify

Recency
Relevancy
Representative
Rhetoric
Sample
Spin
Source Based Evidence
Sufficiency`
Variety of Sources
Verifiability

Exercises: Go to Interactive Disc to Complete

1) Look at the following paragraphs and determine what type of evidence each is:

   A) "This gay wedding craze is starting to spread around the country. Today a guy in Utah married five guys (Jay Leno, Tonight Show)." "Leno's joke isn't too far off the mark," says Stanley Kurtz, a scholar at the Hoover Institute, a conservative think tank at Stanford University.

   B) There are now two partial mine bans: the Ottawa Convention, which permits only anti-vehicle mines, and the new U.S. policy that permits only self-destructing mines. Three months later, the U.S. mines would be perfectly safe. But after three months, three years, or three decades, the Ottawa-compliant field will be as dangerous as the day it was laid (LA Times, March 6, 2004).

   C) Doctors, already are required to register to prescribe Accutane, and more than 12,000 dermatologists have done so, according to Hoffman-La Rouche (LA Times, March 8, 2004).

D) A major problem Californians must now face is that Shell recently announced it would close its Bakersfield refinery this year. The Bakersfield plant provides 2% of California's total gasoline supply and 6% of its diesel needs (LA Times, March 11, 2004).

2) Look over these paragraphs and consider which personal qualities of credibility may be at issue in each:

A) After agreeing last week to allow U.S. weapons inspectors unconditional access, Iraq reversed course Saturday and said it would not abide by any new U.N. resolution allowing monitors entry to key presidential compounds ("Iraq Excludes Palaces from Inspection Sites," LA Times, Sept. 22, 2002).

B) An independent special prosecutor is imperative to investigate possible criminal violations by Enron Corp., its officers and its auditor, Anderson Co. Almost every day reveals new ties between the Bush administration and the failed energy company. At the end of last week it was revealed that Vice President Dick Cheney attempted to assist Enron in obtaining a contract to construct a power plant in India. Cheney, who worked in the energy industry before his election, has refused to answer questions about his meetings with Enron officials. The Bush administration has strong ties to Enron. Bush's presidential election bid received $113,800 from Enron and its chairman, Kenneth Lay. Bush received another $300,000 for his inaugural committee. In fact, Attorney General John Ashcroft excused himself from the Enron investigation because of the campaign contributions he received from the company (LA Times, January 11, 2002).

C) Besides denigrating Arabs, Jewish Defense League leader Earl Krugel made racists remarks about African Americans during secretly recorded conversations with an FBI informant, according to defense documents filed in connection with his upcoming bombing conspiracy trial. "The racist expressions used by Mr. Krugel are irrelevant to the bar," defense attorney Mark Werksman declared in his court papers, "And even if somehow relevant, the introduction of such could prejudice the jury, or mislead or confuse them into forming a negative impression of Mr. Krugel and possibly convict him out of distaste for his language, rather than because he is guilty of the offenses charged" ('Defense Seeks to Purge Racists Remarks on JDL Tape,' LA Times, Sept. 20, 2002).

3) Gather each of the types of evidence, both of fact and of opinion. Apply the tests of evidence to the various quotations, examples and statistics.

4) Make three arguments of minimum form, using a claim and some grounds to support it. Then bring your arguments to class and share them with each other. You may find that others may observe error that you yourself have missed.

Sources

1) Perelman, Chaim, and L. Olbrechts-Tyteca (1969). The New Rhetoric. Notre Dame, IN: Univ. of Notre Dame.

   Willebrand, Mary Louise, and Richard D. Rieke. "Strategies of Reasoning In Spontaneous Discourse." (1991) Communication Yearbook. Ed. James A. Anderson. Newbury Park, CA: Sage, pp. 414–440.

2) Solmsen, F. (1954). "The Rhetoric and Poetics of Aristotle." New York: Random House.

3) Fisher, W.R. (1984). "Narration as a Human Communication Paradigm: The Case of Moral Argument." Communication Monographs, 51, pp. 1–22.

   McDonald, K. & J.W. Jarman (1998). "Getting the Story Right: The Role of Narrative Academic Debate." Rostrum, 72.

4) Brownlee, Don (1982). "The Consequences of Quantification." CEDA Yearbook 3, pp. 29–31.

   Spiker, Barry K., Tom D. Daniels, and Lawrence Bernabo (1982). "The Quantitative Quandary in Forensics: The Uses and Abuses of Statistical Evidence." Argumentation and Advocacy 19, pp. 87–96.

   Dahnke, G.L., and G.W. Clatterbuck (1990) Human Communication: Theory and Research. Belmont, CA: Wadsworth.

   Capaldi, Nicholas (1975). The Art of Deception. Buffalo, NY: Prometheus Books.

6) LA Times, "Monitoring of Coast Waters Is Questioned," Aug. 15, 2002.

7) LA Times, "Motor Cars Rated 'Green' In Survey," Feb. 20, 2003.

8) The Associated Press, "Cold Fusion Seen in Lab at University," The Register Guard, 4, April 1990.

9) Reinhard, John C. (1988). "The Empirical Study of the Persuasive Effects of Evidence: The Status After Fifty Years of Research." Human Communication Research, 15, pp. 3–59.

   Reynolds, R. & M. Burgoon (1983). "Belief Processing, Reasoning & Evidence." Communication Yearbook, 7, pp. 83–104.

10) Baudhin, S., & M. Davis (1972), "Scales for the Measurement of Ethos: Another Attempt." Speech Monographs, 39, pp. 296–301.

11) LA Times, "Big Tobacco Curses the Day Expert Witness Took the Oath," August 25, 2002.

12)   LA Times, "Study Finds Misreading in Breast X-Rays," Sept. 18, 2002.

13)   LA Times, "A Supplemental Pitch," August 26, 2002.

14)   LA Times, "Internal Probe Faults Cincinnati Policeman in Shooting," March 20, 2002.

15)   LA Times, "Inspectors Include Man With Leadership Role in Sex Fetish Clubs," November 28, 2002.

16)   LA Times, "On Man's War Against Vietnam," Sept. 23, 2002.

IV
Ways That We Reason and Ways That We Fail

We've discussed propositions, which correlate to Toulmin's "claims," and we've looked at evidence, which relates to Toulmin's "grounds." What about Toulmin's "warrants?" How do we understand and manage the patterns of thinking that relate claim to grounds?

There are many kinds of human thinking—creative thinking, intuitive thinking, physical or kinetic intelligence, even emotional intelligence, the ability to adapt to stress and conflict, most recently prominent in personality testing among businesses. Some school systems are touting an "information competency" requirement, the ability to be facile with computers and the Net.

However, there are a finite number of primarily inductive reasoning patterns that we use in critical thinking.[1] *Inductive* patterns work from specific information and work toward a general understanding. *Deductive* patterns apply known or accepted generalizations as a standard for analyzing particular cases. Reasoning by definition is the only deductive pattern here. We'll call these patterns of reason, for the sake of memory and western movie fans, *"The Magnificent Seven"*:

> Parallel Reasoning
> Generalization
> Reasoning by Definition
> Reasoning from Sign
> Reasoning from Cause to Effect
> Reasoning from Dilemma
> Reasoning by Authority

Often texts like this separate discussion of reasoning from *fallacies,* errors in reason, language, and appeals. Our approach will be to relate the two. There are many more kinds of errors than patterns of reason. (Isn't that the way of things, more ways to do it wrong than to do it well?) We will cover other fallacies in a later chapter, after the you have a handle on these.

Parallel Reasoning (Analogy)

There are several ways to look at this subject, but let's start with what may be the simplest pattern of reasoning to understand, parallel reason, more commonly known as analogy. It may even be our most primary form of reason, comparing like and unlike things. You've practiced it since early grade school, playing "which of these does not belong?" You remember . . . a teapot, a frying pan, and an aardvark?

Parallel reasoning and analogy are like fraternal twins. The action of mind is essentially the same:

$$A = B$$

They both are a matter of comparing things and drawing conclusions from similarities. The difference is how literal the comparisons are.

Analogy is a poetic comparison used to describe something in an interesting way. One feminist graffiti is an example:

> "A woman without a man is like a fish without a bicycle."

A woman is not like a fish in any literal sense, and a man is not much like a bicycle. The point of the comparison is to make a claim in a colorful way: "Women don't need men." These kinds of comparisons may be expressive aspects of style. The literary concepts of metaphor and symbol evolve from analogy, along with some of our most basic tribal rights. Shamanism, for instance, is essentially an act of analogy by which a tribe's spiritual leaders attract hunted animals by imitating them.

While analogies are largely expressive, they are not without rhetorical impact. In a recent quip by a pundit, an analogy was used to make his message as succinctly as possible: The elephant and the donkey are outdated symbols for our political parties. They should be replaced with pit bulls and rabbits.

Another person made this more literal comparison: A Star of David painted on a Palestinian home is like swastikas on a temple back in the U.S.

Parallel reasoning uses literal comparisons, although the essential mental action is still to compare and contrast. For instance, if we were to consider the issue of sending American troops into a foreign conflict, you might see articles asking, "Is this another Gulf War?" "Is this another Balkan episode, or another Somalia?" Most recently, it's been asked, "Is this another Vietnam?" That is, is Iraq a war that will go on and on without success, draining American resources and damaging our international support?

We work this with a ***simple arithmetic formula:*** If A = B, then we can expect similar results in each case.

If we made certain mistakes in a similar war in earlier instances, we can avoid the mistakes with retrospective reasoning. Such reasoning is ***predictive.*** We could not speculate about propositions of fact regarding the future without such reasoning. This is the essence of the old phrase, "He who does not know history is condemned to repeat it."

The language by which we identify such reasoning in everyday discourse includes:

>   At least two things are being compared.

A word or phrase making the comparison clear: "like, as, is similar, compare, resembles, are alike, compared to, by contrast," are all words and phrases that might signal the use of parallel reason.

In a court of law, use of the word "precedent" indicates that the lawyer will refer to another earlier case like the present one to draw conclusions about how the judge should rule now.

In policy discussion, the word "model" may indicate taking what someone has done effectively in a similar situation and applying to the present circumstance.

Let's take a look at some ***examples*** of parallel reason and try to build Toulmin style arguments from them. Also, take note of the language that delivers the comparison:

> Why don't we prosecute white-collar crimes, one economist asks. Ken Lay, William Grasso, Enron and other scandals with corrupt corporations cost tax payers and investors billions, when all the bank robberies and armored car robberies in the country added up to $78 million in 2000, according to the FBI? We jailed a woman who stole $153 worth of videos but not these overly wealthy corporate leaders.[2]

If that is your ***grounds,*** what might your ***warrant*** be? What would you infer from the comparison in the evidence?

The warrant might be: "Evidence compares more favorable treatment of white collar crime against blue collar crime, so it would seem that we have an inconsistent standard for prosecution, one that favors 'business class.'"

In other words, we do it to the poor who steal less, so we should do it to the rich who steal more.

Then, how might one focus this analysis of the warrant in ***a claim. . .?***

It might be a fact claim: "White collar criminals are prosecuted less than blue collar criminals."

It might be a value observation: "We have an unfair standard for criminal prosecution in the U.S.A."

It might also be a proposition of policy: "We should prosecute white collar crimes more rigorously."

Now, read Toulmin's three parts in reverse, and we've invented an argument:

> ***Claim: We have an unfair standard for criminal prosecution.***
>
> ***Warrant: Evidence compares more favorable treatment of white collar crime than blue collar crime. So, it would seem that we***

> ***have an inconsistent standard for prosecution, one that favors 'business class.'***
>
> ***Grounds: As the LA Times noted . . . etc.***

Let's try another regarding fuel standards for the SUV. These are from Carl Zichella, western regional director of Sierra Club:

> ***Grounds:*** The auto industry went crazy when Governor Gray Davis signed California's landmark global warming control bill. Litigation to overturn the new law, which restricts automobile emissions of carbon dioxide and other greenhouse gases, was threatened before the ink on his signature was dry. This is not a new or unexpected response. When government requires new safety or efficiency standards, car manufacturers claim that this will lead to financial ruin, thousands of jobs will disappear and consumer choice will suffer. That industry has been wrong every time, and it's wrong again. Car makers, instead of spending money suing to overturn this law, should simply comply with it. No new or expensive technology is required.[3]
>
> ***Warrant:*** In spite of the fact that no new technology is required to improve emission of greenhouse gases, the auto industry is incorrectly preaching doom and gloom for itself, as it has in the past to avoid similar appropriate laws. They didn't hurt then, they won't hurt now (parallel reasoning). In fact, they may be spending more money in suits than they might in making the changes.

Notice, it's not atypical that the warrant may repeat some of the language from the evidence itself: Here's the point I'm making, and here's someone of authority also making it. That's not to say that the evidence will always offer the pattern of reason for your warrant so clearly. Often you have to make your own inferences to conclusion from less conspicuous evidence. However, we're lucky here.

> ***Claim:*** The auto industry is trying to rationalize their way out of tighter greenhouse gas regulation, which could and should occur.

Remember that we would write and speak the argument to others in reverse order, as a matter of previewing our thinking for easier "digestion" of grounds. The above order, however, represents how arguments are often explored and built. You look at a piece of evidence, and you reason "from the grounds up" to a conclusion, or claim.

Fallacy: False Analogy

There is also a wrong way to work this pattern of reasoning. It's a fallacy, an error in reasoning, called false analogy. This is making comparisons among things that are not really alike. Here's an example:

During a conversation about imprisoning suspected Al Queda members, one American pilot who fought Japanese in WWII argued that we should treat them the same as an enemy on the battlefield. Actually, he was a little more colorful than that. He said that he'd be happy to do the job himself. His comment has been approximated to protect the guilty:

> Having had the privilege of being the executioner of national enemies on other occasions, I would like to offer my services to dispose of Al Queda terrorists currently being held in jail. Over Iwo Jima, when that Japanese zero came after me, I didn't worry about reading him his rights or asking his intentions. I just blasted him right out of the sky and sent him to hell. Why do we delay? Why are we paying to keep these monsters alive in prison, let alone considering the costs of trial? Among them is this guy Maussaoui, however the hell you say that. He would have joined on the flights on 9/11 if he had not been arrested. He wouldn't offer mercy to the three thousand Americans who died on that day. Like the Japanese zeros, he chose to involve himself in an act of war and he deserves to be shot like any other enemy on the battlefield.

He's certainly a passionate American, and he's angry with some just cause, but are there differences between the two conflicts which might make comparison a sketchy thing to do? Consider it among yourselves and answer.

Perspective: There are ways in which the two events are different. World War II was a war declared by Congress, while this war is an executive action. The term "war on terror" is a rhetorical encouragement, like the "war on drugs." It is not the same as a Congressionally declared war. It's also worth noting that a Japanese pilot, firing in the heat of battle and creating an imminent threat, is not the same as someone who most likely conspired in 9/11, yet is sitting unarmed in a cell.

Now, it has to be acknowledged that fallacies are somewhat subjective. Even those who study them regularly are influenced by perspective. Some people with a lot of anger about 9/11 might say, "What's wrong with that analogy?" So, let's flip perspective with this example.

Let's try building another argument, regarding how America jailed Japanese-American citizens in prison camps during WWII. Again, we'll start in reverse order from that in which we might speak:

> **Grounds:** In the word of one protester, "The American public should know the identities of those imprisoned for the 9/11 attacks. We should protest in favor of due process for them, especially those who are U.S. citizens. It's against their constitutional rights to subject them to detention without it. The Manzanar exhibit at the Japanese-American national museum drives the point home. I watched survivors of the WWII detention camp there, and I bemoaned the fact that those violations of human

rights caused by racial profiling that led to that camp were being used today against loyal Arab-Americans. I fear that we mock the very human rights that are the basis of the democracy we defend and export."

Warrant: We've established prison camps for supposed terrorists that are very like camps in which we imprisoned Japanese-American citizens, resurrecting old racial profiling techniques in trying to fight terrorism. We apologized for what we did to Japanese-Americans, therefore, we should also apologize to Arab-Americans falsely detained.

Claim: We should apologize to falsely imprisoned Arab-Americans.

Discuss this analogy from your different points of view. Does this comparison seem apt? Are you inclined to think the comparison fair, or not? Discuss this with your instructor in class.

Someone of more liberal social opinions may find the first comparison inappropriate, but the second one sensible. A more conservative person may look at it from the opposite point of view. Both, however, would have made comparisons of the present with WWII. Might one be contradicting oneself to approve of one comparison, yet not the other?

It's not that superficial, or shouldn't be. The key issue to be decided is if the specific comparison is appropriate. The first analogy doesn't just compare the two wars, but a dogfight in a battle with the execution of a prisoner. The second analogy, though, compares the imprisonment of U.S. citizens in each war based largely upon racial profiling. Hence, the second could more specifically be argued as an apt comparison.

Generalization

When we play "compare and contrast" and make analogies, we're actually beginning to create categories of living things, ideas, and people.

Watch a child learn to talk. It starts with simple categorization. It learns that there are lots of things to label. After it sees something enough times it grasps comparisons. We grow to recognize cats as different than dogs. Toys gradually get classified as something different than food . . . although the two seem interchangeable for a time in the average child's mouth.

Although it is not as simple as parallel reasoning, generalization has a natural relationship with it. Generalization may, in fact, grow from parallel reasoning. Generalization, it might even be said, is an extended case of analogy. It seeks descriptive classifications.

The mental action involves classification and description. Basically, we gather sufficient information about enough individual cases to classify like items into a group, a class. We then attach characteristics to that class, based on our observations of the group:

$$A1 + A2 + A3, \text{ etc.} = \text{Class A}$$

The ***language of generalization*** includes: "After careful study we've concluded, it is generally so, usually so, normally so, customary, even universally so," are all word choices that may indicate a generalization in everyday writing and speaking. It is usually a declaration in a direct and simple manner about what can be expected of a particular group of people, places, and things.

You rent a place where there's a hummingbird feeder in the yard. You fill it and begin to observe the birds. You see that two are alike. You'll discover that they are called martins. Then you notice many martins, which you can classify as a group by their shiny black feathers and their bright yellow eyes, as well as their approximate size. Their forms are the same, and they move in a similar manner. You've generalized them into a class of birds.

As we see more and more martins over a period of time, we can finally generalize that the male differs from the female. You'll notice that the females are a grayer color, and you'll make exceptions to the generalization. Eventually, you notice other birds, and the process of dividing birds into various classes continues.

This might be called ***"Adam and Eve" thinking,*** because of the Biblical story about naming the creatures of Earth. They might have begun with parallel recognition that these things with feathers look alike, but those hairy things are different and look like each other. They could then observe and describe behaviors, further clarifying the various groups.

In one play, the story includes Adam's very literal perspective in naming the animals, "Those are swimmers, those are flyers, and those are crawlers." Eve corrects him, "No, silly. Those are fish, those are birds, and those are animals."

Then, once they had a sense of what went with what, they could watch the characteristics and behavior of each group and refine their classifications with descriptions of what is typical in each group.

What do we know about mammals, as a group?

> That they have fur.
> That they breathe air.
> That they're warm-blooded.
> That they give live birth.

How did we come to know that? By first comparing and categorizing mammals as a group, then carefully observing many cases within each group (Figure 3):

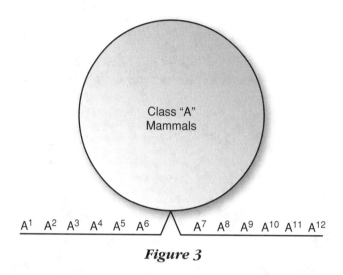

Class "A"
Mammals

A^1 A^2 A^3 A^4 A^5 A^6 A^7 A^8 A^9 A^{10} A^{11} A^{12}

Figure 3

This diagram shows many individual cases at the bottom, moving up into a unified general sense of the class in the circle above them. Circles called Venn Diagrams are sometimes used to illustrate classification. In this one, you could put all the generalizations you have about that class in the circle: furbearing, air-breathing, warm-blooded, live birth.

Generalizing from **studies with statistics** is typical. Envision, not just a dozen individual examples of creatures, but thousands, even millions.

Here's a good example of statistical generalization. Note, it includes the methodology of the study, as was recommended in the last chapter:

> For women aged 55 and older who were followed for eight to eleven years, routinely being screened for tumors reduced the risk of death from breast cancer by 55%, according to a new analysis reported in this week's edition of the international medical journal *The Lancet.* For women who were aged 45 to 54 at the beginning of the study, screening led to a 30% reduction in deaths, the researchers said.[4]

Notice that generalizations may often appear as graphs, pie graphs in particular, like this one entitled "The impacts of mammograms" (Figure 4):

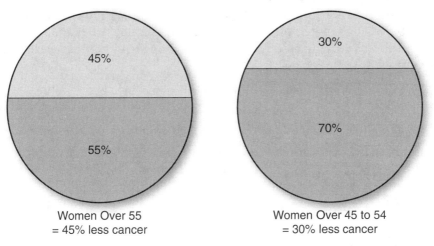

Figure 4

Let's take a real world quotation and see if we can further illustrate the typical mental action of generalization. After refusing for months to divulge its evidence against Iraq, the Bush Administration offered a list of newly declassified intelligence. Like a prosecutor trying to persuade a skeptical jury, Secretary of State Colin Powell offered fresh accusations:

- Baghdad has moved weapons, hidden documents, replaced computer hard drives and even razed buildings and removed topsoil to deceive UN weapons inspectors. In all, Iraq has cleared nearly 30 suspected sites of incriminating material since last fall.

- Iraq's illegal procurement network around the world continues to seek toxins used in biological weapons, precursor chemicals for nerve and blister agents, special tubes and magnets to enrich uranium, and other prohibited materials.

- Hussein's regime built specially designed trailer trucks and railroad cars as clandestine mobile laboratories to develop and produce such germ warfare agents as anthrax and botulinum toxin. In all Iraq has outfitted at least 18 large trucks as mobile production facilities.

- The Iraqi dictator has personally tried to prevent scientists from cooperating with UN inspectors. In December, he had scientists sign documents acknowledging that divulging sensitive information to inspectors is punishable by death. He also warned that any scientist who agreed to be interviewed outside Iraq, as the UN Security Council has demanded, would be treated like a spy.

- Baghdad harbors a terrorist network, including several Al Queda operatives who fled Afghanistan after the 9/11 terrorist attack. Chief among them is Abu Massab Zarqawi, an associate of Osama Bin Laden with expertise in chemical and biological weapons.

- Iraq performed gruesome germ warfare experiments on 1600 condemned prisoners in 1995. A witness saw prisoners tied down to beds while deadly experiments were performed on them.[5]

While this catalogue of specific examples may not reach statistical levels, stacking a lot of examples like these can be quite convincing to an audience. Thus, another clue to identifying generalizations may be a bulleted list like this. Examples like these were enough to justify a war on Iraq, in part because of the emotional tenor of the country after 9/11.

Only later was it discovered that some of these examples, for instance the special tubes to enrich uranium, or the moving anthrax labs, were not true. In fact, they may have been purposeful distortions by an Iraqi informant who wanted us to overthrow Hussein. Yet it was the evidence that was flawed, not the essential mental action.

Fallacy: Hasty Generalization

Hasty Generalization is probably the most commonly used and recognized fallacy. It is simply a case of too few cases counted toward the generalization made. We have an explosive situation with someone of another race or nation, and, because of the emotion involved, we may "jump to conclusions."

The language of hasty generalization may sometimes include statements like, "Well, I know it's true, because I knew this guy who. . . ." It's always a guy they knew, but it's just one guy, and he seldom gets identified.

What we may tend to do instead is base our generalizations on dramatic, difficult social events. My first encounter with black persons, where I lived in Inglewood, California, was to be beat up on my way home from kindergarten and to have my silly yellow raincoat ripped. It was traumatic, but I fortunately did not generalize my experience. I was exposed to many more positive experiences among blacks, and I was able to avoid the fear response that may come when we're inexperienced with another race.

* * * * *

In boxing, there's a concept called ***"combination punching."*** That means that, instead of simply swinging for a knockout punch with one, big roundhouse right, you use a variety of weapons—uppercuts, jabs, and body punches—to avoid hasty generalizations.

This relates to what we told you earlier: certain combinations of evidence are stronger than others. Consider a case example to make the point in terms of avoiding hasty generalization:

We sometimes overreact to a few emotional or traumatic situations and fix an attitude about some other group based on very few examples. We get frustrated with an older person driving, so we think to ourselves:

> "All old people should be forbidden to drive."

The sample is extremely small, the guy ahead of you on the freeway, so that does not necessarily generalize into a reliable blanket criticism.

However, **add statistics** to an example or two, and you have something more reliable than your subjective, personal reaction. One national sample by Auto Club reports that the elderly have surpassed teenagers as the age group with the most accidents.

Then, use examples. Add a face to the story to dramatize the point, something other than your personal experience, something verifiable in the press.

Recently, in Orange County, an elderly woman let her foot slip onto the gas pedal while stopped at a ferry to the Newport Peninsula. My wife and I happened to be kayaking by at the time when she hit several people and knocked a car into the bay. In Santa Monica, not too long later in the same year, an elderly gentleman plowed his car, without braking, into a couple of dozen people at an open market.

If we **describe the signs** of age and how they generally affect reflexes and accidents, we're closer still.

Still, we would not have supported the claim "all old people should be forbidden to drive." We may have started a case for the qualified position:

> "Elderly drivers require closer scrutiny and regulation."

Reasoning by Definition

The natural counterpart to the inductive process of generalization is the deductive process, often called reasoning by definition. Once we've generalized about a group, we've also defined it. "Mammals are that group of animals which are furbearing, breathe air, are warm-blooded and give live child birth."

Because of this handy catalogue of mammals, even very small children know animals as exotic as hippos and giraffes, two mammals that don't look remotely alike.

But how do we reason about things that are new to us, for instance, a new species not already in our handy catalogue?

We go to our biological checklist to see where this new species might fit. We use the general definitions established in various groups of animals and apply them to individual cases of things we can't identify.

If it has all the necessary characteristics—fur, air breathing, etc.—we would say that "by definition" it is a mammal.

Let's see, this new creature has fur. Check one. It is warm-blooded. Check two. But wait! It lays eggs! That's on other checklists, the one for fowl, for fish, and reptiles, too. What do we call this thing?

You may already know that this is an actual creature. It's called a platypus, and it's a partial exception to the rule of mammals.

We would classify it as a mammal, because most of its features are mammalian. We would note the exception visually in a Venn diagram, in which "M" stands for mammals, and "P" stands for platypus. It has features both inside and outside of the class of mammals (Figure 5):

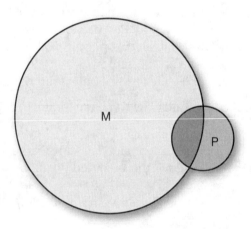

Figure 5

Venn diagrams, usually used in algebra and syllogistic logic, can help us visualize the nature of the situation. This one also reminds us to watch our qualifiers carefully in our claims. It would not be technically correct to say "All mammals give live birth," as we've found at least one exception. We might modify this claim to, "With small exception, mammals give live birth."

Here's another Venn diagram to illustrate the essential ***mental action*** of definition. If it has the characteristics of the class, it is a member of the class. By definition, we would say, this can be classified with the group (Figure 6):

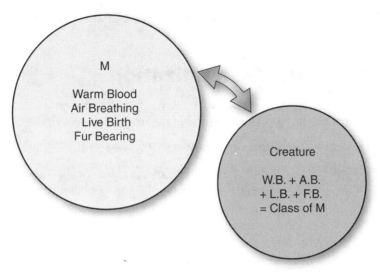

Figure 6

We could call this form of reason ***"Sherlock Holmes" thinking.*** Holmes was the master of deductive reasoning. He looks at a crime scene beneath the window of a murder victim, observes some footprints, picks up a cigar butt, then declares:

> "It was a tall man, injured, perhaps during the recent war, and he just arrived from India."

> "Good grief," says Dr Watson, "However did you know that, Holmes."

> "Elementary, my dear Watson," Holmes would say, then explain.

The footprints, he reasons, were from military boots, as he recognized the sole print from his studies of footwear. Also, the indentations were uneven, indicating a limp. He knew from its smell that the cigar tobacco came from only one place, India.

Holmes's great gift was knowledge. He knew about many, many classes of objects and actions relevant to crime. Thus, he could deduce from his knowledge of groups to his conclusions about individual clues.

Think of your key areas of knowledge, the subjects you know about, then consider the seemingly intuitive leaps you make. If you know about horses, then you can glance up without really thinking and say, "Oh, yes, that's an appaloosa." You learned a long time ago that an appaloosa is not an Arabian and is not a quarter horse. Perhaps you spot the larger head as a key element, along with the spots, typical characteristics of an appaloosa.

If sports are your interest, you know how a basketball differs from a soccer ball from a volleyball, even though they are all round and of roughly similar size. At least, we hope that you soccer players don't run onto the basketball court and kick the wrong ball.

Fallacy: Sweeping Generalization

This is the deductive counterpart to hasty generalization. It applies a generalization overmuch to an individual within the group, who may have exceptional features.

Think about the earliest men and how they might have reasoned:

> "Og" is a typical Neanderthal man. He comes out of his cave, sees his neighbor "Ooga," and waves to him. Suddenly, Ooga hollers out in pain. Og runs over to check on his friend and finds Ooga quivering, then grimacing in death. Og sees a long squiggly creature near Ooga, what we would know as a snake, baring its fangs. Og, a direct type, takes a rock and flattens the snake into a belt. He later crushes every snake that he sees, creating great fear in the land with his tales of deadly, squiggly beasts.

What Og, the overenthusiastic naturalist, lacked was a reasonable sample from the group examined. He committed both a hasty generalization, that all snakes are deadly, then a sweeping generalization that lead to his murder of all snakes. It is not unusual that a hasty generalization may lead to a sweeping one, but they are not the same thing.

Are all snakes poisonous? Of course not, and even snakes that are poisonous break down into two distinct subgroups, "krates" including cobras, and "vipers" including rattle snakes. As we know, some snakes are not poisonous and, in fact, contain rodent populations. Yet Og is out decimating king snakes and other helpful species, reasoning that all snakes are the same.

We call that sweeping generalization, applying overmuch something that may be partially true, or true in some cases, as if it were always true.

The mental action of sweeping generalization is the error of not recognizing, or oversimplifying individual differences in a group.

For instance, we might believe that Asian-Americans are generally good students, and statistics would support that, but would we then assume that every Asian-America is good in school?

You might believe that people from Hawaii are generally peaceful, and you may have evidence in the fact that Hawaii posts the highest age longevity of any state. Would you then be astonished to meet a bad-tempered guy from Hawaii, or one who died young, for that matter?

You might think that blacks are good runners, and we could find support in the history of successful Kenyan runners who dominate world marathon competitions. Yet would we then encounter a single black man and say justifiably, "Oh, you're black, so you must be a good runner?" Hardly.

As for **the language,** the words "always" and "never" are pretty good companions to this fallacy and should be watched carefully.

In a real world example, this country has had a problem with surging anti-Arab bigotry in the wake of 9/11. Of course, everybody knows that anyone wearing a burnoose or a veil is a terrorist, right? That's simply terrible cultural ignorance. Beyond that, we've even had an instance of someone being killed for wearing a turban. Some people can't even distinguish among the various kinds of Asian clothes.

We had a local city council meeting that offended Mexican-Americans in the area. One councilman voted against adding some lawn area at the edge of the beach, as he thought it would bring Mexicans with blankets who would stay all day.[6] Boy, you know those Mexicans! They see a lawn, they bring a blanket and move in! Quite the politician, eh?

The acts and words described here are fueled by sweeping generalizations about other people. In fact, it's not too daring to say that sweeping generalizations and hasty generalizations are at the very root of racist thinking.

Reasoning by Sign

Signs are a matter of recognizing how objects or traces of action are associated with related events. I sometimes call it **"almanac reasoning,"** as an almanac is full of such natural portents about how phases of the moon may indicate when to plant crops. One could argue that it's just as simple as parallel reasoning, although it does require following the sequence of things, not just a comparison of two objects or events.

Think of **"Ground Hog Day."** In snowy areas, people wait for the ground hog to stick its head out of its hole. The myth goes that, if the ground hog peeks out and sees his shadow and ducks back into its hole, it's still too cold to plant.

This seems a little hokey, yet farmers have raised successful crops for many years, based on careful observation of natural phenomenon by sign, well before there were weather channels and weather men named "Johnny Sunshine," or the like.

When we see apples fall, we take that as a sign the fruit is ripe. Sir Isaac Newton saw a falling apple and realized that it meant more than a sign of ripe fruit. He reasoned beyond sign that there was something that caused the apple fall, and he inferred the existence of gravity as such a cause. History doesn't tell us whether he bothered to eat the apple.

When we see clouds in the sky, we wonder if it's a sign of rain, as the one tends to go along with the other. Older people sometimes have "geezer radar." When their joints ache, it's sometimes a sign of rain, as increasing moisture in the air affects them.

The recent movie "XXX" was employed as a sign in the *Los Angeles Times,* August 22, 2002. They reasoned that the popularity of the hero, played by Vin Diesel as a kind of underground, American James Bond, was a sign that young people were in a patriotic mood the year after 9/11.

"Where there's smoke, there's fire," is an example of sign. It's usually used to suggest that two people are striking off romantic sparks in public. More literally, if you were a backpacker looking for a companion who had gone ahead, and you saw a column of smoke, you might then infer that there's a fire ahead, hopefully warming a companion you seek.

The formula for **mental action** is "A tends to go along with B," or (Figure 7):

Figure 7

The **language of sign** may be quite literal in everyday discourse: "is a sign of, signifies, indicates, marks, is an omen, a portent," may frequently suggest reasoning by sign. By the way, another word for "signs" would be "clues," as in signs of the crime. This victim suffered multiple wounds, possibly signifying an angry crime of passion.

In everyday discourse, you might see a list of **bulleted signs,** like this one about the national housing crisis for middle-income families:

- The number of middle-income families spending more than half of their income on housing increased by 74% between 1997 and 1999. More than 14 million Americans are now forced to spend more than half their income on housing.

- In no state today does a full-time minimum-wage job enable most families to pay fair market rent for a moderate two-bedroom apartment. Congress would have to double today's minimum wage in order to enable families leaving the welfare rolls to afford a two-bedroom apartment.

- Janitors are able to afford rent on a one-bedroom apartment in only 6 of the 60 largest housing markets in the country. Retail salespeople are able to afford rent in only three of these markets.

- Teachers and police officers cannot afford to buy a median-priced home in most major housing markets.

- According to a recent poll, 41% of Americans believe that the lack of affordable homes is a very big or fairly big problem, slightly more than the 39% who express similar concerns about health-care costs.[7]

This is simply a list of signs leading to a **claim: "the housing market is outpacing the ability of middle class families to buy a home."**

When we see a headline like, "Economy Shows Signs of Hope," *Los Angeles Times,* August 27, 2001, we are hearing from people who know about such things, seeing events that are hopeful for the economy. There may be an increase in housing starts, a sign of confidence by lenders who provide the construction money.

We use the term "economic indicators." There may be high employment, stable interest rates, any number of things that, in and of themselves, can't cause an economy to recover, yet tend to go along with recovery.

This leads us to a key point about reasoning from sign; it isn't the same as reasoning from cause. One phenomenon may tend to appear at the same time as another, without either being the cause or the effect of that other.

Fallacy: False Sign

Human behavior is observable and, to a certain degree, predictable from sign. Yet there are at least two ways that this kind of reasoning goes wrong. **Superstition** is one.

People come to believe that breaking mirrors is unlucky, as is a black cat crossing your path. Some baseball players will refuse to change socks, or to shave during a playoff series. They fixate on what seems lucky as a way of coping with stress. All cultures have deep mythology that transcends reason.

Such errors have been seen early in American History. During the Salem witch trials, a physical anomaly like a third nipple was sometimes seen as a sign that one is a witch and might put you on a trial for your life. Suspected witches were tied to dunking chairs, chairs at the end of a pole on a fulcrum, by which they were dunked into the river. If one drowned, it would be accepted as a sign of guilt.

A local event in my town suggests the potential danger of **False Signs.** Clues in a crime are signs, but clues can be misread.

A middle-aged man was roller-blading near the Upper Newport Bay on a road used by joggers, bikers, and skaters. He was found on the road knocked near lifeless with severe injuries to his eye and head. Splattered about him was paint from a paintball gun.

People thought he'd been hit in the eye with a paint ball, fallen and cracked his head. It was even implied in letters to the editor that paintball shooters were lurking in the bushes of the bay firing at unsuspecting skaters.

Police cited witnesses who reported that three "youthful males" were seen in the area with paintball guns. This was initially taken as evidence that paintball shooters had caused the fall, a serious matter since the man later died.[8]

However, an autopsy found that the eye injury was the result of the fall itself. The impact of falling backwards on his head caused his eye to leave its socket and be damaged. Local papers had to retract the incendiary headline.

Consider the practical impact of this: innocent youths might have been arrested and held responsible for a death, had the scientific evidence of the autopsy not corrected a superficial reading of signs. A general distaste for paintballs might ensue. Perhaps even legal restrictions would become an issue.

Cause to Effect

The mental action is A leads to B (Figure 8):

Figure 8

For example, discussion of the economy often involves reasoning by cause, even reasoning about what present events might cause later.

> A newly projected four-year shortfall of $452 billion is ***linked*** to a sharp drop in revenue. Red ink ***could effect*** fall elections. Congressional budget experts warned Tuesday that the government's fiscal outlook is deteriorating.[9]

This relates the problem to a "sharp drop in revenue." Debate continues about what lowered revenue. Some argue that tax cuts caused it. Others differ:

> The late lamented boom left a legacy of business overinvestment and debt-financed over-consumption that are now depressing new spending, which after all is the propellant of production, jobs and income. Last week's attacks compound these pressures by damaging some industries (airline, tourism), and creating new uncertainties.[10]

The language in everyday argument is easily observable: "causes, leads to, produces, activates, provokes, generates, brings about, results in" are active verbs suggesting a relationship between cause and effect. The ***"causal link"*** is the factor that establishes the connection.

For instance, complaints about Ephedra inspired studies. One was reported under the headline, "No Link to Improved Performance, but a Clear Link to Effects on the Body." The two uses of the word "link" explains that Ephedra's claims for athletic prowess are false, but that other dangerous effects are linked.[11]

The word "linked" may also, in other contexts indicate sign, rather than cause. We'll explain further below under fallacy of correlation vs. causation. Phrases like, "is a result of, as a result, was brought about by," are passive versions of the language of cause.

Reasoning from cause to effect is perhaps the most challenging, yet useful of tasks in argumentation. While the burden of proof may be weighty, it is pretty much impossible to solve social problems without causal reasoning.

Let's look at a few real world illustrations of cause to effect reasoning, to point out some of the challenges that may be typical. Sometimes sorting cause out is the source of great social conflict and uncertainty:

> In a 1999 study by the National Cancer Institute, breast cancer death rates in Marin were among the highest 10% of counties in the nation. . . . Those figures are not necessarily a surprise. Breast cancer rates rise with age, and Marin County's residents are substantially older than average. Rates are also higher among women who never had children or who had their children late in life—characteristics often found in women living in this collection of affluent suburbs. But for many women, those statistical explanations for the disease do not suffice. . . "We've got to take a closer look at the environment. . . . For all those scientists who have written off the idea of a cancer cluster, I say, you go tell that to a community where six women in a three block area have come down with the disease".[12]

So, the **mental action** in difficult social, medical, and technological issues is not only (Figure 9):

A ⟹ B

Figure 9

More often, it's **multiple causation,** and we have to sort through the various causes to see which is most influential and what we can practically do about each (Figure 10):

A & B & C ⟹ D

Figure 10

It's possible, though, that the reverse can occur, that a single cause can lead to many effects . . . not all of them good:

> The powerful drug cocktails that have enabled AIDS patients to live longer, healthier lives are now suspected of causing heart disease in some of the very people they've saved. . . . Researchers are struggling to determine whether the cardiac complications are a consequence of the medication, the inflammation caused by chronic HIV, or some combination of the two.[13]

Remember Murphy's 13th Law? Every solution breeds new problems.

In any case, the researchers are practicing good reasoning by cause, not because it's certain, but because it admits its own limits. They know what their future burden of proof will be.

Fallacies of Cause

There are four common ways that we error in the manufacture of causal reasoning.

Oversimplification

This is simply a matter of overlooking multiple causes for something, focusing on one cause to the exclusion of others. Under the influence of this fallacy, we may make misguided judgments about complex social issues. Someone who thinks ill of immigrants, for instance, may blame them for the cost of social services, though there are many reasons social security, Medicare, or other systems are strained.

Here is an example of intelligent reporting avoiding oversimplification:

> A new report on the death of a man stabbed outside a Riverside gay bar in an alleged hate crime reveals that the man may have bled to death because of a hospital error. A nurse accidentally gave Owens 100,000 units of an anticoagulant drug, 100 times the recommended dose, according to a report issued this week by the Riverside coroner's office. With blood unable to clot, Owens bled to death. Prosecutors said Tuesday the hospital error does not lessen the culpability of five Riverside alleged gang members charged with Owen's murder.[14]

A man is stabbed by a gang, but a nurse accidentally gives him a huge dose of an anticoagulant, and he bleeds to death. Who is responsible? Who caused the death? In auto accidents, we have the concept of "contributory negligence," recognizing that each person in an accident, for all their pleading, may be part of the cause.

Correlation (Sign) vs. Causation

We've discussed both sign and cause previously, and this fallacy is simply a confusion of the two in a given case. While parallel reason and generalization are like fraternal twins, in which the action of one is multiplied many times by the other, correlation (reasoning by sign) and causation are just distant cousins who happen to look alike. Their mental actions are fundamentally different.

If one sees a phenomena in the vicinity of another phenomena often enough, one is likely to think of them as connected somehow. However, A going along with B is not the same as saying A is causing B (Figure 11) :

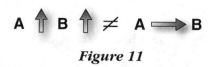

Figure 11

Go back to "Groundhog's Day." The groundhog coming out of its hole is a sign of early spring. Does the groundhog cause spring? No. "Where there's smoke there's fire," an old saying suggesting that, if it looks like something, it probably is that something. Think of it literally, though. Yes, fire generates smoke, so smoke is a sign of fire, but does the smoke cause the fire? We need not answer the obvious.

We may say that housing starts, or the interest rates, or any individual feature of the economy is a sign of financial improvement or decline, but could interest rates in themselves cause an upswing in the economy by itself? Probably not. At this writing, we have very low interest rates, but the economy is moving very slowly, and unemployment is very high.

False Cause

Go back to old "Og," the caveman:

> He comes out of his cave and accidentally stubs his toe on a rock imbedded in the soil. Even as he is hopping about, by pure coincidence, there's a total eclipse of the sun. Og is horrified. In his primitive mind he's certain that he has disturbed the spirit of a very powerful rock, and he is being punished for his offense by the loss of the sun. He falls on his knees and begs the rock to forgive him. Others see him and join in his lament. As the sun comes back into view, the people are greatly relieved. They build a little fence around the rock and offer it regular worship, even (gulp) human sacrifices.

Don't laugh. It may not be far from how some tribal religions were created.

The classic ***"propter hoc" fallacy,*** before this, therefore because of this, means that just because something A happens before something B doesn't mean that A caused B.

False cause has often been a ***result of superstition.*** Early Americans who lacked our body of scientific evidence and expert opinion had to rely on crude interpretations of sign as cause. For instance, in the Salem witch trials, a citizen might testify:

> "Goody Proctor walked by my house, scowled at me, and an hour later I miscarried."

To them, such reasoning was just cause for conviction for witchcraft. Goody Proctor's scowl may have been a sign . . . a sign that Goody Proctor didn't much like her neighbor.

Slippery Slope

This is a term that is often misused in public circles. You'll hear it in congressional speeches and from pundits on the news:

> "I'm not going down that slippery slope."

> "We're on a slippery slope to A. Once we do, that will lead to B, and that will lead to C. Then D is inevitable."

They speak as though a literal landside of bad effects would come from one event. The term is actually a fallacy, for which these phrases are typical models. People project intricate lines of causes and effects, without really establishing each causal link.

Frequently **the language** is extreme, reactive, even fearful. During the recent debate on gay marriage, a typical argument has been that allowing it would lead to other terrible things.

One man wrote in his letter to the editor, "What's next, polygamy? Marriage with animals?" Whatever you believe about gay marriage, there is no evidence that a gay marriage leads to polygamy, let alone bestiality. The statement is an emotional expression of the writer, not a logical argument. Jay Leno even made a joke about it on the "Tonight Show."

> "Boy, this Gay Marriage thing is really catching on. Just yesterday somebody married sixteen guys in Utah."

This error in reasoning has had considerable impact on U.S. history in the twentieth century. The cold war between the Soviet Union and the U.S. was largely defined, from our point of view, by the concept of ***"the domino theory."***

Ever set a series of dominos up on their ends, just to tip one and see the others automatically fall?

In the domino theory, however, countries were supposed fall, one after another, to the communist threat. We used to wonder, as kids, when the Red Chinese would show up in Catalina. This was the justification for the war in Vietnam, but we've yet to have the Red Chinese invade our beaches.

Here's another example, based on some commentary I hear in steam rooms near my home:

> I'm totally repulsed about the weak approach we take in wielding our military power in response to the most violent attack since Pearl Harbor. I knew from the start that we would never capture Bin Laden or put terrorists out of business. The nation is run by guilt-ridden, upper-middle class white people, we are afraid to be tough, afraid of being called racists. This culture of political correctness affects the military, affects our entire judicial system, our immigration enforcement, our education, and the way we distribute jobs. White people in authority in such institutions are totally incapable of calling a spade a spade. They can't tell the difference between good and evil. Political correctness is poisonous to this country's resolve.

First, we have a ***hidden presumption*** that we're lead by "guilt-ridden, upper-middle class Caucasians, who are unable to be tough because they fear being racist." That's actually five presumptions. Count them.

Though few would argue that Caucasians don't dominate leadership positions, how many upper-middle-class persons can afford a campaign? In any case, this critique of leadership is the initiating event in a slippery slope (Figure 12):

Politically Correct Leadership → hesitant military → hesitant judicial →

poor immigration enforcement → problems in education → problems in

workplaces → the inability to distinguish good from evil

Figure 12

Apart from the fact that this is a lot to blame on political correctness, each of the arrows above represents a causal link. Each link obligates you to proof. You can't just assert the other connections.

There's nothing wrong with a good emotional rant to let off some steam. That's what letters to the editor tend to be. It might be better, if you actually want to influence social causes, to blow off steam in private, then consider and construct a better quality, error-free argument.

Reasoning from Dilemma

Choices in public debate are not always clear-cut. There are advantages and problems to both sides in most typical debates. Sometimes, though, in the words of an old blues song, you've got ***"two bad roads and you still got to choose."*** Then, you argue from dilemma, counting the best and worst points from each available position against each other to make a decision, seeking the "lesser of two evils."

Or you may have two good roads and have to choose between apparently equal options. In either case, you have to choose, as they are ***mutually exclusive.*** That is, you can't have both.

Environmental issues are frequently a dilemma:

> Some value the Alaska roadless wilderness as is. Others value it for what it could yield. The Tongass, at 17 million acres, America's largest national forest, is in a league of its own in the national debate over roadless areas. Some say it is foolish to include the Tongass in a federal policy restricting logging

and road building in roadless areas. It would shut down Alaska's whole timber industry. Others say, that's the point: If everything else has had roads graded through it, if there's just one big American rainforest left, why send bulldozers and logging trucks.[15]

Sometimes these are moral dilemmas, requiring an assessment of values for their resolution. Take the case of a Georgia woman, Carol Carr, 63, who was widowed by Huntington's Disease. Huntington's is a terrible disease with long suffering effects she bore until her husband's death. She shot her two adult sons, also suffering from the disease, for which she was charged with murder. Her third son, 38, is in the early stages of the disease. Supporters say Carr could not stand to see her children endure more. She told one friend after the shooting that Andy was writhing and tearfully tugging at the sheets when she entered the room that day.[16]

One's sense of logos may conflict with the pathos of the situation. On one hand, she has broken the literal word of the law. Logos, by the way, literally means "word." Mercy killing is not legally permitted.

On the other, it is difficult to not feel sympathy for a woman who is aging and has already been through so much. Further, it's hard to forget the image of the son himself writhing and clutching the sheets in pain. Put yourself on her jury. How would you vote? Perhaps more importantly for our studies, why would you choose that way? Go to the exercises and discuss this issue further.

The *language* of dilemma would include words and phrases like: "either/or, must choose between, it's a question between, dilemma, or paradox." Be aware that a paradox is not technically the same as a dilemma. Paradox has the connotation of an insoluble mystery, those pesky "which came first, the chicken or the egg" kind of questions, or a Zen verse.

Dilemma is a tough choice, but we can chose, based on costs vs. gains analysis.

Costs vs. gains analysis is simply listing the assets and downsides of the two positions in question, then creating a value standard to decide between the two. This will become even more important during discussions of value and policy.

For example, the war against terrorism has placed our Coast Guard in a dilemma:

> The service's new anti-terrorism focus has come at the expense of its traditional charges, a congressional study concludes. The Coast Guard spent 2,263 fewer duty hours on search and rescue this spring and 4,322 fewer hours than last year on drug interdiction, fanning concerns that port security duties will diminish traditional missions. Instead, Coast Guard units spent 30,805 additional hours on port security more than an eight fold increase.[17]

On this Coast Guard issue, you'd have to decide which functions are more important, the traditional functions of drug interdiction and search and rescue, or the function of port security to check terrorists.

To decide, what standard would you use? You might decide that whichever does more to protect human life was the better choice. You could then calculate how many lives were actually saved, or how many Americans have died because of drugs the Coast Guard might intercept. You might ask, are potential lives lost really measurable against actual lives lost at sea? On the other hand, you may decide that you don't have to choose, but that you can balance the programs more equitably. Maybe they aren't mutually exclusive. What do you think?

"The Dark Side"

Not everything is a "for it or against it" proposition. There are ranges of opinion along a scale on many social problems. When you force a yes or no response, you may be committing the following fallacy.

Forcing the dichotomy is the "dark side" of reasoning from dilemma. When committing this fallacy, one forces someone to make a choice between two mutually exclusive extremes, when there is a third, or more, choices available. Consider this viewpoint:

> So, there's a police brutality charge against an Inglewood policeman, and an Inglewood policeman tries to enforce the law against some kid who is resisting arrest, and he gets a fund raiser, while the officer gets a suspension. Representative Maxine Waters even protested the event, while seeking $10,000 in fundraising for the so-called victim. On the same day, 300 protesters staged a march to protest gang violence. Days later, in the same city, many FBI, police and sheriffs hunted for the murderer of a child, a known sexual predator. Now, ask yourself, all of you who worry so much about the rights of a lone offender, What are the real threats to your peace and existence? Gang violence and sexual predators, or a few overzealous, maybe even racist cops? Make a choice tonight after your prayers for your children.

The writer provides us with an unnecessary choice: Choose either gangs and sexual predators as real social problems, OR police brutality. Why do we have to choose? We can seek a balanced program among all three issues.

The further implication here, if we draw the argument out to its furthest logical extent, is that we have to allow police brutality in order for our streets to be safe. Also, is the author associating the reputed victim with gangs and sexual predators? He also leaves out, rather significantly, the fact that the beaten boy was retarded. So, this seems like another emotional expression, perhaps a racially tinted one, but it is clearly forcing the dichotomy.

Another version of this fallacy is the ***complex question,*** when somebody tries to force you to a yes or no answer on a question that has a hidden presumption in it.

For instance, take the old, "Have you stopped beating your wife? Yes or no!" The hidden presumption is that you beat your wife to begin with, also perhaps that you're married. These are three separate questions, parading as one. Answer with a direct statement: "I never beat my wife." Or, perhaps, "I've never married."

Arguing from Authority

We've saved this for last, because it's the easiest to manage. ***The mental action*** of this pattern is simply: it's so because the best and the brightest in a specific area of expertise assert their own authority as the main reason for acceptance of the claim. Their analysis of the evidence at hand is sufficiently superior to ours as to be a cause acceptance of their conclusions.

A typical pattern of this kind of argument would take an authority's opinion, then state his conclusion as the claim. The quoted opinion becomes the grounds. The warrant is that authority has sufficient expertise to be trusted for his conclusion.

Different authorities in the same field may conclude differently. So arguments from authority should be submitted to the common tests we use on source-based proof: sufficiently specific expertise in the field, public recognitions of his authority, a lack of bias, first-hand observation, etc.

The language typically would include phrases like: "in the words of, as was established by, according to," and other indications of authorship, along with source qualifications.

This is an age of great specialization. It tends to be this way, because we've experienced an enormous information explosion. It's impossible for everyone to be an authority on everything. (I myself have a separate doctor for each part of my body. . . and, boy, are they confused!)

In some respects, one might regard this as a pattern that can be overly relied upon. We sometimes criticize arguments based solely on ***conclusionary evidence.***

> Someone claims "There's new rage against immigrants of all types."
>
> The grounds consists of a pundit saying, "There's a new rage against . . . etc."
>
> He simply makes the conclusion without explaining how he got there.

These sources are using patterns of reason themselves. It would be good if you could identify the pattern of reason used by the expert, as well, instead of merely relying on their judgment. With regard to social problems, there's a lot of room to observe and question even the best and brightest.

Students sometimes, when asked to identify the pattern of reason in warrants, will say over and over, "That's from authority," simply because there's a source.

First, not all sources are authoritative witnesses, as we see in the fallacy below. Second, it's foolish in many cases to rely solely on this kind of evidence and reason, once you have the knowledge offered in this text.

Granted, when a quantum physicist tries to explain worm-holes to me, I take his word for it, but I try to understand what those doctors are telling me, from the grounds on up, about my own various illnesses.

Fallacy of Appeal to Authority

The fallacy associated with argument from authority is "appeal to authority." It's an odd label, as we know it's okay, in fact necessary, to mention authorities. It should really be called *appeal to fame,* since it consists of using celebrity to persuade. Not everyone famous is an expert.

We hear from celebrities all the time in sales and politics. In sales, there's a parade of at least recognizable faces in commercials, while key spots may be occupied with Academy Award winners. Do you imagine that Katherine Zeta Jones really knows a lot about cell phones? Arnold Schwarzenegger is the governor of my state. He's in the news right now because he wants a part-time state legislature, as they make "strange bills" when they have too much time on their hands. It's not clear what an operational definition of "strange bills" is, but the governor should probably be considered an inexperienced, if popular, politician.

Even someone more closely linked to the subject is not necessarily an authority on the subject. A "distinguished scientist" may be a chemist talking about quantum physics.

* * * * *

So, these are the "magnificent seven" of reasoning. You still won't understand everything about warrants, but you can begin to examine your reasons for why you believe something to be true. That's a good start.

More specifically, *remember that there are certain word clues* for the patterns of reason, and that they can generally be found in *the language of the grounds* itself:

For *analogy,* be able to identify the two things compared and look for words and phrases that include: like, as, is similar, are alike, resembles, compared to, by contrast, as well as precedent or model.

For *generalization,* language includes: it is generally so, usually so, normally so, customary, even universally so, or we've concluded that.

For *definition,* you may read or hear: given that, since we know that, this case is typical of most, or simply by definition this is so.

Language of **sign** may be quite literal: is a sign of, signifies, indicates, marks, is an omen, a portent, or a clue.

Causation language may also be quite literal: causes, leads to, produces, activates, provokes, generates, brings about, or results in are active verbs suggesting a relationship between cause and effect.

Dilemma language would mostly be: either/or, must choose between, it's a question of A or B, or it's a dilemma.

Authority language is often: in the opinion of, as concluded by, as established by, and according to, along with the particular qualifications of the authority involved.

Vocabulary

Causal Link (not "casual" link)
Costs vs. Gains Analysis
Reason vs. Fallacy
    Arguing from Authority vs. Appeal to Fame
    Arguing from Cause and Effect vs. Correlation/Causation
                False Cause
                Oversimplification (Multiple Causation)
                Slippery Slope
    Arguing from Definition vs. Sweeping Generalization
    Arguing from Dilemma vs. Forcing the Dichotomy
    Arguing from Generalization vs. Hasty Generalization
    Arguing from Parallel Reasoning vs. False Analogy
    Arguing from Sign vs. False Sign and Superstition

Exercises: Go to Interactive Disc to Complete

1) Discuss the woman who killed her sick children. You're on the jury. How do you vote, guilty of first degree murder, or not? Divide the class between the two verdicts. Explain your positions to each other using Toulmin's argument format. In other words, sketch out your ideas before the next class. Your instructor can help you identify the parts, the kinds of propositions, and the evidence that might be appropriate for your argument.

2) The structure typical of fact manuscripts and some examples will appear in the next chapter. You may want to look through the sample outlines of student manuscripts before you read the chapter.

3) Now that you've seen all three basic parts of Toulmin in action together, along with qualifiers from his secondary triad, you should be building arguments for a proposition of fact manuscript. As a starting discipline, you should label the Toulmin parts in your arguments. Be aware of the pat-

terns of reason you use in your warrants and label them for your instructor, as well.

4) Look at the following paragraphs and identify the ***patterns of reason*** within them.

A) "This week an advisory panel in New Orleans will recommend whether the government should loosen its grip on the nation's stockpile of small pox vaccine, which has been under wraps since the disease was eradicated world wide in 1980. In light of the Sept. 11 terrorist attacks on the World Trade Center and The Pentagon, and subsequent anthrax mailings, government officials are debating whether to release the vaccine to health and emergency workers, and, perhaps millions of other Americans. 'This is a difficult decision to make,' said D.A. Henderson, one of the world's leading authorities on smallpox, during a forum Saturday in Washington. 'There is no right answer. It's a matter of balance. . . .' (T)aking the vaccine isn't a simple choice. There's an estimated 1 to 2 in a million shot that the vaccine itself could kill them, and a 1-in-100,000 chance of causing serious illness, such as severe rash, infection, or brain inflammation" ("U.S Weighs Risk of Smallpox," *LA Times,* June 16, 2002).

B) The Justice Department, it is argued, has not adopted consistent principles in its prosecution of terrorist suspects.

- John Walker Lindh, born in California but captured in Afghanistan among Taliban forces, was tried and convicted in civil court.

- Yasser Esam Hamdl, born in Lousiana and captured in the same Afghan prison rebellion as Lindh, is being detained at the Norfolk Naval Station without being charged.

- Zacarias Moussaoui, a French citizen of Moroccan descent, was arrested in Minnesota as the '20th hijacker.' He has been charged and is being tried in civil court.

- Richard C. Reid, the British shoe bomber, was tried and convicted in civil court.

- Jose Padilla, born in New York, was held as a suspect in a plot to detonate a dirty bomb in the United States. Although arrested by the FBI on May 8, 2002, and incarcerated since then, he has yet to be charged with a crime (*LA Times,* Feb, 2, 2003).

C) Concerning pedophile charges against Catholic priests: "When Cardinal Roger M. Mahoney's attorneys failed to persuade a Los Angeles judge to block media outlets from publishing some of Mahoney's confidential e-mails, the cardinal met the same fate as many powerful interests over the past 70 years. Since the landmark 1931 U.S. Supreme Court decision in Near vs.

Minnesota, it has been very difficult for individuals from large corporations or even the U.S. government to get 'prior restraint' against the press" (*LA Times,* April 8, 2002).

D) "The nation's unemployment rate hung at 5.9% in July as U.S. employers reacted to a plummeting stock market and weakening consumer demand by adding only 6,000 new workers, the Labor Department said Friday ('Economy Suffers Another Cutback,' *LA Times,* August 3, 2002)."

E) "A UCLA team has apparently found the Iceland home of Snorri Thorfinnsson, the first person of European descent born in the New World. Icelandic sagas from the 13th century tell the story of how Snorri's parents led the first Scandinavian group that attempted to settle in Vinland (Greenland) on the Canadian coast about AD 1000. The attempt failed, and the family move to Iceland, but Snorri was born while they were in North America. The building is a classic German fortress longhouse like the Great Hall of Beowulf ("Home May Prove Viking Saga," *LA Times,* September 16, 2002)."

F) "Instead of the three-year, $322 billion dollar shortfall predicted by the White House last month, the government will post four consecutive deficits totaling $452 billion, according to the Congressional Budget Office. The main factor in recent months has been a sharp drop in federal tax collections, the biggest in percentage terms since special wartime levies were lifted in 1946. The falloff has been caused in large part by the effect of the stock market's decline on payments of capital gains taxes. At today's prices, fewer shareholders are recording profits when they sell ("Federal Deficit Grows Deeper Than Expected," *LA Times,* August 28, 2002)."

5) Now, identify the ***fallacies*** in these paragraphs:

A) In America, the works of the national authors are in practically every home and they are read by about everybody. My mother reads Mark Twain. This case in itself proves little; however, I have talked with several people of the lower class who knew their authors and read them.

B) Criticism was made of the Nike Corporation's connection's with Southland's high school basketball team, suggesting that Nike's gifts to such schools as Crenshaw, Fairfax, and Westchester is the reason that they are successful. Locals retorted that, in fact, coaches Willie West, Harvey Kitani, and Ed Azzam, excellent coaches and teachers, all had highly successful programs long before Nike looked their way. The notion is that the criticism had it backward. Nike's attention was attracted precisely because they were successful. What fallacy are the locals invoking?

C) So, when will you stop kicking your dog?

Sources

1) Ehninger, D.E. (1974). Influence, Belief and Argument. Glenview, IL: Scott, Foresman.

   Golden, J.L., Berquist, G.F., & Coleman, W.E. (2001). The Rhetoric of Western Thought. Dubuque, IA: Kendall-Hunt.

   Toulmin, S., Rieke, R., & Janik, A. An Introduction to Reasoning. New York: MacMillan

2) LA Times, "White Collars, Black Hats," April 3, 2003.

3) Carl Zichella, Regional Director of the Environmental Protection Agency "Stop Your Grousing, Auto Makers, and Get the Gases Out," LA Times, August 8, 2002.

4) LA Times, "New Study Defends Mammograms," Feb. 1, 2002.

5) NY Times, "Secretary Lays Out Case," Feb. 6, 2003.

6) LA Times, "Leaders Deny Racism Is Part of Newport Life," June 23, 2003.

7) LA Times, "US Needs to Get It's House in Order," July 31, 2002.

8) The Daily Pilot, "Paintball Assault Leaves Skater Critical," April 19, 2002.

   LA Times, "Newport Paint-Ball Victim Declared Dead," April 8, 2002.

   Tony Dodero, Daily Pilot, "Sometimes Hasty Writing Requires Corrections," August 19, 2002.

9) LA Times, "Federal Deficit Grows," August 28, 2002.

10) LA Times, "The Attacks Worsened a Plummeting Economy," Sept. 18, 2001.

11) LA Times, "Risks of Ephedra Usage in Spotlight," August 27, 2001.

12) LA Times, "Breast Cancer Survivors on a Crusade," March 18, 2002.

13) LA Times, "AIDS Drugs May Cause Other Illnesses," February 4, 2003.

14) LA Times, "Hospital Error Cited in Man's Death," August 28, 2002.

15) LA Times, "Clear Cut Debate Gets Cloudy," September 2, 2001.

16) NY Times, "Georgia Widow Charged with Murder in Deaths of Ailing Sons," August 24, 2002.

17) LA Times, "Coast Guard Lists Toward Security Duty," August 24, 2002.

V

Arguing Issues of Fact

Now we have some idea about argument form. We understand claims, a particular kind of proposition used by Toulmin. We've learned about how **qualifiers** and definitions clarify these claims and shape argumentative territory. We've discovered the different kinds of evidence needed to formulate **grounds.** Finally, we've acquainted ourselves with the patterns of reason we use with **warrants,** as well as some fallacies that can lead our thinking astray.

Let's now look at these four parts of Toulmin's model in action together. We're going to build some arguments, then assemble those arguments into a text. We'll keep this text fairly brief, as our primary purpose at this time is learning how to craft arguments well.

The first text we'll build will defend a proposition of fact. Issues of fact include what has and has not happened; what is and is not true; or what may or may not occur in the future. Issues of fact may focus on descriptions of cause and effect in natural phenomena, in mechanical or in scientific discovery or matters of events, but every field, even value focused fields like churches, have issues of fact to decide.

Is a manned American flight to the moon feasible?

Are we close to a cure for HIV?

Does X product help people to lose weight?

By now, we have some idea about the differences among the various types of propositions. However, let's look at some more sample **propositions of fact.**

It is likely that Celtic sailors arrived in America before Columbus.

Tobacco companies have deliberately targeted youths in ad campaigns.

Talking on a cell phone while driving increases the chances of accident.

Fossil fuels will be seriously depleted by 2030.

These deal with past, present, and future reality. The tense of the verb is one way of recognizing the time frame of your argumentative territory. Notice that they are mostly short, declarative sentences, easy to grasp. Also, there's no attempt to color the language with persuasive adjectives and exaggerations. Remember the rule of neutrality when fashioning propositions.

Yet our purpose is more than fashioning and supporting propositions. We are also concerned with knowing enough about the issue to arrive at the best possible approximation of the truth.

Why do we bother to argue facts? We argue because there's confusion, controversy, or conflict about some matter of fact. We have new knowledge to describe, unanswered questions about the cause of significant phenomena, or we have questions of guilt or innocence in some legal matter. When these factors are present, we have **rhetorical demand,** a reason to speak.

We are using argumentation as a framework for seeking and framing knowledge. This emphasizes that we not allow the errors typical in **pre-critical thinking.** We need to be as objective and open-minded as possible, keeping our culturally conditioned prejudices and reactionary tendencies in check. We'll try not to jump to conclusions. We'll remember to look at the issue, not only through the eyes of someone trying to prove a point, but also from the viewpoint of your **imaginary opponent.** For every argument you make, consider what an adversary would argue against it.

What exactly is the **framework for inquiry,** though? We know we'll put together some claims with warrants and grounds, but how do we figure the order of arguments?[1]

In writing text, conventions of the common **"five-paragraph essay"** or speech are appropriate: you'll have an introduction setting up the issue; a thesis proposition with a clear definition of terms; three or more paragraphs, a Toulmin argument supporting the proposition in each; and a conclusion, evaluating and summarizing how the arguments demonstrate the thesis proposition.

That's an outer framework you're probably familiar with, but what happens with your internal organization. How do we invent the three or more argumentative paragraphs which are key to a persuasive defense of your thesis. To know what the internal organization will be, we have to **assess the issues,** the questions to be answered with regard to the thesis proposition.

Stock Issues for Fact

We sometimes call stock issues **"inventional systems,"** because they help us to invent arguments. They do so by raising specific questions, or issues, that have to be answered to make a complete, or prima facie case. Let's explore the stock issues for fact, in the context of a speech building process.[2]

As with any speech or paper, you first formulate your thesis proposition. You use qualifiers and definitions to focus the discussion, determine your burden of proof, and specify a threshold for acceptance of the thesis.

Once the proposition is determined for you and your opponent, there is a stock issue called **topicality.** Basically, that means that each side must stay on the topic, or lose.

There are **two basic stock issues** to be concerned with now:

ONE: A SIGNIFICANT PHENOMENON EXISTS.

A) A PHENOMENON EXISTS.

B) IT HAS SIGNIFICANT IMPACT.

TWO: THE PHENOMENON'S CAUSE CAN BE IDENTIFIED.

We commonly reduce these two issues to the handy terms **"significance"** and **"in-herency,"** another word for cause. They may also be re-ordered, depending on the particular topic and the way the evidence flows from point to point.

Real World Example I

Let's say we've formulated this proposition: "Talking on a cell phone while driving increases risk of accident." To be "topical," then, we can only talk about the impacts of cell phone use in moving cars.

Definition is fairly easy. We know what "talking on a cell phone while driving" is, though we may have to clarify if we mean both talking directly into the phone unit, or through a headset with both hands on the wheel.

We should recognize that "cell phone" is also the causal agent of an effect in this phrase. So our burden of proof is to find proof of cause for the second term to be defined, "increases risk of accident." We'd then characterize the typical effects we've found in our research.

"Talking on a cell phone while driving" is a causal agent yielding . . .

"Increased risk of accident."

Notice that we have **limited our burden of proof** with "a" causal agent, as opposed to "the" causal agent. We certainly wouldn't want to imply that cell phone use in cars is the sole cause of accidents. That would be an unreasonable **threshold** to establish your case, as there are many causes for an accident. Our threshold now is that we must show an increased risk by adding one to the many.

You could further limit your burden by suggesting, not cause, but correlation. In other words, you'd argue that cell phones are a sign of possible, though not necessarily probable, accident.

In approaching typical stock issues, we can break effect significance down into two steps. **A phenomenon exists argument** might seem obvious, even unnecessary. We can infer the presence of something through its effect. For instance, initially, we were only able to infer the existence of acid rain as a cause by reasoning back from the presence of its corrosive effects. Nobody even knew what to call it. We just saw that a significant phenomenon was happening and looked for a cause.

Practically, though, there is reason to start with a separate argument that a phenomenon exists. People may argue significant effect from a phenomenon that is really a hidden presumption. For example:

> The American preoccupation with sports dominates the media.

"Dominates the media" is a significant effect, in terms of dollars if nothing else. Yet do we really know that America is preoccupied by sports, or are we merely assuming it from personal experience?

Our point is simply, don't assume that your audience acknowledges the existence of something that you take for granted. Show it. You'll find it's actually reasonable to begin with an argument that simply says:

> Americans are preoccupied with sports.

For the cell phone issue, one could suppose that it's not too much to assume that there's a lot of cell phone use, since we're likely to have seen it in cars around us. Nonetheless, confirm that there is frequent cell phone use in moving cars.

I. Claim: Many Americans talk on cell phones while driving.

> Warrant A: We know this because of statistics about cell phone use, as well as our common experience (reasoning by generalization).

> Grounds A1: According to industry sources at ATT, over 50 million cell phones were in use in America by the year 2000.

> Grounds A2: We have probably all seen people use such phones in their cars. Perhaps we have done it ourselves, receiving a call in the car, if not dialing one.

> Warrant B: We also know because makers have adapted multiple accessories for the cell phone which tempt drivers to use them in cars (reasoning by sign).

> Grounds B: Earphones designed for hands free office work, as well as cars, is a clear temptation to use phones in cars. The additional functions of e-mail, voice messaging, even cameras, offer the driver many chances to use phones in traffic. This was noted in a Department of California Highway Patrol Study "On Cell Phones & Driving," issued in 2000.

Notice three particular things about this argument. First, there's the use of both testimony and statistics as proof, a balanced "combination punch." Second, there is more than one warrant and more than one grounds under the first warrant. We can call these **argument chains.** We could even diagram an argument somewhat like we might molecules in chemistry (Figure 13):

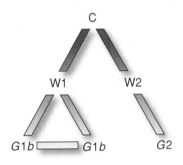

Figure 13

Notice, also, that we're working our source citations into the grounds in simple, everyday language. *Your audience can't hear a footnote* from the back of your text, so it's necessary to integrate it. There are many *phrases to note citation:* "in the words of," "as was noted in," "according to," "as was suggested by," along with the obvious combination of the speaker or publication name with "stated that," "said that," "observed that," etc. Be creative. Try not to repeat yourself too much.

Inherency examines the causes of the social phenomenon's impact. The order is somewhat interchangeable between inherency and significance, as one can argue from cause to effect, or effect to cause. The issue here is, is there a clear correlation between cell use and potential danger?

II. Claim: Cell phone use while driving creates a risky distraction.

   Warrant: There are correlations between cell phone use and auto accidents (sign). It doesn't matter if the cell is hand-held or not; it's the distraction that contributes to accidents.

   Grounds A: According to a report in the February 12, 1997, issue of the *New England Journal of Medicine,* "talking on cellular phones is nearly as risky as driving drunk."

   Grounds B: Alm and Nilsson as early as this study in 1990 had found "Driver inattention to the driving task is the key safety-relevant outcome of driver distraction. Has been implicated in many traffic accidents."

   Grounds C: As Fairclough et al found in their 1991 study, "Others who may not be inclined to use a cellular phone at all in a moving vehicle may do so with hands-free technology. The consequent increase in use among the driving public can therefore increase overall crash hazard exposure. Thus, with hands-free manipulation, more drivers may now be engaged in conversation, which has been shown to be distracting in itself."

This argument—once again, fashioned from student arguments as models for you—is all right structurally, but there are some weaknesses. Can you spot them? Stop reading and try.

* * * * *

OK. If you applied **tests of evidence,** you may have found some weaknesses. The proof is a little old, although newer findings would continue to support and further refine the claim. Further, this is almost all testimony. We see no statistics, except in the first quotation, and we don't really have an idea of the specific percentages nor how they were calculated.

When you rely on testimony, the ethos of the source, their credibility, matters a great deal. To the extent that the *New England Journal of Medicine* is a reliable source, one might be persuaded that there's a likelihood of a causal link to accident.

In fact, with some additional statistics, you could argue for cause rather than sign as the warrant. Weak cause, however, may draw more scrutiny—and rightfully so—than a strong sign. It's wise, sometimes, to limit the burden of proof. It's better not to overextend claims beyond the available evidence.

Effect significance is an examination of the impact of a phenomenon.

The effect significance could be statistics illustrating the frequency of accidents, their costs and injuries. With that approach, which would be ideal, we might place the argument before inherency, as the effect would stand clearly on its own. Here, the impact flows naturally from the cause.

III.   Claim: Cell phones may injure users with accidents

Grounds A: The same study from the *New England Journal of Medicine* also said that the risk of a collision quadruples when talking on the phone.

Warrant A: It stands to reason then, that cell phone users are more prone to the financial and physical damages of auto accident than those who are not. By cause and effect, the grounds suggests that cell phone drivers are four times more likely to have a crash.

Notice that we may sometimes wish to follow Toulmin's original order, perhaps simply to vary our style and not be robotic by repeating the same order of parts over and over. Here, the grounds are brief and singular, and the explanation of the grounds flows well in this order. It would also be good to have some specific examples at this point.

Some particular sectors of the population may suffer more than others.

IV. Claim: Cell phone risk is particularly dangerous for the elderly.

Warrant: Normal age-related problems may be worsened by introducing a distracting, concurrent task (cause).

Grounds: B.C. Hayes says in his 1989 study, "Age Related Decrements in Automobile Instrument Panel Task Performance," "Older drivers will often find it more challenging to operate cellular phones that tend toward small displays and controls designed to specifications drawn from a younger population." This may be especially significant, since elderly drivers have more recently passed teens as the most accident-plagued segment of the population.

This, then, could be the basic interior structure for this proposition of fact speech. It would be good to have some specific statistics about how many accidents, either in sum or per year, have been actually linked to driver cell phone use. Yet it's not a bad start.

A last argument may grow out of a look at the issues from an ***imaginary opponent.*** What might he or she argue on the other side? Typically, an opponent might argue that cell phones enhance traffic safety as emergency communication devices. Offering this preemptive argument first would undermine the reply before it has a chance. Recall that one feature of evidence is that it tends to "inoculate" audiences against subsequent evidence.

V. Claim: Even the most beneficial safety aspects of cell phones can lead to social damage.

Warrant: While cell phones are handy in a roadside emergency, unnecessary calls to 911 create problems for police.

Grounds: "Some emergency response networks have reported in excess of one hundred 911 calls for the same incident, making networks unavailable for reporting other emergencies," according to the Highway Patrol study cited above. They continue, "traffic safety itself may be degraded somewhat if more drivers are distracted while making such calls in hazardous driving conditions, e.g. slowed or stop-and-go traffic."

Given this order, our next practical purpose would be to frame this material with a brief introduction and conclusion, rehearse the presentation and deliver it. That's correct, write the introductions and conclusions after you've completed the body of the text. How else do you really know what you're introducing?

One caution about ***introductions and conclusions.*** There is a tendency to stray into assertions and emotional diatribes that may go beyond the parameters of the proposition you've chosen to defend. For instance, this is a proposition of fact, so you will not go on and on about how cell phones in cars are wrong, or what you want to do about it, making them illegal or placing serious restrictions on their use. Those are issues of value and policy.

For the moment, think of yourself as a ***news reporter,*** one who simply reports the facts of the moment, ***not a news commentator*** who editorializes and offers opinion on the matter.

Real World Example II

Let's text one more proposition of fact, to emphasize understanding of the stock issues, and how they lead us into argument building.

Formulate the Proposition

Tobacco companies have deliberately targeted youth in ad campaigns.

Define the Terms

The key terms are "tobacco companies," "deliberately targeted," and "effective ad campaigns." What companies do we mean? U.S.? Worldwide? What do we mean by "deliberately?" They sat in board rooms and intentionally sought ways to create the next generation of smokers? And what constitutes an ad campaign? Flyers? A concentrated, multi-media effort targeted on a particular audience? Propose basic definitions, then adjust them according to the research.

For this discussion, let's set the goal at a fairly difficult level. We'll limit the topic by defining tobacco companies as "U.S. and British companies," as they control the market affecting us. We'll define "deliberately targeted" as "planned intentionally to start the next generation of smokers," and effective ad campaign as, "use of wide-spread national print and billboard medium to influence purchase that impact youth."

Determine the Burden of Proof

The key burdens of proof include demonstrating the term "intentionally targeted." How do you demonstrate the internal planning of major tobacco companies? We may manage by inference from the content of national campaigns. Perhaps there's expert testimony from a "whistle blower," who might reveal expressed intent in internal memos. We also have to show that the campaigns are effective.

What's the ***threshold?*** To the extent that we can correlate a pattern of specific advertising with youth-oriented imagery to either A) greater name brand recognition among youths, or B) significant increase in cigarette use by the young, we should meet our burden. Also, note that the past tense, "Have targeted" as opposed to "are targeting," limits our burden to past intentions. We don't necessarily have to prove that it's the current approach.

Phenomena Existence Issue

I.   Claim: Tobacco companies spend significant amounts of money on campaigns that at least appear to target the young.

Warrants: We know this through government reports and other expert opinion (reasoning by authority).

Grounds A: According to the January 1992 "Journal of Marketing," "The tobacco industry spends four billion dollars a year in advertising and promotional campaigns through the widespread use of cartoon characters, rock stars, young and attractive models to advertise tobacco products and promote the sale of cigarettes."

Grounds B: In her 1994 "Annual Report," Surgeon General Jocelyn Elder noted, "This strategy is directly aimed at new, young customers since cigarette smoking, of all addictive behaviors, is the one most likely to take hold during adolescence and almost all adult smokers took their first drag before graduating from high school."

Inherency Issue

We might take that second grounds as fairly strong testimony that the thesis is true. Yet the evidence is really circumstantial. She implies a correlation between the ad content and the fact that most smokers start young. I also know that my stepfather was smoking corn silk behind the barn at thirteen during the depression when no such campaigns existed. We need more. We need a ***sense of a trend*** in the tobacco company intent.

II.   Claim: Targeting youth is ongoing, particularly among large companies which rely on a constant flow of new customers for a stable profit margin.

Warrant: These companies know, as a matter of statistics, that a majority of smokers start by the age of 18, and begin significant smoking by 21. So, from a marketing point of view, it makes sense to target them before that. Once one big company started, it was likely that others would follow to compete. Ads make a very specific point about the issue of "being cool," and suggest that smoking itself is cool. So, if you smoke, you'll be cool, they try to say (generalization about the ads). The examples certainly appear intentional.

Grounds A: As was noted in the Jan/Feb 1992 *Multinational Monitor,* "Phillip Morris introduced a cartoon promotional character, a stylized puffin logo for its Benson & Hedges brand in the United Kingdom. The symbol resembles the bird used by the Puffin Books Company, a children's books publisher."

Grounds B: *Advertising Age,* April 7, 1992, noted—along with the rest of America, the prominence of another cartoon character campaign featuring

"Joe Camel" for Camel cigarettes, created in 1988. There were gift coupons in packs that could be collected for teen-oriented merchandise.

Grounds C: "Brown and Williamson, a U.S. company owned by British Tobacco created a cartoon character which is a penguin that has a buzz-cut hair style, day-glo sneakers, sunglasses, and is very conscious of being cool." The ad copy was described in *Multinational Monitor,* January 1992. "The campaign is written in the voice of the penguin who explains, 'My older cousin, Willie the Penguin, represented Kool for three decades. Let's face it, he's gotten on in years. That, and the fact that I'm unique, colorful, good looking, and very modest. Some people think I'm a little irreverent. So what if I have a little fun on the job? I will admit to being just a bit unconventional.' The ads play on the word 'cool.' One ad shows four varieties of Kool cigarettes. The text concludes, 'Now you got four chances to get Kool. Don't blow it.'"

Effect Significance Issue

The last argument reveals that the impacts of these campaigns are significant, in that the campaigns cause more smoking among youths.

III.   Claim: Both in number and in behavioral response, these ads have impact.

Warrant: We can tell this by statistics (generalizations) reporting the success of the campaigns that suggest a cause and effect relationship.

Grounds A: "In a survey prepared exclusively for *Advertising Age* by BKG Youth, a research and marketing company, results showed that when 8 to 13 year olds were asked to name familiar name brands, 90 percent named Camel: 73 percent cited Marlboro." Those results were posted April 27, 1992.

Grounds B: The same issue of *Advertising Age* noted that the impact was even high among pre-school age children. "One third of 3-year olds correctly identified the Joe Camel cartoon character as representing cigarettes. Joe was recognized at the same rate as the Mickey Mouse logo used for the Disney Channel. Among secondary school students, 94 percent were able to identify Joe, compared to only 58 percent of adults."

Grounds C: "Prior to this new marketing strategy," the earlier cited issue of the *Multinational Monitor* said, "Camel cigarettes were smoked by less than one percent of smokers under the age of 18. By 1990, the figure increased to 33 percent."

Then perhaps, one might make an argument about the number of deaths and loss of dollars in productivity that result from cigarette addiction. It would make the impact stronger. Yet that might lead us to push the parameters of your central proposition.

Remember that your explicit purpose is not to make value judgments about the morality of this, not even in your conclusion. The student who wrote the outline above could just as well make the judgment that, "This is a matter of personal choice," as "this is wrong, even evil." We save that conversation for a value issue.

Neither do you argue, even in your conclusion, that "We must ban this insidious and harmful campaign." Save that for discussions of policy.

Since we have all these things we can't do in a conclusion, what kind of things can we do? First, you want to summarize what you've argued, but not in detail or in redundancy. Just mention the claims you feel you've proven. Then relate that back to the thesis. Remember, this is your "Joe Friday" type speech. As he used to say on "Dragnet":

> "Just the facts, ma'am, just the facts."

Let's apply ourselves to the text from **the viewpoint of our imaginary opponent.** This will help us to strengthen our arguments by seeing weak points, as well as offering us an opportunity to **anticipate and preempt adversary arguments:**

What would you argue against the first position on **phenomenon existence?** The obvious attack would be on the recency of evidence. However, the thesis has said "have done," not "presently do." So, older evidence may be not only admissible, but necessary from a historical viewpoint. Nonetheless, we should look for more recent evidence in the area of inherency to further establish an ongoing trend.

On **inherency,** as with the first argument, there are a couple of different sources. They seem pretty persuasive, as the examples suggest some ongoing intent to target youth. Remember your burden is that the campaigns are intentional.

Yet we're also generalizing that these three examples are typical of the whole industry. It would be possible to argue that these are exceptions to the rule and press the advocate to show that this intent is industry wide.

In response, the advocate might even limit his definition of tobacco companies to "such companies spending more than X amount on advertising," excluding smaller companies, some of whom may not target children. You wouldn't want to give an opponent the chance to say, "a majority of companies do not do such advertising, so you've made a hasty generalization, based on only a few major companies."

An imaginary opponent might also argue **alternative causation** to smoking. Recall that multiple causation is typical of social issues. Is advertising the real cause, or just a reminder of other impulses that are already present? Is advertising more a cause of smoking than, say, parental or peer modeling? How many of these young smokers grew up in smoking households?

Significance is perhaps the most vulnerable argument presented. There are three grounds, and there's a strong suggestion that ads got young people's attention and a fair number of them smoked that brand. We don't know if they were already smokers and just switched brands. More importantly, the grounds are all about Camel cigarettes. There's mention of Marlboros, but the advocate has made no case about Marlboros focusing ads on children. Those ads tend to sell a more manly image, with cowboys and the like. What about Philip Morris and Brown & Williamson? Where's the impact of their campaigns?

Having completed a draft, we test its evidence, and look at it through the eyes of our imaginary opponent. We may return to the library and look for additional research, so that we don't stop with Joe Camel. There may be other similar studies on other similar campaigns. Also, there is whistle blower information about tobacco companies, internal memos revealing strategic intent. Go find it.

Prima Facie Case

These outlines, based on a stock issues approach, are an operational definition of the term "prima facie case." "***Prima facie,***" in Latin, means "first face." Such a case, "on the face of it," or at first glance, is strong enough to **satisfy the burden of proof** on the necessary stock issues. It is strong enough that we can **temporarily suspend presumption,** the opponent's advantage in the debate.

Again, consider our **legal analogy.** The prosecutor, our advocate, challenges the public presumption, at least the official line from tobacco companies, that tobacco companies advertise to adults. He must show the judge a sufficient case that he will say, "Yes, this must go to trial." At that point, presumption must be reestablished by the defense attorney, the opposition, or they lose their advantage, and the debate.

On the other hand, know this. The advocate's burden of proof requires that all the basic "elements of the crime," the stock issues, must be answered in his favor. The advocate must win all the stock issues. Otherwise, "the case is dismissed." All the opponent has to do is defeat one of your stock issues to win. So, make sure that your case is balanced and your evidence is sufficient.

In sum, you've established your prima facie case of fact if you meet these stock issues:

> Your arguments are topical.

> You've defined your terms in a specific enough way that we can determine the threshold of your burden of proof.

> You've established the presence of a phenomenon.

> You've presented the effect significance of the phenomenon.

> And you've demonstrated the inherent causes of these effects.

A few final reminders before you actually write your proposition of fact text:

1) Do not balk at returning to the library, or the net, to find additional pieces of evidence. Students are sometimes tempted to go once for an assignment and, rather than do more research at weak points, try to stretch the evidence to fit their purposes. Often, this leads to an only partially complete "prima facie" case, as well as claims that lean well over the actual foundation of the grounds.

2) This is not a merely informative text. It does not offer information for the sake of interest or the usefulness of the information itself. It is argumentative text restricted to controversies of fact.

   Present no evidence that does not relate directly to a claim. Carefully apply the test of relevance to each item. If you have evidence that doesn't apply to a specific argument, but it makes a good point about the topic on its own, you might find an opportunity to use it in an introduction or conclusion.

   Yet most good writers will tell you: go back through your text and look very carefully at what excites you as "good stuff." It may be exactly the thing you need to edit. If you leave all the good stuff in, the text will be too long.

3) Begin putting your text together in the outline form offered above. The system of enumerating arguments is the same as any outline form. This outline is a little like a legal brief. On the outline, it is good to identify the parts as we have done above. You may even signal the parts as you speak, since we're all trying to learn to both speak and listen to arguments.

   You could speak in extemporaneous style, filling in transitions spontaneously to flesh out the text. It could be an outline for fully expressed prose on the page, as well.

Vocabulary

Five Paragraph Essay	Rhetorical Demand	Threshold
Inherency	Significance	
Prima Facie Case	Stock Issues	

Exercises: Go to Interactive Disc to Complete

1) Build your proposition of fact text. It should be three, possibly four typed pages. It should take no more than 3–5 minutes to deliver orally. Actually

rehearse and time the text, don't guess. Organize your speech by the stock issue system described above.

Your teacher may, of course, change this assignment. This, however, would be a reasonable task at this time.

2) Go back to the first sample text in this chapter and respond to it as the imaginary opponent. What would you attack? How? Then describe improvements the advocate might make. (We call this *"a critique,"* an intelligent attempt to better appreciate text.)

3) In the appendices there are additional examples of whole fact texts. Review them to model your own assignment.

Sources

1) There are a wide variety of ways to organize or structure text. See the appendix in the back of back on "speech formats."

2) McKau, J.M. (1990). Reasoning and Communication. Belmont, CA: Wadsworth.

McKerrow, R.E., ed, (1993). Argument and the Postmodern Challenge: Proceedings of the Eighth SCA/AFA Conference on Argumentation. Annandale,VA: Speech-Communication Association.

Meiland, J.W. (1989). Argument as Inquiry and Argument as Persuasion. Argumentation, 3, pp.185–196.

Zarefsky, David (1980). Criteria for Evaluating Non-Policy Argument. CEDA Yearbook 1, pp. 9–16.

VI
A Brief Word about Oral Address

It's important that critical thinking be spoken, not just written. This brings up the rhetorical concern of **audience interaction.** We can understand that concept better by looking at the different settings in which argument can occur.

Private writing, in which only you and a teacher interact, is the vital first step. One learns to synthesize, organize, and express one's thoughts in that setting. One builds arguments as a matter of **intrapersonal communication,** dueling with an imaginary opponent. One can also receive written and some spoken interaction. Yet there is no real external challenge from multiple points of view.

Writing in a public medium, like **journalism,** draws the kind of active interaction that promotes better testing of arguments. Multiple points of view from a wide variety of sources is a norm in that broader environment. The writer is also subject to criticism from the public at large, as well as other equally skilled professional writers.

Speaking before a live audience is a more dynamic, immediate process of interaction, though no less likely to draw contradiction from many points of views (sometimes in raucous, overlapping chorus). This is the level at which we learn to defend our ideas, backed with the preparation we've achieved in private writing. Yet, merely writing alone diminishes maximum opportunity for new information and perspectives. More considered and objective thought can emerge from the process of speaking, questioning, and answering.[1]

Speaking in public **promotes thinking on our feet.** When we have a disagreement at work or in the public, we don't get to go away and write something down over hours and days. We must stand and deliver our thoughts in the moment, hopefully disciplined by this training. Further, speaking text out loud brings a different sense to arguments than perceiving them through private writing. Hidden presumptions and errors in language accuracy tend to show up to the ear in a way that the eyes don't perceive.

This process **benefits the audience,** as well. Not only does the speaker have a chance to hone his own thinking, the audience is forced to look at their presumptions and attitudes in the light of new knowledge and ideas. Sometimes student see things from a new angle, perhaps even more readily than one well versed in the subject.

They may be less conditioned to certain assumptions about an issue, seeing it with fresh eyes. Therefore, no matter if it is a panel discussion, an open class discussion, or individual oral address, texts should be supplemented and tested in open conversation and critique.

So, there are many reasons for speaking text, rather than merely writing it. However, that doesn't keep you from being a little nervous about the process.

When one stands or even sits to speak before an audience of peers, there's often a touch of stage fright, or what is commonly called **speaker apprehension.**[2]

Don't worry so much! You're in good company. Most of us feel this apprehension. A little bit of well directed apprehension can even be a good thing, as it excites the energy of speech delivery. The key to overcoming this is a system of mental and physical discipline used to prepare for delivery.[3]

Mental Techniques

So, let's go over some basic **mental techniques** that can aid good delivery.

1) Do not put off the work. ***Do it now.*** Do a little every day. One of the worst enemies of good delivery is waiting until the last minute to write or rehearse. No matter if you've chosen to read from a manuscript, or deliver extemporaneously, rehearsal improves performance. This means to actually speak out loud, at full volume, while standing somewhere in our home.

   This also means don't continue rewrites right up to the time of delivery. If you see something serious, fine. Adjust. Merely fussing with a text can be a form of procrastination, like cleaning your desk before you write a paper.

2) ***Focus on the content, not yourself.*** There are three basic parts of any speaking experience, according to Aristotle: ***audience, speaker, and message,*** or, in more modern communication parlance, a sender, receivers, and message. Each is really equally important, yet beginners tend to focus on themselves in the process. Do I look all right? Do I sound all right? Am I making mistakes? Do I sound stupid?

   In some respects, beyond a healthy discipline of self-preparation, you might think of yourself as the least important of the three parts of a speech act. The audience, the face of your community, is the object of the address. An important message is the point of the encounter. The speaker is the agent of the message and should submit himself to that role, rather than making the moment all about himself.

Speakers make themselves the focus in one of two ways. They may take such pride in their own delivery—"strutting their stuff," affecting their voice in overly dramatic ways, that the audience sees less of the message and more of your personality. This is beneficial . . . to someone with a weak message that won't bear much scrutiny.

The other way a speaker dominates the process is by being so nervous in the self that they require the sympathy of the audience to get through the process, further distracting from the object of the exercise, the message. So, don't draw attention to yourself with comments like:

> I messed up. Can I start over?
> Oh, I'm so nervous.
> I'm sorry.
> I should have practiced more.
> What's wrong? Did I screw up?

You ask because you're projecting your own paranoia on an audience member who is doing nothing more than listening intently. You're so nervous, though, that you think you're doing badly. Speakers may believe that the audience can see them shaking. We'll ask the audience if anyone's noticed, and generally they haven't. The speaker is simply struggling with themselves in their own mind. In the meantime, again, the message gets lost.

Think of it this way: Nervousness is not the audience's problem. Their problem is to understand the arguments. So, ***get out of the way of the message and let it reach the audience.***

How do you do this? By concentrating on the message yourself, leading the audience to similar focus. Minimize extraneous physical activity. Read the text. Think the thoughts as you speak them. Don't give way to an inner monologue criticizing yourself. Remember, they're not really looking at you with the critical eye you may think they are . . . at least until you make your nervousness obvious to them by emphasizing it with extraneous comments.

Notice, we do not recommend that you envision your audience in their underwear, as some have suggested, only partially in jest. That's a distraction you may never return from.

3) The above are easier to manage if you ***know the text.*** The only way to do this is to ***practice, practice, practice.*** Stand up, don't sit down, and deliver the text at full volume, several times over several days.

Lying back on the bed and mumbling the words is helpful to memory, but you can't even time the material accurately without a full volume reading.

When ***projecting your voice,*** the speech will often slow down the material, and you'll wind up with an overtime presentation. Part of your responsibility is to ***time the message*** with a watch, so you do not take more than your share of audience attention.

Lying back on your bed or in the tub and reciting the words is not a bad idea, nor is saying them when you're driving the car. It's just not sufficient practice until you've replicated the physical activity of speaking. It gives us a sense of the energy it takes to deliver the speech. Also, repeating a speech at full volume can even condition your voice and articulation for the event (see exercises).

Finally, it's ***a matter of relaxing the body over time,*** like stretching before a race, so that the nonverbal aspects of communication can properly frame the verbal content. Physical delivery is either supportive of a message, or it distracts with fidgets and nervousness, undermining audience attention toward the message.

If they're distracted by you, you'll be distracted by their reactions.

4) It's also true that writing style can impact your delivery. There is a distinct difference between ***writing for the ear and writing for the eye.*** In other words, although it's good to expand our vocabulary and to experiment with it in written text, the ear is not the eye. Listeners may hear and recall as little as 25% of the average ten-minute talk.[4]

When ***reading a text to yourself,*** like a book or a magazine, you can stop, muse about a thought or image, look up a word in the dictionary, then go on at your own pace. Not so when an audience listens. The language is coming at them in a linear manner, one word at a time. We can't skip back to the previous paragraph if we miss a few words.

Therefore, we need a shorter, simpler writing style than we might use when writing research papers.

Reading the text aloud will help you to understand this. You'll realize that you're not only writing for the ear, ***you're writing for the mouth.*** If you're not, it will affect ***the smoothness of your delivery.***

There are some words in written text that are difficult to speak out loud. If a word, phrase, or sentence doesn't "fit in your mouth"—that is, it causes you to slip, to mumble, or to stop mid sentence because you've run out of breath—then it's time to abbreviate your language.

Read a little, then look in a thesaurus for simpler or more easily pronounced words. "Don't spend a dollar, when a dime will do" when you're dealing with word choice. That is, don't try to impress anybody with big words. Make every effort that your language be both clear and handily enunciated. Even Aristotle said, "To speak in the language that is common for the day."

It will be necessary to speak the technical language of an expert's field. You should be looking up all the words you don't understand, anyway. It can be embarrassing, as well as damaging to your credibility, when you mispronounce something before an audience who knows the word. If you can't figure out how to pronounce a word with the dictionary, or it's a proper name that you're not sure about, ask your instructor.

This is an important, even calming refinement that can boost your confidence. The very ritual of it can become a source of confidence: "I know this. I can do this." Rewriting, thus, is a part of the rehearsal process. In fact, you really can't complete your writing without the oral delivery of the text.`

5) When you deliver the speech, ***enjoy your interaction with the audience.*** Look them in the eye, individuals, one at a time, rather than a blurry crowd. If you've rehearsed as advised above, you should be able to spend more time with the audience than the text itself. Look at them. Smile as you would when greeting a friend.

The whole dynamic of public speaking is interactive. The sum of you is much greater than the individual parts in creating a total atmosphere for interaction. So, don't take it all on. It's not all about you. Just be standing for a moment among the people you sit with, whom will also be speaking in a little awhile.

Many times even a well-rehearsed person will hide from the audience in the text, even if they know it well enough. Don't hide in the text. Believe it or not, that will make you more nervous. You'll miss the supportive, even appreciative nonverbal communication of your audience. That can be a confidence booster, to notice that they're listening to you.

Think of it as a conversation, like a chat over lunch with a group of friends.

Talk with people, not at them.

Physical Techniques

Now, consider some practical physical techniques for delivery, as well as reinforce the above mental approaches. Our ***nonverbal communication*** can be even more important to persuasion than text content. It frames the message in a way that it's accessible and understandable:

1) Just as you build good arguments ***"from the grounds up,"*** you build good speaking from your feet up. Nonverbal behavior communicates both inwards and outwards. It can help your confidence and maintain enough equilibrium to help you remember the appropriate mental approaches.

   The stance you begin with may affect both your sense of yourself and the audience's sense of you. Take a stable stance. Put your feet about shoulder width apart, but stagger one foot slightly forward. This three pointed stance, heel, toe, and toe, forms a kind of tripod, the most stable plane of all. As you center yourself in the stance, take a pause to center and calm your mind.

   Simply "stand and deliver." Don't pace back and forth like some television evangelist trying to rouse the crowd. As you wander about, kicking your feet, you may distract yourself as well as the audience.

2) ***Footwork.*** Do you never walk then when speaking? Sure, you do. The longer the speech, the more points made, the more appropriate it is that you walk several times. Yet you will not wander aimlessly. Three points matter:

   A) ***Choose when to walk.*** A good plan is to, literally, "move to the next point." Take a silent step or two, so that's there's a pause between issues. This quiet walk will draw the eye to you, if people have drifted during the last point. You draw eyes with the nonverbal, then deliver the verbal message.

      As said before, the nonverbal works best when it frames, or sets up the verbal. Timing matters. Audience attention will be drawn by the last thing that you do. If you speak the next point, then walk, it will be an interruption of your own message.

   B) Lead with the foot that is pointed in the direction that you wish to go. ***Don't cross your legs.*** Don't cross your right leg over your left to move left, nor your left leg over your right to move right. You walk to the sides on a slight diagonal, which is easier to handle gracefully than moving up and back. If you have four arguments, walk four times, two in alternation toward each direction. Remember to start far enough away from the audience so that you don't run into them during your talk. This walking reinforcement of your points should be a part of your rehearsal, as well.

   C) Return to your three-point stance as soon as you arrive from taking a step or two. ***Pause between points.*** Set the stance before you speak again. These ways of reinforcing breaks in thought are a kind of visual paragraphing.

Pauses matter for audience comprehension. If we run sentences together, as though they were all of equal importance, it is harder for an audience to comprehend. Pausing before key points helps.

3) **Eye contact** is very important in communication with others. Looking at each audience member is the gateway that opens to our talk. Eye contact is used to achieve some bonding with the groups. It's a positive persuasion factor. So, the next thing you do after setting your three-point stance, is to **look directly at the audience.**

We mentioned the importance of eye contact as a part of your mental tactics. Let's carefully define "look directly," as particular behavior, since this is the real point of nervousness for some. We'll use an exclusive/inclusive definition. It does not mean to look over the heads of the audience, nor at their forehead. Well-meaning teachers sometimes offer such ideas, but there is no replacement for the interactive warmth of genuine eye contact.

The lack of it affects the audience. You know when someone isn't looking at you. You can feel it, just as surely as you can feel someone staring at your back in a public place. It's a way that people pass energy and support back and forth. If you're not looking at the audience, why should they look at you? Just standing and reading into your text is like treating your audience to a radio show. Who looks at a radio? It's in the background, but we give attention to something else.

Since nonverbal communication communicates both inside you and out from you, your **eye contact has an effect on you,** as surely as it does the audience. At first, you may be very nervous to look, but try this.

Look at one person, maybe someone you know and feel comfortable with, then another, then another from there. Don't look at "the crowd" in fuzzy outline. Pick individuals and talk to them, no differently than you would if waiting in the hall for class, passing the time. If you do this, you may be surprised how much support you feel from the others. You may feel energized by **the synergy of your mutual focus with the audience.**

There's an exercise at the end of the chapter to help you with this. Do it. No matter how silly it may seem, do it.

4) **Voice** is our next concern in delivery. We'll keep this very simple. Use your own voice, not an impersonation of something you've heard in media. Don't force it. Don't try to sound like a radio announcer by lowering your pitch. Be yourself. However, you do have **two minimum obligations.**

A) You must **speak loudly enough to be heard** in the last row of the audience. We don't yell at people. We use a technique called "projection." ***Rather than shout, breathe it out.*** That's right. Repeat the idea in your mind and practice it with your text. Rather than shout, breathe it out.

Our voices carry when we breathe the sentence out. It will be louder, but it will not sound harsh or angry. There's an old saying about this kind of delivery: "Breathe in the thought, hold the thought," that is, feel the sense of it, "then breathe out the thought."

In other words, you look down at your text for your next line, "inhale it," look at your audience, then exhale as you speak. It will feel artificial initially, perhaps mechanical, but the more you practice it, the smoother your vocal will be, and your eye contact will be regulated by the practice.

B) ***You must speak clearly enough to be understood.*** Students are sometimes surprised, especially if they're not prepared, at how much work it is to articulate properly. We tend to be a little lazy in our private speech, slurring words in the local vernacular. ("'Sup?") It's harder to hear slurred language in public speaking situations.

That doesn't pass muster in more public conversation. Though you may be used to speaking only by dropping the lower jaw, you will need to activate both lips in the process to make sounds clearly, and it's work to do it right. Your mouth itself can get tired with it. So, practice your diction. Don't be surprised by a cramp in your jaw, if you don't. There's an exercise at the end of the chapter to help you with this.

Those are the two minimums, but ***vocal emphasis*** is also important. We are not very effective if we drone on in the same flat pitch, pace, and volume, making every word of equal value. Some phrases and words are more important than others. If we only typically hear and remember 25% of a ten-minute talk, maybe we should make choices about the most important 25% and emphasize that language with our delivery.

Find that language, perhaps underline it in the text you're going to deliver from, and decide how to emphasize the key points.

You may do so by bringing volume up or down at those points. Sometimes a well-projected whisper is as good as a shout. You can pause to set off the point. You can keep a certain pace, then slow down the rate to emphasize a key point. There are many possible ways to say a single thing. Experiment with it.

You may find, once again, the rehearsal process can affect the rewriting process.

5) **Gesture,** the use of your hands to accent a point, is worth brief mention . . . but only a mention. We may complain that we don't know what to do with our hands in front of the room. We do. We gesture all the time, some more than others, but normally in the flow of conversation. We just forget when we fail to relax, or have an unrehearsed manuscript in our hands.

If we're to think of this as a conversation with the audience, we should allow ourselves to gesture as we would in other conversations, as we feel like it.

Believe it, unless you stand around with your hands in your pocket all the time, you've learned how to use your hands. So, give them a chance. Don't tie them up behind your back, or in front of you like a fig leaf on Adam. Don't clutch your elbows rigidly at your side. Let them come out from your body and reach toward the audience.

We may also make some decisions about using gestures to emphasize points. Don't be trapped into rehearsing in front of a mirror. A little is fine, to get a sense of what you look like, but beware of over rehearsing, or locking into planned gestures in a mechanical way.

The key, here as well, is to be familiar with your text. Rehearse with the manuscript. Grasp it with the left hand, if you're right handed, or visa versa. Then use the opposite hand to gesture naturally, as the impulse or decision finds its way into your rehearsal process.

* * * * *

In sum, these are ten quick areas in which you can improve delivery with practice. Try them. Maybe hook up with someone in the class and practice for each other. Get some objective input about how you're coming across. Most folks don't notice their own fidgets and idiosyncrasies, since they're a matter of habit. With objective input, though, habits can be broken.

Vocabulary

Audience, Speaker, and Message
Delivery
    Three-Point Stance
    Eye Contact
    Natural Footwork and Gesture

Vocal Articulation, Projection, and
    Emphasis
Intrapersonal Communication
Nonverbal Communication
Speaker Apprehension

Exercises: Go to Interactive Disc to Complete

1) Do the following tongue twisters in class. You'll discover you need to do them again at home. Think of them as vocal gymnastics. Repeat each several times before you speak, like stretching before a race.

   Isn't it horrid, Harold, when you're hot and in a hurry, and you have to hold your hat on with your hand.

   Marvin, a marvelous man with a muffler shop, makes muffins every Monday.

   Rugged rubber baby bumpers.

   She sells seashells by the seashore.

   Six thick thistles thrust through her thumb.

   Tommy G. Thompson, Secretary of Health and Human Services, spoke at the Senate subcommittee.

   How much wood would a woodchuck chuck if a woodchuck could chop wood? He'd chuck all the wood that a woodchuck could if a wood chuck could chuck wood.

2) This is the silent exercise. Each member of the class goes to the front of the room one at a time. You are to set your feet in a three-point stance and spend one minute looking at everyone in the room. Make authentic eye contact. Don't rush up or back to your seat. Take your time. Actually see them and see them seeing you.

3) Once your speech is prepared or delivered, go on to the next three chapters, as others are finishing the assignment. Begin to consider values worth discussing for your next assignment.

Sources

1) Kortner, A.N. (1990). Debate and Communication Skills, ERIC Digest. Bloomington, IN: ERIC Clearing House on Reading and Communication Skills.

2) Brownell, W., and Richard, K., (1985). The Communication Apprehension and Speech Anxiety Peak Experience. Paper delivered at the Annual meeting of Eastern Communication Association. Hartford, Conn: ERIC.

   MacIntyre, P.D., Thivierge, K. (1995). "The Effects of Speaker Personality on Anticipated Reactions to Public Speaking." Communication Research Reports 12–2, pp. 125–33.

3) Campbell, K.K (1996). The Rhetorical Act. Belmont, CA: Wadsworth.

   Rybacki, K.C., & Rybacki, D.J. (2002). Communication Criticism: Approaches and Genres. Boston, MA: Pearson.

   Sonntag, L. Speeches for All Occasions (1993). U.S., New Jersey: Mimosa Books.

4) Adler, R.B., Proctor, R.F., & Towne, N. (2005). Looking Out/Looking In. Belmont, CA: Thompson/Wadsworth.

VII
More Fallacies

Now that you're doing your proposition of fact speech, you've probably discovered that there are yet other ways arguments can go wrong.

Fallacies are actually of various types besides the logical fallacies discussed before. There are other *logical fallacies,* along with fallacies of *relevance.* There are fallacies of *appeal* and fallacies of *language,* which may become especially important for your value speeches coming up.

More Logical Fallacies

The first we'll mention is the *"non sequitur,"* which means "does not necessarily follow." It occurs when an argument makes a huge inferential leap, which doesn't make sense because steps in the thought process are missing.

Sometimes ideas will pop out of us that aren't really connected, though they may seem to make sense to us at the time. A recent phone call from an animal lover to a talk radio show used this argument:

> Grounds: Now that Saddam Hussein is gone, Iraq is a hotbed of looting, crime and rebellion. There's even dog fighting.
>
> Claim: I say, "Bring back Saddam!"

Notice there's no warrant. That's common with non sequiturs. There is no connective thinking linking the grounds to the conclusion drawn in the claim. It makes perfect sense to the speaker, in the midst of his disgust about dog fighting, but it's not a logical argument about Hussein.

Sometimes quotations from very famous speakers are peppered with non sequiturs.[1] Here's one from former senator and presidential candidate, Barry Goldwater, speaking before the National Inter-Fraternity Conference:

> Claim: Where fraternities are not allowed, communism flourishes.

No particular grounds or warrant was in evidence. One could perhaps be reasoning the other side of the probability that communists ban fraternities. Yet it still seems like quite an inferential leap.

Consider Mayor Daly's observations about crime in Chicago during his tenure:

> Claim: The more killing and homicides you have, the more havoc it prevents.

Let's be kind. Maybe Mayor Daly misspoke and intended to say "creates" instead of "prevents." Yet assuming that he meant to say exactly this, what would you imagine his warrant to be?

> Warrant: Heck, it's just statistical. If the general crime producing population winnows itself down, then there's all the less work for police to do (?!).

A couple of other people have been unwittingly disconnected on the issue of crime. Mayor of Washington, D.C., Marion Berry, who was himself convicted on drug charges, argued:

> Claim: Outside of the killings, (Washington) has one of the lowest crime rates in the country.

Do you think their Chamber of Commerce picked that up for a slogan? "Sure, you'll be killed, but you'll be otherwise safe from crime."

A similar disconnect came from Frank Risso, former police chief and mayor of Philadelphia:

> Claim: The streets are safe in Philadelphia, it's only the people who make them unsafe.

Now, that's a relief. I always go to a new city worrying that the streets themselves will rise up and beat me.

And of course, we can't leave Dan Quayle out of this mix. Here is a famous non sequiter from a speech before the United Negro College Fund, whose motto is "A mind is a terrible thing to waste":

> Claim: What a waste it is to lose one's mind—or not to have a mind. How true that is.

Whether you have a mind or not, that's difficult to follow.

* * * * *

Transfer fallacies are inference errors, in some respects close enough to hasty and sweeping generalization fallacies to be mistaken for them.

Transfer/Composition fallacies conclude that because a part of something is a certain way, the whole of that something is that way, too. Simply recall the phrase, ***"the part for the whole."***

For instance, if one were buying cars, and wound up being taken in by cool rims and snappy leather interior—and it's red, too—one might tend to infer that the appearance of the car is reflected in the whole car, though it may not necessarily be so.

Appearances may be deceiving with people, too. You fall in love with his or her beauty, but discover that the packaging is deceptive. They turn out needing some work on their interior.

If I ran across a really good teacher at school, I wouldn't necessarily infer that it was a really good department, or a really good school. Not by that detail alone.

It's easy to see that this is **close to hasty generalization.** In fact, sometimes both fallacies could be applied to a single piece of discourse. The difference is in the tightness, the integrity of the whole. The example about car parts for a car is apt, or a single department for a corporation. It isn't just that the sample is small. It's that someone may perceive a singular characteristic as improperly representative of the whole.

One of the better examples of dual error—both hasty generalization and a fallacy of transfer/composition—came from an exercise in the first edition of Rybacki and Rybacki's "Advocacy & Opposition." I'll vary the subject slightly, but the design is theirs.[2]

> Claim: Sports is a veritable shopping center of designer steroids.

> Grounds: Why, just last week, three baseball players were suspended for steroids.

Again, there is no specific warrant. If there were, the reasoning errors would be clear.

> Warrant: Three is a significant number and baseball is representative of all sports.

There is hasty generalization as three players are not a particularly large sample for baseball, let alone sports. Further, sports is a super-class including several small sub-classes, football, baseball, basketball, soccer, etc. To characterize baseball is not to characterize all of sports, and that's the transfer fallacy of composition.

One of the hottest topics in the new century is the separation of church and state. As religious people frequently assume articles of faith (values), they may identify so strongly with their religion that they project the truth of their religion as the truth for the general population.

Some Muslims believe that God, named Allah, is on their side, and that the U.S. is "the great Satan." Christians and Jews believe that God, traditionally named Yaweh, is on their side, and that many Muslims are part of "an axis of evil." Who can say which speaks most accurately for the whole of divinity. Yet some Americans feel like this:

> I recently read that the vast majority of Americans believe in God. The words "in God we trust" are on our money. I've pledged allegiance to the flag with the words "one nation under God" included. Our founding fathers

clearly had God in mind, yet we have controversy over having a wooden cross on a hill above a town, and the ACLU goes after a southern courthouse for posting the ten commandments. Maybe it's time for the Godless minority to just shut up.

However, there is a mistaken hidden presumption. Someone who believes in God is not necessarily a Christian. Their proper title is "theist." Some of our founding fathers were theists and Masons, though not Christian. So, what is true of Christianity, which is a subclass of theism, is not necessarily true of theism as a whole. Ask Hindus, or Buddhists, or any member of the global population who believe in God, per se, but call him by another name, just as they have other words for "coffee" or "love."

Here's an illustration for how this hidden presumption would constitute a transfer/composition fallacy, in which T stands for theism and C stands for Christianity, and the arrow illustrates the transference from **subclass to the superclass** (Figure 14):

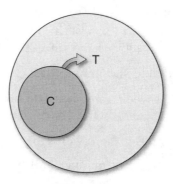

Figure 14

The fallacy **transfer/division is the reverse,** it infers that what is true of the whole is necessarily true of the parts. Remember the phrase "**whole for the part.**" The transference here is **from superclass to subclass** (Figure 15):

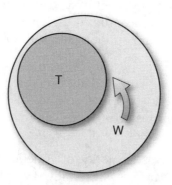

Figure 15

This mental action is a similar to sweeping generalization. Again the difference is the integrity, the unity of the classes involved and whether the whole is representative of all its parts. If I have an idea that Ford is a good brand of car, does that mean that every car I get from Ford will be a good car? Or if I like an individual model as a whole, does that mean I like every aspect of it. I've driven Ford Mustangs for years and have generally been satisfied, but I know that, no matter how well I care for it, it's going to leak oil some day and make noises like a wounded rhinoceros.

Are you in a committed relationship or a marriage? Do you like them, love them? All parts of them? If you do, you may be very early in the relationship, you've been enormously blessed. . . . or you're fibbing under pressure. Relationships of any depth tend to have conflict over habits, values, or personal characteristics. While the relationship may tend to be greater than the sum of its parts, some of its parts are less desirable than others.

How do we distinguish between sweeping generalization and transfer division. If I say, "Any Mustang is a good Mustang," that would be a sweeping generalization. If I say, however, that "My Mustang has a great engine, therefore, all its engineered parts are good," I'd be committing a transfer/division fallacy.

The third kind of transfer fallacy has a slightly different dynamic than composition or division. It may make as much sense to think of **"red herring,"** also called "straw man," as a fallacy of relevance. It is a transfer in the fact that we transfer attention from one thing to another. A red herring is a fish with a pungent odor that was often spread across a trail to mislead tracking dogs.[3] Today the term, popularized as a mystery story metaphor, is used to denote a deliberately misleading argument. While composition and division may be accidentally committed, red herring suggests some intent to distract or deceive.

One famous red herring came from **Richard Nixon's "Checkers Speech."** He was being scrutinized for taking favors when he was Vice President under Eisenhower. While he redressed no particular questions, he used distracting images to create sympathy. In fact, he committed two fallacies, including "appeal to pity" which we'll discuss below. The numerous ellipses edit out some ramblings that are, in themselves, a distraction:

> One other thing I probably should tell you, because if I don't they will probably be saying this about me, too. We did get something, a gift after the election. A man down in Texas heard Pat on the radio mention that our two youngsters would like to have a dog. . . . The day before we left . . . we got a message from Union Station . . . saying they had a package for us. . . . It was a cocker spaniel . . . from Texas, black and white, spotted, and . . . Tricia . . . named it Checkers. And, you know, the kids . . . loved the dog, and I just want to say this . . . regardless of what they say about it, we're going to keep it.

The dog was the only favor Nixon really acknowledged, though others were indicated. He also went on at some length about his wife's old cloth coat, a contrast to the mink of Mamie Eisenhower and other Washington wives. The red herring is in his making an issue of "they," some conspiracy of hateful people who want to take his daughter's dog. His appeal to pity is fairly common, involving mention of little dogs and children. People who would look down on perks for White House members certainly wouldn't begrudge a little girl a dog.

We prefer "red herring," but **straw man** is also used to label this fallacy. The metaphor suggests that, instead of attacking the actual arguments made by an equal opponent, we create a "scarecrow," an irrelevant and distracting issue, and beat it up to make ourselves look good.

Notice in political debates how this gets set up. Panel members from the news corps will ask a pointed question, and the candidate will reply: "That's not the real question. The real question is. . . ." Then the candidate goes his merry way arguing some tangential issue, for which he is better prepared.

* * * * *

Sometimes our reason runs in a circle, chasing its own tail, not unlike a little dog. This is called, appropriately enough, **circular reasoning.** The mental action can be defined easily in terms of Toulmin. Circular reasoning is when warrants merely repeat claims. Your moms and dads probably used this one to exert authority:

> Claim: "I want you to do X."
>
> "Why, mom?"
>
> Warrant (claim repeated): "Because I said so."

She wouldn't put it this way, but her warrant, her reason why the claim is true, simply refers again to the claim. Other examples are:

> "All of us cannot be famous, because all of us cannot be well known." So, what's wrong with that? "Well known" is just a synonym for "famous."
>
> "I'm all for women having equal rights, but women should not fight bulls, because a bullfighter is and should be a man." That is, a bullfighter is a man, so a bullfighter should be . . . well, male!

The language pretty much consists of a repetition of the same thought with slightly altered word choice or grammar. It may seem redundant. That's why another common name for this fallacy is, **"Begging the Question,"** repeating the claim over and over, as if to persuade by sheer force of repetition. We prefer "circular reasoning" as "begging the question" is another term commonly misused today. People say, "That begs the question, where was he at the time of crime." They use it positively, in other words, as a way of saying, "this issue demands our attention."

* * * * *

Actually, there's a fair amount of truth in the notion that **repetition persuades,** though it isn't logical in argumentation. Advertisers make hay with our being hypnotized into name brand recognition. Sadly, but rather humanly, fallacies are sometimes effective.

I ask my students every year, "What brand of toothpaste do you use?" There's usually very little diversity in answer. The companies that are first and second in advertising dominate the selection, though virtually nobody seems to be able to tell why they get any better use out of those toothpastes.

Fallacies of Appeal

Perhaps the most obvious and easily detectable of all fallacies are fallacies of appeal. **These will become especially important as we go on to look at value propositions.** Any evening of watching television commercials will give you many examples.

The most common fallacy may be **Ad Hominem** attack, literally "to the man," or "to the person," in more modern terms. As we said earlier, the main distinction between being argumentative and aggressive is that argumentative people address issues, but aggressive people attack their opponents. Ad Hominem is inherently aggressive.

A common example in real world terms would be the efforts of a defense attorney focusing on lurid details of a rape victim's past, to suggest that "she was asking for it."

Ad hominem may appear in the **language of name-calling.** So, we commonly see it in tough political campaigns. California Governor Schwartzenneger, unable to pass a budget, called his congress "girlie men." It was an ill-considered reference to an old Saturday Night Live skit spoofing the governor himself. Women were particularly offended by the reference.

Ad hominem can also be visual imagery that degrades the object of the communication:

A congressional advocate of curbs on immigration was criticized for using an "anti-Hispanic" prop at a news conference to denounce the widening acceptance of Mexican identification cards. Rep. G. Tancredo (R-Colo) and several of his colleagues stood beside a large poster to dramatize their concern that more than 1 million IDs issued by Mexican consulates—and accepted in this country by many local authorities and banks—are a form of amnesty for illegal immigrants. The poster depicted a mock consular ID card with a picture of Mexican President Vincente Fox. It was captioned, "Office for the Issuance of Illegal Alien ID." It listed Fox's occupation as "El Presidente," and the citizenship of his parents as "Unknown. . . ." Tancredo expressed surprise at the criticism and said it was an effort by his opponents to shift debate away from the merits of the issue.[4]

Again, we may have an example of two possible fallacies in one expression. The "unknown" answer to citizenship of parents is a veiled suggestion that Fox is a bastard. There is also a charge by him that other congressmen commit a "red herring" fallacy. Which do you believe? Why?

It might surprise you that this is a fallacy, since name calling is so often in the media, so often a part of our election process. Nonetheless, it shifts audience attention away from the issue that's really at hand to the character of the person. Thus, it's a fallacy.

Don't you wish more people knew that?

* * * * * *

Another commonly used fallacy of appeal is called the ***bandwagon argument,*** in Latin "argumentum ad populum," or argument to the people, specifically in the sense of the crowd. This is familiar to you, as those TV commercials mentioned earlier are full of such appeals.

They show a lone guy with Brand X beer, looking across at a Budweiser party, all gorgeous (by a certain standard) girls in bikinis . . . in the snow. The Swedish Bikini Team, or the like, cavorting around in sub-freezing temperatures. (Yeah. That always happens.) And the Brand X beer guy is all alone. The appeal is to our need to belong, our desire not to be different. It doesn't necessarily make Brand X any worse than Bud.

In the case of popularity, as defined in polls, it can be both deceptive and unreliable. Popularity tends to come and go. Look at general approval ratings for presidents. They may move up and down rather dynamically, according to people's satisfaction with the most recent events.

Further, that a majority believes something does not necessarily make it true or right. The majority believed that the world was flat. The majority thought Dewey would beat President Truman in a landslide. A majority of Americans seem to enjoy so-called "reality programming." I pray for their recovery daily.

Don't get me started on "talk" shows. Jerry Springer seems to be a professional platform for the advancement of ad hominem.

* * * * *

The Appeal to ***Pity and Fear*** is an exploitation of pathos, one of Aristotle's three appeals. There's a point at which pathos goes beyond itself to "bathos," insincere and excessively sentimental pathos.

My favorite example comes from judicial history. A teenage male murdered his parents, rather viciously. His attorney argued for mercy on the grounds that his client was an orphan.

I learned the hard way how often this fallacy is used as a persuasive tool by public agencies, and businesses. As a high school student, I agreed to chair a youth drive for a certain famous charity. I spent many hours getting other young people to join the drive and spoke for the drive, equipped with the usual, touching poster of a child on crutches in leg braces. Only after the drive did I discover that 96% of the money raised actually went back into the organization running the drive, while only 4% wound up with the children pictured in the posters. Basically, it was an employment program and an excuse for travel junkets.

The names have been excluded to protect the guilty, since they've cleaned up their act considerably.

More modern charities, like the United Way, have a better balance in expenditure, but there are still many scams and manipulations that rely on your fear or your sympathy. There was an incident at my college during a demonstration against the Vietnam war. A group of fairly radical protesters distributed a handbill that said they would napalm a dog in the college square to show what we were doing to people over there.

A large group of people gathered, shaking their fists, in total ire over the threat to a dumb animal. Of course, there was no dog. There was only a guy at the mike, telling us, "Look at how angry you got over one dog. Why aren't you angry about the thousands of human lives lost in Vietnam?"

A few people thought it was creative. Others stayed around, somewhat skeptically, to hear what the guy had to say. Most of us were repulsed and left, because we felt manipulated by an unfair appeal to sympathy and an event based on a lie.

The use of children and dogs continues to be useful in exerting influence on the public:

> A new cache of videotapes showing the apparent training of Al Queda operatives in Afghan terrorist camps offers graphic confirmation of the long held belief that Osama Bin Laden's network has experimented with chemical weapons. . . . The 64 tapes obtained by CNN in Afghanistan and airing through the week on the cable network, appear to show terrorist camp trainees using poison gas to kill dogs.[5]

Was this a real tape? Where did it come from? Wasn't this about the same time that we were being told Iraq was stockpiling chemical weapons, only later to find that this was false? Is this, possibly, an appeal to fear? Or is this an authentic glimpse into testing of gas? Discussions in Congress at this moment are exploring these and other unanswered questions. To my knowledge, no particular verification has been offered.

* * * * *

The mental action of **Appeal to Tradition** is simple: "we should continue to do something merely because we've always done it this way." By that analysis, we should stay away from all new schools of art, all new scientific discovery, virtually any new manufacturing process, even if it creates both jobs and cheaper products, simply because it's new. This is not to imply that new ideas are always better. In fact, to argue, "let's do it because it's new," is equally unreliable. Old ideas aren't necessarily better. New ideas aren't necessarily better. Better ideas are better, as measured by their effect and benefits.

* * * * *

The fallacy of **Appeal to Ignorance** is easy for students to misunderstand. They'll hear something they think is dumb, and they'll say, "That's appeal to ignorance, because it's an ignorant argument." Not quite. The mental action can be described as a reversal of the burden of proof. The language typically looks like this: one makes a claim, then, in lieu of providing grounds, asks another to prove the claim wrong. It often is seen in discussions of the super-natural and speculations about the unknown.

You can almost hear Leonard Nimoy intoning on one of those unsolved mystery shows: "But as for the yeti, nobody has yet to prove it doesn't exist."

You see, though, it's not our burden to prove that the yeti does not exist. If you are the one who proposes that something exists that is not generally accepted, the burden of proof is yours. So, while it is often mistaken, the mental action is very specific.

Fallacies of Relevance

Apart from using grounds that do not support a claim, there are several ways to distract people from the issues at hand, or to offer arguments that don't belong in the discussion.

There is **simple avoidance** of the issue. Trying to avoid talking about it at all. This is the "no comment" response we often see from public figures, or "I don't recall" when questioned before judges or congressional committees.

My wife has perfected this method: I ask her how much money she's spent, but she ignores me and goes on to a different subject.

You may also **seize on a trivial point.** For instance, you focus on a picky detail that isn't the main thrust of your opponent's argument. For instance, your opponent reads a piece of evidence that defeats your position, but you notice that there's a clerical error on the date of the magazine cited. So, you say, "that was printed on the 15th not the 16th!"

True, it was sloppy scholarship, and one should try to keep the original materials you quote from available. Remember our suggestions that you copy original articles twice, one to cut for cards and one to keep in tact. Yet the point of the evidence remains the same. Also, you've just admitted that the evidence exists.

Finally, **shifting ground** is another way to avoid an issue one is stuck on. Recall our conversations about argumentative ground and the metaphor of a specific fort that we've defined and are defending. Let's say that you're the opponent, successfully laying siege upon your adversary's fort. You've cornered him in a weak position for which he has no answer, but he shifts to a different position. He may either retreat to a tighter position in the fort, abandoning a portion of his burden, or he may leave the fort entirely and pretend that his position is closer to yours than it really is. Doing either, he will hope that you don't notice that he's altered the original proposition. You'll watch for that, however, and hold him to his original position.

The question of the moment in journalism is whether there's been a shift of ground on the justifications for an Iraq invasion. The initial justifications offered were that there was a likelihood that Iraq had WMD (weapons of mass destruction) and would use them, and it was connected to Al Queda and 9/11.

After Hussein was overthrown and was captured, no evidence was discovered of either WMD or an Al Queda connection. The justification shifted to the position that we'd overthrown a despot and liberated Iraq's people. One could certainly make a case for either justification. However, Congress was talked into buying the first one. Is that a shift of ground?

Fallacies of Language

Fallacies of language involve words that distort meaning or incite emotions in an unreasonable way.

Equivocation, using words and phrases that can be interpreted in at least two ways, can be a significant source of interpersonal and argumentative misunderstanding. For our purposes, clarity of definition is an essential part of debate. We must understand one agreed upon sense of the terms in contention.

There are always the innocent daily human misunderstandings we may all have. For instance, people aren't always careful with their pronouns. Talking about two female friends, we might tell a story that goes something like, "Well, she did this, but then she did that, so she got really upset." Which she is she, one might ask?

Equivocation can even be used intentionally as an unethical tactic. An advocate presents an idea that can be seen as meaning a couple of different things. The opponent may try to pin the advocate down to a clearer definition, but the advocate stays "slippery." Then, after the opponent has committed to a particular version of the advocate's position in his counterargument, the advocate stands up and pleads, "But that is not what I truly meant. You've misinterpreted what I've said." Thus, intentional equivocations may be used to support an intentional shifting of grounds as a strategic effort to waste your time while you make "irrelevant" counterattacks.

For instance, consider a case in which an advocate wants to rely on "law enforcement agencies" to enforce a new program of anti-terrorism. As his opponent, you press him for a clearer definition of "law enforcement agencies." He tells you that he'll "rely primarily on police." You then use your time on the floor arguing why police are inadequate to meet the terrorist threat, especially because they are not sufficiently interconnected to respond. He then replies that his position has been misunderstood. Yes he's using mainly police, but that he's using "Interpol," though not exclusively. Since he's used the plural form "agencies," he can also rely on the FBI.

The point is not that these agencies are not vulnerable to criticism. The point is that the advocate has been intentionally vague, luring you to waste a significant portion of your allotted time on an irrelevant position.

Emotive language involves using what we might call "hot words," words that provoke or incite negative emotion. Most people probably have some "hot words." It may be something as simple as being called "a girl" when you want to be acknowledged as a woman with equal status to the speaker.

At our campus, I've learned that there is no such thing as a "secretary" anymore. We only have "office supervisors," an innocuous euphemism. If you call someone a secretary, though, it's a hot word, a word that excites disagreement unnecessarily.

They may be something more incendiary like ***racial epithets.*** I spent enough time in parts of the south to have heard the "N" word enough for a lifetime. To the present day when I hear it, even among blacks teasing other blacks, it makes me very uncomfortable. When I'm uncomfortable, I don't always think straight, and I suspect it's much the same for most.

What words set you off defensively? "Fat?" "Short?" "Stupid?" How about "taxes" or "terrorist?" "Conservative" or "liberal?" Consider the times you have felt uncomfortable or irritated around these words, perhaps even been thrown into an internal monologue of angry and distracted thoughts.

Some of this language may be intentional. People who use emotive language against us "win" by throwing us off our composure. Recognize these words for what they are, and try to keep to your own center.

It's possible, if we get reactive about a hot word, that we lose our own perspective and get drug down to a lower level of argument. When we're incited to unreasoning emotion, we may return the favor, with hot words of our own, rather than finding an argument best phrased for clarity. There's an old saying, "Never wrestle with a pig. You'll get muddy, and the pig likes it."

Finally, there's ***jargonese,*** the use of specialized terms to confuse an opponent, or to create an illusion of superiority. This may happen when a specialist in a field describes something in such complex terms that you can only take his word for it. Doctors who are more interested in your compliance than your understanding may sometimes overwhelm you with new terms, then ask you to simply trust him that certain treatments are necessary. Yet research will indicate that there's a fair amount of unnecessary medical tests that are administered, as well as unnecessary surgery.

Garage mechanics may also dazzle you with technical terms about why you need a lot of engine repairs, or new suspension, or whatever. The chances are good that you have paid for at least some unnecessary repair.

In a practical debate situation, you may be given highly technical definitions that the advocate refuses to clarify or simplify technical definitions from expert testimony. Remember what Dr. Albert Schweitzer suggested about scientific explanation: if you can't explain it to a five year old child, then you don't really know what you're talking about.

* * * * *

Not only are fallacies, especially fallacies of appeal, remarkably persuasive to the mass public, some fallacies may even be taken for good style. A little humor, for instance, even when dealing with serious issues, can be very persuasive. However, like sheer force of repetition, it may be persuasive for illogical reasons.

When humor is used to distract us from the fact that the speaker or writer has no particular support for their position, nor an answer to someone's counterargument, then it's the fallacy of ***reductio ad absurdum, or appeal to humor.*** These often attempt to reduce an argument to the point of being absurd, laughable. One makes an attempt to somehow laugh off the issue, or ridicule an opponent's argument. There's often a tone of sarcasm or irony. For instance:

Any individual owning an SUV must report to the Department of Defense immediately. Why not? We're fighting the war for their fuel. Just think of what we could do by sending the drivers of these gas-guzzling monsters off to some desert in 120 degree heat. They've already trained to drive tanks, so they could go right to the front lines. Our national fuel efficiency would double at least, as well as pushing the gas prices down where they belong. Our air would be twice as clean, burning half the fuel we used to. The streets would be less busy. Talk about a solution to unemployment. Millions of jobs created, now that we've sent all those ambassadors of good will to the Middle East to win those hearts and minds. You say the auto industry would be hurt? No, I say. We would simply be educating the next generation of car buyers that the decisions we make today affect every American tomorrow. Can't you see the ads? Buy a

Lincoln Navigator and win a free, all-expense-paid trip to Iraq! Or how about: Buy a giant GMC and personally meet Osama Bin Laden!

From one point of view, if you believe we went into Iraq because of oil, this is funny. Would it convince anyone to actually send SUV drivers to the draft? Of course not. That's not even really the author's claim, is it? His purpose is to skewer both SUV drivers and the war in Iraq as an energy industry scam.

As with all things rhetorical, the effect of this is in the mind of the audience. Some may find both the subject matter and the sarcasm offensive, especially if they have a more patriotic vision of the war in Iraq.

And this reminds us of an important point about all fallacies. They are perceived in a somewhat subjective manner, and there is often disagreement about what they mean.

I recall 1988, when Vice Presidential candidate Lloyd Bentson confronted Dan Quayle in a national debate. Quayle had been claiming, in defense of his youth, that John Kennedy was also a young man when he went to the White House. Bentson retorted, "Sir, I knew John Kennedy, I worked with John Kennedy, and you are no John Kennedy." Half the live audience applauded and laughed, while the other half booed. I'll let you guess the halves.

Quayle had no particularly effective retort, except to say, "That was totally uncalled for." Yet Bentson's efforts were not effective in persuading the American public to vote for Michael Dukakis over Ronald Reagan.

There's no denying, though, that some reductio ad absurdum is effective as an aspect of style, as long as we identify with the person using it. For instance, projecting an adversary's idea out to its furthest logical extent, but in a humorous way, can be a way of making their argument seem trivial.

Recall our earlier conversation about Goldwater's claim that "Where fraternities are not allowed, communism flourishes." Apart from pointing out that it was a non-sequitur, we ran the idea out to its furthest logical extension: if this is true, then we should have sent fraternities to Eastern Europe during the Cold War and all would have been well.

Historically, a lot of reductio ad absurdum could be classified as wit. In a duel in British Parliament, Disraeli faced off with an adversary who said:

> "Sir, you will either die of syphilis, or on the gallows!"
>
> Disraeli coolly replied, "That depends, sir, on whether I embrace your mistress, or your principles."

Game. Set. Match. While Disraeli did nothing more than return an ad hominem with an ad hominem, his had humor, was a better insult, and—perhaps, most importantly—he did not strike first. As a well-timed rejoinder, reductio ad absurdum may work.

Winston Churchill also had a wicked sense of humor and had a way with rejoinder. At a formal dinner with Lady Astor, a very proper and high bred lady, it is said that Churchill was asked:

"Winston, what part of the turkey do you prefer?"

"I'd like some of the breast," Winston said.

Lady Astor flushed and reprimanded, "We don't say breast in this house."

"Well, then, what do you call it?"

"We call it 'White Meat.'"

"Fine," he said, smiling to himself, "I'll have white meat."

The next day, Lady Astor received a corsage from Winston with this equivocal, but humorous note:

"I hope that you will pin this on your 'white meat.'"

However, some issues don't bear joking, and humor works best when there's a well constructed argument underneath. Arguments are the meal. Humor is dessert. Or as Aristotle put it, "Humor is the only test of gravity, and gravity of humor, for a subject which will not bear raillery is suspicious, and a jest which will not bear serious examination is false wit."

Vocabulary

Fallacies of Appeal:
    Ad Hominem
    Appeal to Ignorance
    Appeal to Pity and Fear
    Appeal to Tradition
    Bandwagon Argument
    Reductio ad Absurdum (Appeal to
        Humor)
Fallacies of Language:
    Equivocation
    Emotive Language
    "Jargonese"

Fallacies of Logic:
    Circular Reason
    Non Sequitur
    Transfer Fallacy
        Composition
        Division
        "Red Herring"
Fallacies of Relevance:
    Avoiding the Issue
    Shifting Ground
    Seizing on a Trivial Point

Exercises: Go to Interactive Disc to Complete

Identify the fallacies represented below:

1)   "A prominent Saudi Arabian editor Tuesday disavowed an article that appeared in his own newspaper Al Riydh, that repeated the century old fiction

that Jews use the blood of Christians and Muslims to make holiday foods ("Saudi Editor Retracts Article That Defamed Jews," *LA Times,* March 20, 2002)."

2) "Conservative U.S. preacher Jerry Falwell apologized Saturday for calling the prophet Mohammed a terrorist, saying he meant no offense to 'any sincere law abiding Muslim' (*LA Times,* Oct. 13, 2002)."

3) We can't all be smart, because we can't all be intelligent.

4) The Spanish Inquisition, with all its torture, must have been justified, if whole peoples invoked and defended it.

5) In 1950, Senator Joseph McCarthy claimed that he had 81 case histories of communists in the State Department: "Of case number 40 I do not have much information, except the general statement of the agency that there is nothing in their files to prove he has no Communist connections."

6) "I'll fight him for nothing, if the price is right," said Morton Starling, WBA welterweight, talking about fighting titlist Lloyd Honeyghan.

7) "Please, I know I'm late with my assignment and I'm supposed to get a one grade reduction, but I've really had a lot of problems lately."

8) Admiral David Jeremiah, a former vice chairman of the Joint Chiefs of Staff, hints at a fallacy argued by local congressman in his editorial, "Closing Bases Can Bolster U.S. Forces," *LA Times,* September 3, 2002. He argues that Congressmen who claim to be on the side of our military forces should support closing some bases. By cutting unnecessary costs, we can use the savings to improve the readiness and modernization of the U.S. defenses. As Secretary of Defense Rumsfeld recently said, "No organization can say that it's doing a good job with the taxpayer's dollars if it's maintaining some 20% to 25% excess capacity." Yet similar legislation has often died. Members of Congress are understandably reluctant to cast the vote that may temporarily cause economic upheaval or cost local jobs. Elected officials focused on serving their constituents ought to be mindful of all the constituents that they serve nationwide, including those in uniform. . . . What fallacy can you see in the congressional thinking?

9) A national poll indicates that 70% of Americans oppose increases in military spending. Therefore, 70% of homeowners oppose such spending increases, as well.

10) Many women fear getting old, thinking that their husbands will lose interest in them. An archeologist, therefore, is the best kind of husband. They love old things. So, the older the archeologist's wife gets, the more interesting she will be.

Sources

1) Petros, R. and C. (1993). "The 776 Stupidest Things Ever Said," New York: Doubleday.

2) Rybacki, K.C., and Rybacki, D.J. (2004). Advocacy and Opposition: An Introduction to Argumentation. Pearson Publishing: Allyn & Bacon.

3) "The 365 Dogs Calendar," Sept 30, 2003, Workman Publishing.

4) LA Times, "Congressman Tactics Under Fire," May 23, 2003.

5) LA Times, "Tapes Seen as Poison Proof," August 20, 2002.

See also sources for Chapter IV "Ways That We Reason and Ways That We Fail."

VIII
Arguing Issues of Value

By now, you've completed a proposition of fact speech and learned something about structuring arguments. While issues of fact are controversial, nothing brings more controversy than issues of value, questions of what is right or wrong, ethical or unethical, even good and evil. Especially, though, value arguments are concerned with **how to determine our priorities among important, yet often conflicting values.**

At the most basic, personal level, you might explore your own values by asking yourself what do you think is important in life? If you haven't explored your values, this is a good opportunity for you to do so.

How does one explain one's value judgments? It's difficult. Most deeply held values simply seem, to those who hold them, obvious and true. We've been taught that value by people we respect, lived with it on an ongoing basis, seen evidence for it in our own experience, and it seems ingrained into our very personalities.

What does one say, however, when asked, "how do you know that?" Often we fall back on begging the question: "It's so because it's so." Maybe we throw in a bandwagon argument: "Everybody knows it's so."

Yet **values are not facts.**[1] They are neither true, nor false. They are simply felt and believed. They are informed by facts, may begin as natural reactions to facts, but they are not themselves facts. This is one of the most difficult points of critical thinking, especially when exercised in practical social discussion. The idea that values are subjective may be easy for educated people, yet even they may get red-faced with anger when pressed to defend a value.

It's very important that we understand something about values. They may not be facts, but they are **the eyeglass through which we interpret facts.** If our eyeglasses are tarnished by prejudice or propaganda, then we may not be seeing facts for what they are. We may be projecting our subjective feelings and beliefs over the situation examined. We may only be able to see things one way, unable to perceive multiple viewpoints on the subject with empathy.

That's understandable when we consider **how people accumulate their values.** Often, a value is less a considered conclusion than something that you've always been told. They were the assumption of the family, of peers, of significant others who have influenced you. In other words, at least some values were given to you in tact as a matter of the **cultural conditioning** discussed earlier. So, we have been trained to have an innate, yet inherent sense of what's right and wrong. We know this is good, and that is evil. This is fair, and that is not.

Values may include **personal habits** that were developed when we were young, like being on time, being a hard worker, or being an honest person. We might express those values as proper nouns: punctuality, industry, and honesty, respectively. Men may still recall their Boy Scout oath, the recitation of which reminds us of our short-comings: "thrifty, clean, brave, reverent, etc."

Some unconsidered values may be **glittering generalities,** words that sound good, almost like obligations of our culture, but which may look better in the abstract than in real life action. Take a commonly used phrase in politics like **"family values."** On one hand, one feels guilty saying that they're against such a thing, but what does that really mean? Whose family? Which particular values? Does one simply mean that all families are to be honored as an institution?

Often, in politics, it means much more: that one party has the real family values, while the other has undermined the institution of family itself. This sounds good, to one side or the other, but it is historically naïve.

The last U.S. census says that only 20% of American families have children with both parents living in the same household. The single parent household has become more the norm. Yet that doesn't fit handily into our traditional view of "family values." Is this the responsibility of a particular political party? Families used to be born, lived, and died in the same locations, stabilizing what "family values" might have meant.

The truth is that this phenomena of fractured families has been evolving since at least the 1930s, when the depression forced many farming families away from the de-stroyed lands of the "Great Dust Bowl" looking for work. Steinbeck's novel "The Grapes of Wrath" depicts the situation in which individual family members were dropped along the way on a journey west, as soon as anyone found work. The pattern of moving to find new work has become an American norm.

WWII kicked in another emergent pattern of growth, traveling as a source of enter-tainment and personal growth. Johnny went marching to Europe, but he didn't always return as the same person. He'd encountered other fascinating places with new values of their own. There was a popular song about it, "How You Gonna Keep Him Down on the Farm, After He's Seen Paree?" When he did come home, he told his family about these world wide wonders.

With the emergence of commercial airlines in the 1950s, this travel impulse became in-stitutionalized, and families became fragmented as a natural matter of increased mo-bility. Both political parties had been in place during those times, from Hoover through Eisenhower. So, who does one blame? Certainly not a particular political party, television, or video games, or any of the other things often held responsible. Historical and economic events—like the necessity of two parents working to cover the cost of living—may have much more impact on the family.

Speaking of WWII, how about ***Hitler's idea of "racial purity"*** as an example of glittering generality. As a matter of vanity and a need to feel good about themselves after their defeat in WWI, many Germans came to believe in this ideal. History has shown them the folly of that value, and no nation today wants more to keep neo-Nazism in check. Through life experience, they have come to know the real meaning of euphemistic values like "racial purity."

In sum, the very language we tend to use to express our values may hide their real meaning from us, as well as their impact on society. The language of value tends to be very abstract. Only by concretizing the values in real world experience can we really make sense of their usefulness. If we can't see values in action, then how can we judge their impact on our culture?

This is one reason we'll be emphasizing that ***the proof of the value is in living it, not merely in saying it.*** Otherwise, values just live in some rarified place in our minds, or as meaningless utterances from our mouths. We must really consider whether there is benefit from the value, not only for ourselves, but for the greatest possible good. Considering the social impact of our choices is the very essence of good will, a key factor of credibility.

Old Sayings

The values of a people are often imbedded in the colloquial sayings of their language. "A stitch in time saves nine," for instance, is an expression of handling problems before they get out of hand. "A rolling stone gathers no moss" advises us to keep active by way of preventing sloth. Your folks have probably used a few on you.

Test out the following old sayings and see if you can imagine the real world effects of obeying or not obeying them:

> Honesty is the best policy.
>
> A bird in the hand is worth two in the bush.
>
> Neither a borrower nor a lender be.

Honesty, most have probably been taught, is certainly an important value. Yet, are people really all that honest? Research among college students indicates that, in a recorded day of statements made among peers, less than a third were entirely true.

Is there another arguable side to honesty then? Perhaps honesty is not the best policy all of the time. Some courtesies require that we not be honest. We don't always tell people the truth about how they look. Aren't there times when to know the truth is enough, and your expression of it to others is not required?

The point is not to undermine the value of honesty, but to show that, although these phrases have been repeated to the point of cliché, there are potential issues of conflict in each. There is no reason to argue, unless conflict, confusion, or controversy exists.

"A bird in the hand?" Isn't that, at least potentially, the fallacy of appeal to tradition, one might ask? If we did not journey out "into the bush" from safe territory, would we ever have harnessed electricity? If we listened to this phrase, we'd still be clutching candles, or even torches against the terrors of night. And one, of course, could just as easily argue that prudence is a terrific value and that mere adventurism is a lure to self-deception.

"Neither a borrower nor a lender be." This makes practical sense. You pull your weight, and they can pull their own. Arguments over money can spoil friendships. Yet in what context do we ask the question? Think of it on a more universal, perhaps economic level. Without lenders we could not own homes as common people, and without borrowers, how would those same banks sustain a profit so they can continue to finance our buildings and institutions?

* * * * *

From even these examples, we can see that values are ***an important moral compass for social action.*** Therefore, they are deeply involved in the policy issues that we'll discuss later. There may be many choices of how to respond to an issue that have workable mechanics, yet violate our community sense of right and wrong. It made a certain mechanical sense to limit the threat of spies during WWII by putting Japanese-Americans into prison camps, ***in the name of security.*** Now, our values have changed, and we have museums dedicated to the reminder that this was not an ethical thing to do.

Values Resist Change

Although we've mentioned some value changes in our historical examples above, we have some real challenges in attempting to persuade people to consider new values. The truth is that some values are so deeply held that it is next to impossible to alter them. Others are less resistant.

Milton Rokeach, a social psychologist, defines values as specific sets of beliefs and attitudes that act as long term goals. He discusses two kinds. ***Terminal values*** are ultimate life goals, like "I want to be rich," "I want to help the environment somehow," "I want to accomplish something significant," or "I just want to be happy."

Our **Instrumental Values** are more changeable and immediate values that help us to achieve our terminal values. "In order to be rich, I must be industrious." "In order to be happy, I need leisure time."

Rokeach argues that these values are interwoven and fall into **a hierarchy, like the layers of an onion.** Some are at the core and some are closer to the surface. The closer one gets to the core, the more difficult it is to change a value.

Rokeach says there are *five layers of belief:*

A) **Primitive Beliefs (unanimous consensus)** are core beliefs we've gathered from personal experience, backed up by consensus from our peers. These rarely change. So fundamental a belief as "killing is wrong" might be representative.

B) **Primitive Beliefs (zero consensus)** are similarly gathered by social experience, but not backed up by others. These are idiosyncratic and privately held. They may include perceptions about our own worth and capacity, or our value of self. "I'm not special," or "I'm the bomb!" "I'm popular," or "Nobody likes me." These are not much more likely to change, but may be influenced somewhat.

   (You may have had an interpersonal communication class in which your beliefs about yourself were nudged into a somewhat different direction.)

C) **Authority Beliefs** are often controversial and depend upon our interaction with figures of authority, our parents or teachers, for instance. "You should show respect for your elders," or "don't talk out of turn," might be examples. These are potentially changeable, but only through extended forms of persuasion and experience.

D) **Derived Beliefs** is taken from secondhand information from media figures, books and other reading materials, or public speech. We derive personal beliefs from such information, without necessarily examining the ideas themselves with any particular depth. By offering other credible evidence, it is possible to change such values.

E) **Inconsequential Beliefs** are usually individual preferences and tastes and are quite changeable.[2]

It's also true, though, that even widely supported **values do change.** We may receive **new information** that forces reassessment. When Columbus showed Europeans that they wouldn't sail off the end of the planet heading west, interest for "New World" emerged. It made a value of exploration itself, and that became a motive principle for European economics and politics. Living that value out, in part, contributed to the creation of our country.

New technology inspires value changes. Consider the impact on modern values that resulted from the invention of the cotton gin, or the automobile and mass production, the dropping of the A bomb on Hiroshima and Nagasaki, or our recent discovery that fetal tissue could perhaps be used to cure certain illnesses. Few value struggles have been more vigorous than this and other biomedical issues.

There is also ***erosion of values through time.*** People take them for granted. They pass away as people tire of them, and they come back into vogue, like a pendulum swinging back and forth across the face of history. So, there are times when rhetorical demand is very high for intelligent discussion of values.

Core American Values

What lies at the very core of our principles as Americans? Steele and Redding mention several, among them these:[3]

> ***The value of the individual***—We rank the rights and welfare of the single citizen above those of government.
>
> ***The value of achievement and success***—We believe that citizens should be able to accumulate money, power, and status. We are an upwardly mobile population.
>
> ***The value of change and progress***—We believe in new actions leading to ever more positive change. Our very free market economy is based on the notion of growth.
>
> ***The value of ethical equality***—We believe that "all men were created equal" and should be treated accordingly.
>
> ***The value of effort and optimism***—We believe that even the most unattainable goals can be reached through hard work and positive attitudes.
>
> ***The value of pragmatism***—We believe in such things as practicality, common sense, efficiency, and function. Terms like "Yankee Ingenuity" have represented this value historically.

I would have to add, from my own experience as a forensic coach, as well as a sports fan and a witness to several wars, that Americans ***believe in winning and winners.*** We find it hard to accept losing. When the Dream Team doesn't make it to the basketball finals of the Olympics, it surprises and disappoints us. We hold winners up as media icons and invite them to our most prestigious talk shows, even the White House. The Vietnam War went on for longer than it might have, since Presidents Johnson and Nixon were each reluctant to be "the first American President to lose a war."

These are certainly among our values, but there is probably considerable disagreement among Americans about the degree to which we achieve them. Which of these values do you think we represent well, and which do you think are "lip service?" What other American values do you think should appear on the list?

* * * * *

Let's look at some issues in the news involving values. Try to identify the values in conflict in each. Compare the above core American values above:

There's a belt that issues a 50,000 volt shock to unruly prisoners in court, a shock that drops them to the ground in front of judge and jurors, and often causes involuntary urination and defecation.[4] The practice was sent to the Supreme Court. You're on that court. What are the values in conflict? How do you decide?

Consider Taylor Hess, a young Texan who was expelled from school, because a bread knife from his grandma's good will donation box fell out into the bed of his truck. The principal, responding to the school's zero tolerance for weapons policy, expelled Taylor. What values are in conflict here? Do you agree with the principal? Why or why not?

Much is in the news about differences of opinion over separation of church and state. On one hand, an atheist citizen has sued the U.S., on his daughter's behalf, over the inclusion of the phrase "under God" in the Pledge of Allegiance. He argues that it violates his daughter's right to pledge to the country, though not God.[5] The Supreme Court didn't make a judgment, but dismissed the case on the basis that the father couldn't represent the daughter. What would you have decided?

On the other hand, Red Cross wouldn't let a school choral group sing "America the Beautiful" at a Red Cross function. Some reacted negatively to that action. Yet Red Cross is an international organization that is allowed into conflict zones in part because of its political neutrality. Again, identify the values in collision.

Stock Issues

We need a larger framework within which to sort those values out. We've sparred a bit to give you a sense of some of the things that might be discussed in conversations of value. How does that evolve into *a text?* It proceeds, like fact, from *stock issues:*[6]

1) *First, as with fact, define the terms.* It's very important to be clear about what you mean by a value. You're for "love?" What do you mean? Platonic love? Brotherly love? Marital love? Sexual love? Love of country? What?

2) *Create a value standard, a hierarchy by which to judge the issue.* There should be a clear rationale for this choice. Suggest *a specific threshold, or criterion,* for the acceptance of the case.

3) *Measure the values against the standard.* And remember to consider the value in social action. Don't get lost in a cloud of abstract words. Bring values down to earth. Offer examples of the idea that the proof of the value is in the actual living results.

Practical Standards for Arguing Values

For the practical purposes we pursue, we're not really looking for some abstract, absolute philosophical truth. We're dealing with **the relative world of practical social issues** and probabilities rather than certainties. There usually isn't an absolute right or wrong in most value debates, unless we're talking about something so odious that everyone but a pathological criminal rejects the idea. The case of child molestation comes to mind.

The mental action is to discover a sense of priority among our principles, even among ineffable qualities, like "love," "courtesy," "loyalty," or "courage."

To express a sense of priority, it's often easier to compare two values against each other, a thesis against an antithesis.

To build opposition into the proposition helps to clarify the debate. You can define and sharpen each concept against the other.

So, **the language** is often something like **"X is more important than Y."**

> It is better to give than receive.
>
> Faith, love, and hope, but the greatest of these is love.
>
> Democracy is better for mankind than socialism.

If we don't want to be reduced to silly utterances like, "My idea is just as good as yours," we need to understand and create some **objective standards, or criteria,** for evaluating the relative weight of values. We might think of this as "ethical weight," being determined on an old fashioned scale (Figure 16):

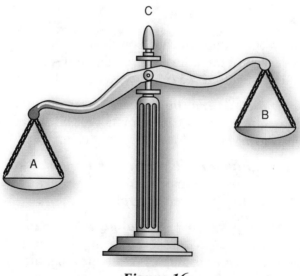

Figure 16

In this illustration, we have value A against value B, but they are weighed against each other on a fulcrum, a point of balance, value standard C.

*A **value standard*** is either a framework of priorities that you develop yourself, with objective justification, or it's a framework already established and accepted by members of your community.[7]

> The Ten Commandments
>
> The Constitution of the United States
>
> Maslow's Hierarchy of Needs

For instance, Maslow said that we value our survival above all things.[8] It's only When our survival is guaranteed that we can value love. It's only when we have love that we are primarily concerned with social respect. Then it's only when we have some sense of social respect are we really likely to value issues of higher self-development, what Maslow calls self actualization. Only a fully realized self can consider altruism, like sacrifice for the common good. It's certainly an idea that can be and has been challenged.

By that analysis, however, we could make "survival" the basic standard for a value struggle: "Whichever value best supports human survival is the better value, because without survival all other values become moot. Without survival we cannot exercise or support any other value." That is arguable, but it's a typical analysis.

However, we also need a specific criterion by which we can determine, if we've met that standard. How do we determine what "best supports human survival?" Do we mean long run or short run? What may save mankind in the long run may possibly kill hundreds of thousands in the short run. Consider the casualties of WWII in stopping fascism from taking over Europe and Asia. A criterion, from this perspective, might be that that which helps the species as a whole survive, rather than the short-term survival of individuals, best meets the standard. Other examples of people sacrificing themselves for their children or their peoples would then be used to support the idea.

A pacifist might argue that all taking of human life is not only wrong, but counterproductive. Killing simply leads to more killing. By that perspective, the criterion might become that "that which involves persons and nations in no killing at all is best." Concepts of total nonviolence and passive resistance best satisfy the standard of survival. Examples like Gandhi or Martin Luther King might be used to support this idea.

What's clear is that different standards can be applied to a real world situation. Different criteria can be applied to the same standard. Differing standards and criteria are the essence of value discussions and debates.

A Typical Value Discussion

Sometimes questions of value are terrible ***dilemmas.*** Both sides of a struggle between values have merit, may even both be essential to the republic's conduct. For instance, the various elements of our Bill of Rights sometimes come into conflict. What is more important to you, **the right to free press or the right to fair trial?** More importantly, how would you decide between the two in a situation in which one must take priority? Stop now and discuss the question among yourselves.

* * * * *

Now, let's create a typical value discussion in the form of an interior dialogue. We'll use the structural format of **Thesis, Antithesis and Synthesis,** as the advocate, the imaginary opponent, and a reasonable referee to wrestle with these values. This **reasonable referee** is a point of view from which you look at both sides of an issue and try to arrive at a balanced view among ideas, a synthesis. This is the point of view from which we notice fallacies or the untenable social impacts of an idea. We could consider that viewpoint the fulcrum on which our scale balances.

Here's an **interior dialogue,** based on the above notion, one might use to work through a proposition. Let's go back to our **free press vs. fair trial** idea:

> **Thesis:** On one hand, there are surely arguments to be made for the right to a fair trial. The idea of being locked away in prison without due process, based on some political mood of the moment, is terrifying.

> **Antithesis:** On the other hand, imagine a world without freedom of the press, in which the truth would be manufactured daily by some government news agency. We'd act on misinformation and propaganda all the time. We could be persuaded to do anything, on the basis of "the facts." That, too, is scary.

> **Thesis:** Well, there are historical examples of what happens when we lose fair trial. The Romans imprisoned and persecuted Christians. In the American west, local judges like Roy Bean hung people summarily, on a whim. You could die for insulting his favorite actress, Lilly Langtry. In the 20th century, Germany, the Soviet Union, China, Cambodia, and Argentina, have all imprisoned large numbers of their population for political or racial reasons. A more recent example is the American imprisonment of 9/11 suspects, without specific charges or due process.

> **Antithesis:** Those are prisoners of war.

> **Synthesis:** We'll accept that some are, for the moment.

> **Antithesis:** There are also historical examples of what happens when free press is set aside. Let's take a couple of the very situations you mention. Could Germany have achieved the holocaust without the dominance of Nazi propaganda? Could China have managed its cultural revolution if it hadn't cast aside the press and replaced it with Mao's "Little Red Book?"

Synthesis: Okay, but how can we decide? What standard shall we use? I think we have to look at how the two values relate somehow, since each has historical reasons for its existence.

Antithesis: Is the individual damaged at trial more important than a whole deceived public? Aren't the many more important than the one (Mr. Spock, "Star Trek II: The Wrath of Khan")?

Thesis: But it isn't just individuals. It's the very principle of fair trial. Once one is put away unfairly, it's a precedent for more of the same. The single human sacrifice becomes the motive force of many sacrifices. So, "the needs of the one can outweigh the many (Captain Kirk, Ibid.)." That's so, at least to the degree that the individual becomes a precedent for the many.

Antithesis: But how does that happen? It cannot happen without compliance from a tainted press, otherwise you get "Free the Chicago Seven" style protests. The press covers it, then we know something is wrong. Free press becomes the guardian of all human rights. Aren't the sum of human rights more important than any individual right in itself? Therefore, a guardian of all human rights should take precedence.

Thesis: I admit you have a point, but you seem to be contradicting yourself when you say that no human right can take precedence, then try to argue freedom of the press as supreme?

Synthesis: We'll agree to that. The standard seems self-contradictory.

Thesis: Can you give me a real world example of what you're trying to say?

Antitheses: Let's go back to another of your own cases, the Soviet Union. Did you know that the Soviet constitution is based upon that of the United States? It includes a right to fair trial, but there was only one government news source, "Pravda." So, you wouldn't know why your husband or neighbor was sent to a Gulag. You'd just know that they went. So, Soviets were free to listen to news, but only to the government point of view. The right to free press doesn't matter, unless there's actually free press. Thus, freedom of information through a free press is vital.

Thesis: One more thing concerns me. There are unreasonable intrusions by the press on the individual on trial, which might serve either the prosecution or the defense in an unfair way. Scott Peterson, accused of killing his wife and her unborn child on Christmas Eve in Modesto, CA, has sought changes of venue because of press. The press tells the story, the public watches, decides they don't like Scott Peterson, and the defense delays because they can argue that Peterson can't get a fair trial in Modesto. The freedom of press may have given an innocent man a chance for fair trial, yet it may also be a technique used by a guilty man to delay trial in his favor.

Antithesis: I guess we should **define "free press" more carefully,** because it's not entirely free, nor should it be. But that's an argument for scrutiny and regulation in the public, which the press informs. It doesn't make free trial more important than free press.

Synthesis: So, it's fair to say then, that the right to fair trial and the right to fair press are at least intertwined. There's also some convincing persuasion that, in some ways, fair trial and other rights may depend on free press. However, it must be noted that free press is not entirely free, but has restrictions that should be enforced to make sure that this guardian of rights doesn't lose perspective in pursuit of a story.

Thesis: Wait. I just thought of something else. If you have fair press, but not free trial, couldn't you simply try all the critical people in the unfair court and intimidate free press away? Then you'd only have a sham version of fair press. Etc.

* * * * *

We don't recommend that you walk around having these kinds of conversations with yourself all the time, especially out loud. People may want to offer you a white coat with very long sleeves. Still, this kind of inner dialogue is useful for testing value arguments against each other. Sometimes, we call it "cost vs. gains analysis."

Costs vs. Gains Analysis

One can use costs vs. gains analysis—a comparison between virtues and detractions of two ideas—to help yourself to find a value standard. In a sense, it's simply a particular variation of reasoning from dilemma. Here's a simple example of costs vs. gains.

Everyone has probably seen salads packaged in plastic bags. They are certainly convenient, and that's a value we seem to hold pretty dearly in modern life. Yet an article about Dole Fresh Vegetables and Fresh Express, the chief competitors in this market, suggests other considerations.

On one hand, packaged lettuce processing allows us to use parts of lettuce heads which would not make it to market on their own. Thus, there's less waste from the field. Lettuce is a volatile commodity crop. It's susceptible to bad weather. Processing salads and getting the best out of whatever is grown makes lettuce "as predictable and stable as floor wax or pretzels."[9]

On the other hand, processing lettuce in this way multiplies by many times the water used to yield a single salad, and it is nearly twice as expensive as buying heads of lettuce and cutting them yourself.

Compare the costs and gains. Create a value standard. But how?

Here's a hint: Which is more important, water or lettuce? How do you know? You know by an almost instinctive standard, **survival needs,** as expressed in Maslow's Hierarchy of Needs.[10] By that standard, you'd have to go with water. It's hard to find a criteria by which convenience overcomes the value of survival. You can survive without lettuce but not without water. Indeed, lettuce itself cannot make it without water, nor any other living thing that we might eat.

Let's consider a less dramatic standard on the same proposition: **What is the best dollar's worth for a typical American shopper?** On one hand, you have convenience, and the lettuce is clean and ready to serve. Time is money, so one could argue that saving the half hour it may take to chop vegetables for the salad gives you time to take care of that much more profitable business that day.

On the other, it's expensive, because it does use a lot of water and you're paying for someone to clean the lettuce for you. Unless the average American shopper is upper-middle class, it might be a bit rich for some. An average head of lettuce costs about a buck and a half, but an average bagged salad costs between three to four at this writing. It's probably best, by this standard, to buy head lettuce, to save money.

Value discussions are sometimes just that simple, at an everyday level.

Real World Example I: Terrorism

One very important national debate highlights how difficult finding a standard can be. After 9/11 in 2001, our disaster at the World Trade Center in New York, we became very concerned with terrorism. Many measures were proposed by Attorney General John Ashcroft to curb terrorism. "The War Against Terror" became a primary national value in and of itself. Simply dropping the term "9/11" ended many public discussions, even in independent news agencies.

However, some claimed that human rights were damaged too much to support certain aspects of these measures. People were held in prison, for instance, without charges for unusually long periods of time. It was advocated that terrorist suspects should be tried in military tribunals, rather than civil courts where rights are viewed very differently. Essentially, they're being treated as prisoners of war, though some were arrested abroad and some were citizens of the U.S. arrested domestically.

Consider some issues for discussion: Should both classes of individuals, citizens and non-citizens, be treated by the same standard? Should either class be treated by a standard applied to "prisoners of war?" Is "The Geneva Convention" still a primary standard for dealing with POWs?

The rhetorical position of the Bush administration was that we were in "a state of war." However, the other position goes, we are not technically at "war with terror" in the sense of a congressional declaration. It's war in a rhetorical sense, a persuasion toward a particular viewpoint, like the "war on drugs," or the "war on crime." The impact of this discussion will be played out in the courts trying terrorist suspects for years to come.

In costs vs. gains analysis, though, it's a national struggle to compare the value of the safety gained by such measures and the threat to human rights. What makes us safe, if you use safety as a standard? The other side of a value discussion might be that diplomacy is superior to independent force in the war against terror.

There are a couple of criteria we might apply to measure this ***standard for safety: long-term and short term gains for the country as a whole.*** Or expand your argumentative territory to what's best for the world, if you like.

The short-term gains for safety may be appealing, but there's also long-range concern among some citizens that we would both erode the rights that make us a democracy worth protecting. Also, there's concern about eroding future international support by the way we treat the concerns of allies, as well as the possibility that our efforts are counter-productive to long-range security. Some have even pointed out that we may be breeding the next generation of terrorists, as they witness the destruction in their country.

Our standard might be, that two criterion must be met to best protect our safety: 1) The best value is that which protects us in the present; yet 2) does not threaten our future. It's not uncommon that such multiple criteria are used. However, we then have to clarify the value hierarchy among these criteria. One might argue that 1 is more important than 2, as not surviving in the present may make survival in the future a moot point.

Real World Example II: Death Penalty

Allen Burlow, author of "Dead Season: A Story of Murder and Revenge," published by Vintage Press in 1996, recently wrote an editorial about mental incompetence and the death penalty. It is a good example of how value standards function in the legal world:

> Kelsey Patterson, a 50-year old convicted murderer is in the Texas prison system, where his behavior is regulated by implants in his brain and else-where on his body. Or so he believes. Patterson is psychotic. Yet the Texas prison system plans to execute him, assuming his appeals are turned down. Regardless of how the courts rule, the larger issue is if people with severe mental illnesses should be subject to the death penalty.

Patterson has a long history of serious mental illness. In fact, he'd been involved in two previous shootings but was never tried because the state considered him legally insane. After each of these incidents Patterson was confined to a state mental hospital where he was given powerful anti-psychotic drugs until his mental "competency" was restored. Each time he was released without supervision and stopped taking his medications.

In October, 1991, he went into a pawn shop and bought a .38 caliber pistol and killed Louis Oates and Dorothy Harris. After he shot them he walked to the home of a friend, told him what he'd done, laid down his weapon, took off his clothes, and wandered aimlessly around the street, shouting crazily until police arrived.

The jury found Patterson competent to stand trial after hearing from the State's psychiatric expert, Dr. James Grigson, also known as "Dr. Death." He earned the name because of the scores of defendants, including at least one innocent man, he has helped to land on death row. Although Patterson's trial was repeatedly interrupted by the defendant's crazy outbursts, which lead to his being evicted from the courtroom for half of the proceedings, the jury found the evidence of mental illness insufficient to spare him.

By law, the state may not execute someone who doesn't understand that his execution is imminent and the reason for the execution. Under present interpretations of this standard, however, very few inmates escape a death sentence. In 2000 a Florida judge found an inmate competent to be executed despite "clear and convincing evidence" that the defendant believed he was being executed because he was Jesus Christ. In January, Arkansas executed Charles Singleton, a paranoid schizophrenic who was delusional and was rendered legally "competent" only when the state forced him to take an anti-psychotic drug.

Patterson's lawyer, Gary Hart, says his client is legally insane because he believes that the court system, controlled by Satan, has granted him a pardon. In short, he doesn't understand that his end is near. Indeed, he has refused to talk to Hart for more than seven years, because he says his attorney doesn't understand "hell law." Hart insists that the U.S. Constitution does not allow the execution of someone whose very mental illness obstructs the legal process and prevents anyone from evaluating him.

He also refers to the U.S. Supreme Court's 2-year old decision banning executions of people with mental retardation. That case, Atkins vs. Virginia, concluded that mentally retarded people have "diminished capacity to understand and process information to communicate, to abstract from mistakes and learn from experience, to engage in logical reasoning, to control impulses, and to understand the reactions of others." As a result, the court found that retarded individuals are less morally culpable and said their executions would contribute to neither retribution nor deterrence, among others, the intended goals of capital punishment.[11]

In other words, the Supreme Court applied a similar standard as the Texas law, but applied more expansive criteria for justifying the standard than Texas does.

In sum, the author compared legal standards, both law and case precedent. Texas law says that they may not execute someone "who doesn't understand that his execution is imminent and the reason for his execution." Yet the criterion for decision against this standard was the judgment of a single expert witness, the so-called Dr. Death, who said the evidence of exceptional circumstances was insufficient to establish incompetence. This criterion was accepted, rather than the patient's behavior, in spite of Constitutional Law that says you can't execute a person whose "very mental illness obstructs the legal process and prevents anyone from evaluating him."

The defense could not offer opposing testimony, as the defendant refused psychiatric and legal advice, which might be considered an acceptable criterion for the standard set by the Supreme Court. He also seems not to understand the charges against him. With his babblings about "hell law" and an imaginary pardon, as well as his nonsensical disruptions of trial, his behavior should be a sufficient criterion to meet even the Texas state standard. Thus, by either standard, if properly applied, this person should be sent to a mental institution for life. It is arguable that he should never have been released after a second failed and unsupervised release.

Now, we've seen more than a real-world example. This example explains how value decisions may be a matter of life and death.

The Examined Life

There is an old saying that, ***"The unexamined life is not worth living."*** The person who examines his own values in contrast to others may evolve more sophisticated, educated, and personally chosen values.

Martin Luther King went so far as to suggest that, if one hasn't found a principle, yet another word for value, that we would die for, then we really haven't discovered a purpose for our lives. The statement was prophetic. He was assassinated very soon after that statement for defending his value of racial equality.

To what extent have you examined your own values? Can you say what they are? What exactly are the principles that you run your life by? Where did they come from? As you're making important choices that will affect the rest of your life, isn't this a good time to consider such questions?

Vocabulary

Costs vs. Gains Analysis
Criteria/Criterion
Hierarchy
Instrumental Values
Put Opposition in the Proposition.
Stock Issues for Value: Define the Terms
                        Create a Standard
                        Apply the Standard to the Value
Terminal Values
The Unexamined Life Is Not Worth Living
Value Standard

Exercises: Go to Interactive Disc to Complete

1) Look at a sample value speech in the appendix. Your instructor may either assign an individual speech like this, or a parliamentary debate as described in the next chapter. Begin choosing opposing values to discuss and start researching either assignment.

2) Consider the standard of survival with the proposition "Democracy is better for mankind than socialism." Which system of values presents a lesser danger to human life? Why? What criteria would you use to determine which system better supports survival? Examine the social actions that have evolved from each.

3) Read the Bill of Rights of the United States of America. Really. We mean it. Look it up. It's not that long. Consider the various values expressed there, then place them in a hierarchy in terms of their relative importance. Which seem most important and which less so? You might make this a class project, with different people defending various aspects of our enumerated rights.

4) Try the "Open Boat" exercise: You're on a cruise. The boat sinks. Too many people, say a dozen, have wound up in a single life boat designed for no more than eight. It has water and food for eight for three days. There is a compass, a half a dozen blankets, a box of matches, a skinning knife, and four pairs of oars. Some of the passengers are injured. The seas are high, and the boat is in danger of being swamped. No other boats are in sight. The fog is near constant. You are many, many miles from your destination. Here are the people:

There is an elderly retired couple. The man is seriously, perhaps fatally, injured.

There is a lone and emotional child of seven, separated from his family.

There is a doctor, a mechanic, a lawyer, a teacher and a lower-class seaman. All are male, except the teacher, and all are able-bodied.

There are two female college students. One of them is seriously injured and has been unconscious for a long time, having been dragged into the boat by her friend.

There is a married couple on their honeymoon.

On the third day, nearing the end of your supplies and with no rescue in sight, how should you collectively handle the situation? By what standard? By what means?

Take your time and think. Realize that you may not be rescued, who is involved, what supplies may be left. Swells continue to threaten to swamp the boat. Discuss your answers with others in the class.

Sources

1) Christian, C.G., and Traber, M., Eds., (1997). Communication Ethics and Universal Values. Thousand Oaks, CA: Sage.

    Jensen, J.V. (1997). Ethical Issues in the Communication Process. Mahwah, NJ: Lawrence Earlbaum.

2) Rokeach, M. (1973). The Nature of Human Values. New York: Free Press.

3) Steele, E.D., and Redding, W.C. (1962). "The American Value System: Premises for Persuasion." Western Speech 26, pp. 83-91.

4) LA Times, "Use of Stun Guns Is Curtailed," August 23, 2002.

5) LA Times, "A Godforsaken Ruling," June 27, 2002.

6) Perella, J. (1987). The Debate Method of Critical Thinking: An Introduction. Dubuque, Iowa: Kendall/Hunt.

7) Johanssen, R.L. (1996). Ethics in Human Communication. Prospect Heights, Ill: Waveland Press.

    Rescher, N. (1969). Introduction to Human Values. Englewood Cliffs, NJ: Prentice-Hall.

8) Maslow, A. (1954). Motivation and Personality. New York: Harper & Row.

9) LA Times, "Lettuce Grows into Processed Food," August 19, 2002.

10) Maslow, 1954.

11) LA Times, Commentary by Allen Burlow, May 12, 2004.

IX

"Spin"

When a story comes out from which someone can benefit, or which alternatively might damage them, various media will spin the story. That is, they will shape perspective on the event by shading the context as positive or negative, by including and excluding certain details, and by so simple a thing as which side of an argument they choose to quote or interview.

Information can get especially distorted, since the famous and powerful people giving the information to the media are spinning the information themselves. It's all an effort to make things more positive or negative, from a certain point of view. In sum, media sources have values and prejudices, no less than we do. At its best, spinning conceals the truth and preserves the images of public figures. ***At its worst, it's a form of propaganda.***

Spinning includes, along with a good strong dose of euphemisms, rationalizations, and appeals, some of the following media behaviors:

- Choosing some information rather than other information as a story focus, some details being more advantageous to an editorial point of view;

- The number of comments and quotations by one or the other side;

- Editorial comments made about those testifying by reporters (personal descriptions and adjectives);

- Blurring the line between news reporting and news commentary, i.e. offering subjective comments during a supposedly objective report, often as an aside to fellow news personnel;

- The timing or possible delay of the information's release;

- What is never released or mentioned;

- Presenting actually untrue comments, as in the case of ***"disinformation,"*** the intentional release of false information to credit or discredit certain groups or individuals;

- Perhaps most importantly, responses by parties involved to negative reactions by the public, which is at the core meaning of "spin."[1]

The problem is that this tendency to use euphemisms, to print or speak only certain facts, while selectively excluding others, has become a much bolder norm for media, making it difficult to determine what is really true.

Media Influence

Media—newspapers, news stations on television and radio, and magazines—are backed by businesses, often huge conglomerate corporations. Each media entity has its own editorial policy, motivated in part by the financial and political aims of the corporations backing them. This affects the objectivity of fact gathering and reporting, which is something of which researchers have to be aware.

It's a dilemma. ***We have to have evidence, yet the evidence is often "slanted"*** in particular directions:

> CNN political analyst William Schneider, an authority on opinion polling, believes that highly charged political issues or campaigns are particularly prone to spin off fictional study results, which then take on a life of their own. . . . Commentary pages are the soft underbelly of American journalism. Their writers, however self-interested, are held to a different, which is to stay lower standard of proof because of their presumed expertise. In fact, they are responsible for regularly injecting false information of this sort into our public discourse. In the marketplace of ideas, and on the used car lot, caveat emptor ("Let the buyer beware") is still the best policy.[2]

Norah Vincent, senior fellow at the Foundation for the Defense of Democracies, a think tank set up after 9/11 to study terrorism, notes that instead of encouraging criticism within the press, ***newsmen who speak out about biased reporting are ostracized*** from the industry. Bernard Goldberg's 2001 book, "Bias," was about liberal bias in the news. He used his own employer, CBS News, as Exhibit A, and was let go soon after. Web pundit Andrew Sullivan met a similar fate at the hands of the *New York Times* for similar comments.[3] In other words, the right to free speech does not necessarily reign when it comes to media as industry.

Sometimes, like a good detective in a mystery novel, one has to follow the money to understand the intentions of news entities.

Another overarching problem in media is its commitment to ***"infotainment,"*** which emphasizes showmanship and personality, yet blurs the lines among reporting, news commentary, and popular entertainment. American news media are no longer run by a separate news division, but by entertainment divisions, so that network "news" includes thinly veiled advertisements for that night's sitcoms, dramas, and reality programming, as well as interviews with their "stars."

Dramatized portions of these programs are sometimes ***simulations of actual news events*** rather than actually videotaped events. Some studies suggest that a majority of television viewers can't tell the difference between live footage and a staged simulation.

Add to that the common use in newspapers of digitally altered photos. Recently, we saw hoax newspaper photos of Abu Ghraib-like pictures of British soldiers, supposedly torturing Iraqi civilians. It was revealed, by photographic experts among other sources, that the photos were staged for political aims. Such printing approaches, along with simulations of news events, project artificially created events as if they'd actually happened.[4]

A translator for CBS, Steve Winfield, put on a fake Arabic accent to translate Saddam Hussein's interview with Dan Rather, creating an illusion that Saddam was talking English.[5]

Can we imagine a world in which news is made up for ratings purposes, and we can't tell the difference? That should remain the stuff of science fiction movies. Unfortunately, we see a very real tendency for news agencies to go even beyond these techniques, to the threshold of printing false stories. Jayson Blair, the reporter who fabricated stories for the *New York Times,* is just one of several similar examples revealed in recent times, along with USA Today's Jack Kelly, its top foreign correspondent.[6]

This chapter's focus on spin emphasizes that we try to ***distribute the risks of bias across a wide variety of sources,*** representing multiple perspectives. That's the minimum objectivity for which we should aim.

Further, it would be useful to actually have a sense of what the range of influences among present sources actually is.

A Method for Understanding

I heard a lecture at the Golden West Debate Institute, held at the University of Redlands each summer, at which I taught for several years. It was offered by Professor Steven Shiffren, later an editor of the *Harvard Law Review.* He illustrated the concept of spin before it was a commonly used media name.

He would raise a single issue, then trace responses in the press from the political right to the political left, from the publications of right wing American militia groups, all the way left to communists in *The Peking Gazette.* The responses were so diverse, it was if we were hearing about several entirely different issues.

Let's consider a recent and important public event and attempt something similar, looking at how a variety of news entities across the political spectrum comment. We'll stop short of *The Peking Gazette,* but we'll consider a wide variety of magazines, newspapers, television news entities, think tanks, and other information sources.

The issue will be our very difficult discussion of the use of torture by American soldiers in Iraq prisons. While much of this discussion is partisan, points of view do cross party lines, making it an interesting subject for media study. Remember, the purpose of this discussion is not to favor any single political entity. If there is a prejudice here, because of our concern with objectivity and perspective taking, it would be toward a centrist point of view which takes all sides and opinions into account. We're simply going to let the various media entities speak for themselves.

The footnote attached here explores stereotypes and sweeping generalizations we tend to make about opposing political parties, especially in an election year.[7] You may read it on a voluntary basis.

The truth is that, except in the most polarized times, ***bipartisanship is a simple necessity of functional government.*** The "two-party" system, as well as the separation of powers, is the way that we institute dialectical thinking into issues that impact us all. There are many factions within any political party. More importantly, there are credible and effective individuals in each.

In examination of the parties, ask yourself this question: exactly which Republican or Democratic party are we referring to? In each party, there are old-liners and new order constituents whom we'll discuss in greater detail later. Republicans have "neocons" and "paleocons," while Democrats, especially since Bill Clinton, have traditional liberals and others who are more centrist in economic values. In a sense, we have at least four mainstream parties among the two, as well as Libertarian and Green Party entities. To that extent, the labels "liberal" and "conservative," traditionally and respectively associated with Democrats and Republicans, are gross oversimplifications.

Let's return to the issue of Abu Ghraib. Of course, few serious publications are likely to say that torture is a good thing, though some make arguments that it's justified under certain special circumstances. Differences among publications, however, have often been less than subtle. Let's start in the political center, then look outward toward left and right. Let's remember that those terms, along with liberal and conservative, are sweeping generalizations. It would take more space than we have here to examine more subtle distinctions.

The Center

What, though, is the center? In some respects, it's a mythical point somewhere between liberal and conservative on the spectrum of political opinion. Abstractly, the center might be seen as the fulcrum for a scale, a point of view that somehow balances the sum of political opinions.

People may consider themselves at the center from various points along that spectrum. We know this because we often hear the word "extreme" from one side or the other while mentioning their opponents. We're center because we have cornered the truly rational perspective, meaning that the other side is "off center" somehow, with all the subjective connotations that may bring.

The center, on any given issue, may involve a more moderate coalition of both slightly liberal and slightly conservative parties from either side of this imagined center. In fact, rather than a specific point along the spectrum, we should probably think of the center more as a flexible zone of thinking than a single point.

However, there are **some organizations and websites** that are not affiliated with any particular political party and claim to be moderate and objective. They attempt a synthesis between the left and the right in an intelligent dialectic. Such groups include the think tank **New American Foundation** (www.newamerica.net), the **Centrist Coalition** (centristcoalition.com), and the website **centrist.org.**

The Centrist Coalition speaks of the center in this way on its homepage:

> The Centrist Coalition is a gathering place for moderate Americans who have a certain distinct vision of political leadership in our country. We believe strong leadership involves a bold mix of views drawn partly from the left and partly from the right. On one hand, we embrace an economic agenda focused on growth and fiscal responsibility. We believe in free trade, fair competition, and limited government. On the other hand, we embrace an inclusive social agenda that celebrates the rich diversity of American life, and seeks to avoid imposing one person's choices on another. We are pro-choice and pro-rights.

In a website survey regarding the presidential race, 50% said they weren't happy about either candidate as a presidential choice. About 20% were yet undecided, suggesting that they don't adhere to party loyalty as the main guideline for their thinking. Many centrists appear to be independents, though they usually distinguish themselves from Libertarians, or any other party.

Centrist.org, on its home page, looks at the center as an alternative to the partisan gridlock:

> The U.S. faces . . . . a gridlock caused by the polarization of our political climate. Extreme political polarization has grave consequences. Democrats rarely talk seriously about the need for Medicare or Social Security reform. Democratic budget policy is dominated by demands for more spending and public programs; however, the wisdom of that spending is infrequently questioned. . . . . Republicans have taken "supply side" economic claims to absurd extremes. Republican orthodoxy now states that cutting taxes (especially for businesses and high income taxpayers) is always and everywhere the best policy. It doesn't matter that sometimes tax cuts don't seem to work, or that the deficits they create are poised to crush the next generation of Americans under a mountain of debt.

Other centrist think tanks will be discussed below. For our purposes here, we'll start our look at the center in the form of moderate **news magazines** commonly found on American coffee tables, in order to regain a sense of the torture employed by U.S. forces abroad.

On May 24, 2004, in an article called "The Roots of Torture," **Newsweek** described congressional response to images of torture, some of which were still classified:

> It's not easy to get a member of Congress to stop talking, much less a room full of them. But as a small group of legislators watched the images flash by in a small, darkened hearing room in the Rayburn Building last week, a sickened silence descended. There were 1800 slides and several videos, and the show went on for three hours. The nightmarish images showed American soldiers at Abu Ghraib Prison forcing prisoners to masturbate. American soldiers sexually assaulting Iraqis with chemical light sticks. American soldiers laughing over dead Iraqis whose bodies had been abused and mutilated. There was simply nothing to say. "It was a very subdued walk back to the House floor," said Rep. James Harmon, the ranking Democrat on the House Intelligence Committee. "People were ashen."

In some respects, even this paragraph, opening what is classified as a news report rather than news commentary, had nonobjective aspects: the use of particular adjectives like "the small darkened room" and "sickened silence" to emphasize the drama of the situation. The parallel structure emphasizes "American Soldiers" three times. Also, the suspension of normal punctuation, periods rather than commas, emphasizes the impact of the individual images. It is written to suggest the rhythm of a slide show.

The White House suggested that this was the work of a few "bad apples," MPs who were poorly supervised.

> But evidence has been mounting that the furor was only going to grow and probably sink some prominent careers. Senate Armed Services Committee chairman John Warner declared the pictures were the worst "military misconduct" he'd seen in 60 years, and he planned more hearings. Republicans on Capital Hill were notably reluctant to back defense secretary Donald Rumsfeld. And *Newsweek* has learned that US soldiers and CIA operatives could be accused of war crimes.

Was it appropriate to anticipate accusations that have not been yet made, one might ask? Were they setting up interest in future issues based on, as of yet, unconfirmed suspicion?

The impact of this *Newsweek* issue was quite strong. It was the second of two publications, just after **New Yorker Magazine,** to break the story. *Newsweek,* however, revealed two new ideas about the matter:

1)   Suggestions by Darius Rejali, "an expert in the use of torture by democracies," that inexperienced MPs did not think to put a hooded man up on a stool with

electrodes attached to his extremities and tell him he'd be executed if he fell. "That's a standard torture. It's called 'The Vietnam.' But it's not common knowledge. Ordinary American soldiers did this, but someone taught them." One may wonder how *NYM* concluded that Rejali was an expert, since his actual credentials are not presented in the article, and he is the only expert cited.

2) A memo suggesting that, "The Bush Administration created a bold legal framework to justify this system of interrogation," suggesting that the Geneva Convention does not apply in Iraq, and that, "Bush, along with Defense Secretary Rumsfeld and Attorney General Ashcroft, signed off on a secret system of detention and interrogation that opened the door to such methods." Yet *Newsweek* also makes the observation that, "It is unlikely that President George W. Bush knew of these specific techniques."

Time, May 17, 2004, initially put their topic focus toward the issue of authority, who knew what when, issues of fact rather than the colorful sense of expose in *Newsweek.* *Time,* perhaps in part because it is associated with a huge corporate conglomerate, took a slightly less incendiary approach. Their initial reserve from direct accusation may be because of corporate limits on editorial policy. Yet, as the details emerged, they joined Newsweek and others in a more accusatory tone. Headlines like "The Scandal's Growing Stain" and "What Happened to the Bush Dream Team?" appeared in their May 17, 2002 edition.

Similarly, **US News and World Report** remained largely fact focused and avoided colorful language. *US News* gives consistent attention to issues of military strength. Yet it contents are objective in the sense that it focuses almost entirely on news, while both other magazines contain a lot of articles on popular culture, especially *Time* with its interest in entertainment.

While it would be something of an overgeneralization, as each magazine tries to include both right and left perspectives, one might think of *Newsweek* as center, but edging slightly left of both *Time* and *US News,* with *US News* slightly to the right of *Time.* Yet *Newsweek* regularly prints one of the most articulate and intelligent of conservative pundits, George F. Will. It's not that simple at the center since, by definition, they have to include multiple points of view, in the name of both objectivity and mass marketing.

Among the most reliable and objective of centrist magazines is **The Economist.** It's a British publication that is less likely to appear on American coffee tables than the other three. With **The New Yorker, Atlantic Magazine,** and **Harpers,** it is more likely to attract an educated audience.

The Economist, in their April 10th–16th, 2004 issue, concentrated not at all on accusations of higher involvement in the scandal. It focused on factual matters, especially the impact of the torture incident on presidential approval rating:

Popular opinion first. The earliest poll (by the Pew Research Centre) taken after the shocking footage from Fallujah showed no erosion of public support for the war. . . . But there are increasing signs of public nervousness about the conduct of policy, even while opinion remains steadfast about the war's justification. Approval of Mr. Bush's handling of Iraq has plummeted to 40% from 59%.

True, there are adjectives like "shocking," and a colorful verb like "plummeted," but that's certainly not extreme, especially compared to the emotionalism of *Newsweek*. There was no initial editorializing whatsoever. The cover simply and objectively reads "The Challenge in Iraq," while the article itself is called "Now What?" Remember, of course, that the British government is an ally in the war, and that may tend to temper an impulse to criticize before the facts are all in. Other European publications were hardly so generous. Public protest in Spain, our only other major ally in the war, was enormous and eventually led to the withdrawal of Spanish troops.

The Atlantic, sometimes associated with The New American Foundation, wasn't particularly focused on the Abu Ghraib situation, either in articles or editorial stance. It concerned itself more on behind-the-scenes election politics, in which Abu Ghraib is mentioned in passing, but not as the main subject. While author Benjamin Wittes, on loan from the Washington Post, argued that the administration—in particular Attorney General Ashcroft—had gone too far, he also asserts that administration critics had, too. It was a balanced approach.

Harpers, on the other hand, printed far riskier articles. *The Atlantic* followed US Marines into Fallujah for five days in April 2004, not long after the other key event of that month, the slaughter and dismemberment of four American civilians. *Harper's* followed insurgents in the Iraqi resistance for a year, posting their findings in June 2004. Patrick Graham offers a sympathetic, yet complex view of insurgents, in which they are at once extremely polite and hospitable to him on a personal level, at the same time that they intend to fight the American government to the death.

* * * * *

Newspapers are a combination of many elements, features, entertainment, news and opinions. Yet they, too, have editorial policies. A majority of major papers try to be centrist, in that they print some of each point of view. Their editorials are revealing, however, as they involve such matters as candidate endorsement, criticism of legislation, and indeed, criticism of the war in Iraq.

The major national papers, based on numbers of Pulitzer Prizes over the last five years and general circulation, include: *The Los Angeles Times, The New York Times, The Washington Post, The Chicago Tribune, The Boston Globe, The Christian Science Monitor and the Wall Street Journal.*[8]

Of these, WSJ is probably the most likely to be perceived as a conservative publication, mostly because of its focus in the world of business. In fact, it would not be unfair to say that most major American newspapers lean slightly left in the center zone. In the words of some more strident conservatives, the media is a "vast liberal conspiracy."

CSM is associated with **The Nation Magazine,** often viewed by conservatives as a liberal publication, though the newspaper takes a less provocative view. While **The Chicago Tribune** only noted that CIA director George Tenet resigned over the controversy in Iraq, *CSM* looked at Tenet as "Bush's Lightening Rod." In other words, he was drawing the heat on the controversy away from the White House.[9]

The Washington Post is famous for exposing the Watergate scandal. They took generous swings at the Bush administration over Iraq and other related matters. In the aftermath of the torture controversy, they wrote on May 4th, 2004, that:

> Deep divisions have arisen at the top of the US military over the Iraq issue, with many top generals believing that while the US is winning battles in Iraq, it is losing the war. A senior general at the Pentagon said he believes the United States is already on the road to defeat. "It is doubtful we can go on much longer like this," he said, "The American people won't stand for it.—and they should not." Asked who was the blame, this General pointed directly at Rumsfeld and Deputy Defense Secretary Paul D. Wolfowitz. "I do not believe we had a clearly defined war strategy, end and exit strategy before we commenced our invasion," he said, "Had someone like Colin Powell been the chairman (of the Joint Chiefs of Staff), he would not have agreed to send troops without a clear exit strategy. The current OSD (Office of the Secretary of Defense) refused to listen or adhere to military advice.[10]

So, here comes another version of Watergate's "deep throat," again, an anonymous yet authoritative source.

The New York Times and **The Los Angeles Times** were similarly critical. As the Abu Ghraib story unfolded, *LAT* reported an internal army investigation that was critical of General Miller's approach, particularly the use of police to "soften up" prisoners for interrogation. *NYT* called for Defense Secretary Rumsfeld's resignation.

Both tended, however, to focus attacks more on Bush himself and the notion that others, like Tenet and Rumsfeld, were falling on their swords to protect him.

The bottom line among these publications, in sum, was that President Bush was caught in **a dilemma:** either he knew that torture was going on and feigned surprise, or he was not sufficiently aware to control critical functions of the administration, either of which would undermine his credibility as a wartime president.

Letters to the editor are also revealing, since most editorial staffs will tend to print letters, not only the basis of interest factor, but roughly in proportion to the number of comments from each side of the issue. Though most are scrupulous about including point and counterpoint from multiple points of view, one can sense that letters to the editor tend to be chosen on the basis of their sympathy toward editorial policy.

In other words, if you have liberal leanings and read a more left/center newspaper, don't be shocked if most of the letters are moderately liberal, or visa versa with a conservative newspaper. Don't be surprised, either, if letters from a different editorial viewpoint are less intelligent or literate and a bit of a set-up for comment by other readers of the paper.[11]

Television news is much like newspaper news in two respects:

1) Mainstream news channels operate on a daily basis, so they're on the cusp of the most recent event. Magazines operate on a weekly to monthly basis, focusing on deeper analysis of events. Yet the Sunday edition of most major newspapers does similar weekly analysis in an opinion section, and networks similarly carry analysis shows like "Meet the Press."

2) Apart from the major networks one is more likely to find truly conservative channels on local news stations. The major networks, like newspapers with national circulation, tend toward the left of the center range. With regard to the Iraq war, however, the networks stepped into line with the official line on the war. There was initially very little criticism, with little focus on "collateral damage." Much of the Iraq coverage focused on personal interviews with the soldiers, human interest stories which personalized the soldiers.

It was the Abu Ghraib story that consolidated a critical angle on network news. They circulated the photos of the incident to mass audiences at a greater speed, as virtually everyone watches some TV, though less than a quarter of Americans read newspapers regularly. This makes the point that television has one advantage over other media. It has **more immediacy for the average household than any other form of communication.**

Even on cable, there tends to be a moderately liberal inclination. CNN and MSNBC are both examples, though each has conservative pundits in their midst. On cable, **only Fox News is a distinctly and consistently conservative news station,** and it's gaining a larger audience, largely at the expense of CNN.

The other television news agency that is very influential internationally is the British **BBC.** Apart from international respect, they tend to be on the front lines of international conflicts in Iraq. Like *The Economist* magazine, they are also noted for their objectivity.[12]

Centrist think tanks, essentially fact finding and policy study institutions, are the deep underbelly of analysis for the long-range view of the news, as well as much government thinking.[13]

The Brookings Institution is one of Washington's oldest think tanks. It is "non-partisan, devoted to research, analysis and public education with an emphasis on economics, foreign policy and governance." Their own position on Iraq on the May 27th website is cautiously centrist. For instance, in "June 30 and Beyond: What Happens After the U.S. Leaves Iraq," analyst Kenneth Pollack writes:

> . . . I think we all have to be very humble in making these kinds of predictions and recommendations, because the honest answer is none of us really knows any more. . . . We've really lost our bearings. We are in a situation now in Iraq where we are really terra incognita. We don't really know what the right answer is. And we all have different theories, but that's all they are.[14]

On the same day, they printed an article by Senator Joseph I. Lieberman, a democratic Senator who is also a hawk on Iraq:

> In short, I'm calling for a bipartisan political truce on the home front that will greatly help us achieve the victory we all desire on the battlefront. From the beginning I was a strong supporter of the war against Saddam Hussein. He was a dictator, warmonger, terrorist, outlaw, murderer, a thief, and a thug. . . . Thanks to the brilliance and bravery of American and allied forces, we won that war. But the final test of war is the quality of the peace that follows. Today, we are clearly engaged in a new war in Iraq.

The Rand Corporation is a non-profit research organization. Their motto is "objective analysis, effective solutions." Their focus on Iraq leans neither left nor right, but is focused on solutions for past intelligence failures. On their May 27th website, in "Why We Didn't Get the Picture," Bruce Berkowitz writes:

> U.S. intelligence analysts have been taking a lot of criticism lately, but when the investigations are completed, we will discover that this wasn't an intelligence analysis failure. Perhaps it is an intelligence collection failure combined with a misunderstanding about how intelligence really works.[15]

Other centrist tanks are more focused on domestic issues. They include the National Center or Policy Analysis, "a non-profit, non-partisan public policy think tank" focused on issues like, "health care, taxes, Social Security, welfare, education, and environment".[16] There is also the Urban Institute, dealing with U.S. social and economic problems such as civil rights, education, health, Medicare, and taxes.[17]

Lean a Little Right

Let's begin again with ***magazines and newspapers,*** remembering that not all conservative pundits write in entirely conservative publications. Nor should it be assumed that all conservatives, any more than all liberals, are in agreement on Iraq. In fact, opinions are quite diverse.

There is no initial mention of Abu Ghraib in ***William F. Buckley's National Review,*** the long-standing conservative stalwart of mainstream magazines. The May 3, 2004, issue does mention the Iraqi beheading of and the "barbarous defilement" of four American civilian contractors on the bridge at Fallujah in several articles. For instance, as was stated in an article called "Kicking the Corpse":

> (T)he joyful scenes in Fullajah send shivers down the spine. By treating those they killed in such a fashion, the participants in the killing denied the common humanity of their victims. They did not merely see them as enemies; they saw them as beings to whom nothing whatever was owed. If it's true that people who burn books will soon burn people, how much truer is it that those who disrespect the dead will soon disrespect the living? This is a very poor (omen) for Iraq's future, and for the region as a whole. After all, people who mutilated four Americans hate not just Americans, but many of their fellow Iraqis of a different religious sect or ethnic group. In fact, they hate everyone who is not them. Peace will not reign when the Americans depart. . . . The joy they expressed during their gruesome performance was in part the joy of having liberated themselves from the irksome restraints of civilization itself.

One might note that the same logic in this quotation could very well be applied to the guards at Abu Ghraib in their smiling photos. It is true that this *NR* edition was on newsstands early in May, a month in which much was revealed about Abu Ghraib. However, the next month again scrupulously avoided mention, except to insist that it was only a handful of soldiers, and that the real scandal was the slaughter and dismemberment of civilians in Fallujah.

Thus, a centerpiece of conservative analysis in response to Abu Ghraib was to hold up Fallujah as worse, while paying little attention to issues of higher responsibility for the scandal. Basically, they followed the line that a few bad apples were responsible.

The article following "Kicking the Corpse" was about the Marines and was called "Few, Proud, Remarkable." Ads include a T-shirt for sale featuring Bush as a cowboy branding a donkey, the national symbol of the Democratic party. Cartoons show John Kerry frowning at recent job recovery statistics. Articles about the job recovery declare the problem over. Further, in "Outsource, outsource, and outsource some more." *NR* argues that we should continue to outsource jobs to foreign countries, since the best jobs stay home anyway and "The jobs that have been lost . . . tend to be lower skilled and lower-paid jobs."

Otherwise, the magazine's approach is "Let's stick to our own ground and not be drawn into defending torture." Instead, ***National Review*** defended the need to get tough on Iraqis to enforce compliance with peace initiatives:

> In light of recent events, however, we should downplay expectations. If we leave Iraq in some sort of orderly condition, with some sort of legiti-

mate, non-dictatorial government and a roughly working economy we will be doing very well. The first step toward this goal is dealing harshly with our enemies.

The American Spectator, while it tends to deal a lot with practical economic issues, extends its analysis to international matters. Its articles are intelligently written and well-considered. Especially interesting in the last week of March 2004, was an in depth interview with John F. Lehman, a former secretary of the Navy under Reagan, who was very critical of intelligence gathering and sharing for the war. They are critical of the administration for overspending (23% of it from Bush tax cuts and 27% from increased federal spending, the rest from a sluggish economy). Yet they actively support Bush for re-election, giving no particular emphasis to Abu Ghraib. They argue that Bush should be elected, among other reasons, so that he can privatize social security. They did say that **torture was "unacceptable and un-American."**

The Week Magazine, however, printed more mixed viewpoints of the administration. After Abu Ghraib, they ran an April 16th issue with the headline "Which Way Out," rather than sticking to the hard line established by *National Review.* These are among the reprints from various publications:

- From an editorial in the ***The Atlanta Journal Constitution:*** The wave of savage uprisings in Fallujah, Baghdad, and other Iraqi cities is making a mockery of the Bush administration's "starry-eyed" fantasy of a pro-Western, democratic Iraq. The architects of this war assured American's that once we toppled Sadam Hussein, Iraqis would become a strong, shining beacon of peace and tolerance for the entire Islamic war. Instead, more than 100,000 Americans are now bogged down "in a brutally inhospitable place," where grievances are settled with "bullets and bombs."

- From an editorial in the ***Weekly Standard:*** In the end, Iraq will be worth what America pays in "blood and treasure." By giving Iraq a chance to move "however fitfully and slowly" toward democratic self-rule, we will create a powerful alternative to the angry, nihilistic ideology of Bin Ladenism and the savagery of pro-Saddam mobs.

- From an editorial in ***Newsday:*** Actually, our best option is to face reality: Iraq is just not "viable as a unitary country." The Colonial British drew its borders artificially, heedless of history. Like Yugoslavia, Iraq will only find peace when it is dissolved into three countries, and the Sunnis, the Shiites and the Kurds can go their own way.

Business Week is a moderately conservative magazine. Yet it is focused almost entirely on economic issues and has taken no particular position about the war and Abu Ghraib, except to the extent that it affects the economy.

Daniel Casse, senior director of the **White House Writer's Group,** a Republican-oriented communication firm, and a special assistant to President Bush says the dissent on Iraq comes from **distinct points along the conservative spectrum:**

> "**Paleoconservatives,**" as he calls them—as opposed to neo-conservatives in the line of Goldwater and Reagan—along with **libertarians and anti-interventionists** such as Patrick Buchanan, have opposed the invasion of Iraq since the beginning and haven't changed. Says Casse, "But more disturbing is a thoughtful group of conservatives that think the war is not being well-managed or has failed to meet anybody's expectations, and that runs from George Will to Mark Helpern."[18]

Conservative **George Will** raised the notion that our Wilsonian efforts in Iraq may be futile. President Wilson, who presided over WWI, believed that America's practical mission is to pacify the world by multiplying free governments. This is a fairly widespread issue among conservatives.

Mark Helpern wrote in the Wall Street Journal on May 17, 2004, calling the mistreatment of Iraqi prisoners "a symbol of the inescapable fact the war has been run incompetently, with an apparently deliberate contempt for history, strategy and thought, and with too little regard for the American soldier, whose mounting casualties seem to have no effect on the boastfulness of the civilian leadership."

William Kristol, vociferously pro-war editor for the Weekly Standard: "I am an unrepentant hawk. On the one hand, the war is right. On the other hand, the administration has botched it. On the third hand, we have to tell them what they've done wrong and how to fix it." He points out that he and his regular writing partner, Robert Kagan, have always been critical of the administration for what they consider to be anemic troop levels, but that doesn't mean that he's changed his mind about the rightness of the war itself.[19]

John Podhoretz, a conservative columnist for the New York Post, often a counterpoint to the more liberal **New York Times,** said: "I find the lack of steadfastness on the part of some people to be intellectually appalling. If they're losing heart it's because they didn't think it would be tough for them. They thought they could dance around and say 'We were right and you were wrong.' Well, people in Iraq have it tougher than the columnists and intellectuals who are having people say mean things to them at cocktail parties."

Television, as we've said, is predominantly left/center on the major networks. On cable, it's a slightly different story, because there is **Fox News.** In "On Cable News It's all Shoutmanship," a commentary by Brian Lowry, he says:

> Fox New Channel's not-so-subtle marketing slogan, "We report, You Decide," has helped frame the cable news tussle in political terms the assumption being that the channel's "fair and balanced" claim is a code for fire-

breathing conservatives, while left-wingers gravitate to that bastion of the liberally biased media, CNN. . . . Maybe Fox News' secret ingredient isn't so much ideology as attitude—a network whose shouting heads and razza-matazz perfectly suits a media culture where news must be rouged up and ready for prime time.[20]

Fox is simply and unabashedly conservative in its editorial stance, though it also presents opposing points of view. Often, though, they're set ups to support the war. ***CNN's conservative reporter Tucker Carlson*** told the New York Times: "I supported the war and now I feel foolish."

Rush Limbaugh told his radio listeners that what happened in Abu Ghraib prison "is no different than what happens at a Skull and Crossbones (fraternity) initiation." Skull and Crossbones was a politically-oriented fraternity at Yale which both Bush and John Kerry joined, though at different times.

Conservative think tanks, like any other think tank, tend toward the long-range view and don't always focus on today's news. There were, however, exceptions when it came to Abu Ghraib.

The American Enterprise Institute is an economic and foreign policy think tank. They are "dedicated to preserving and strengthening the foundations of freedom—limited government, private enterprise, vital cultural and political institutions, and a strong foreign policy and national defense." On their May 27th, 2004, website, there are articles like "No Way Out: Iran Is at War with Us" by Michael A. Ledeen, suggesting that we may have to go on from Iraq to fight Iran before we leave. Also appearing was "Terrorists Have No Geneva Rights," by John Yoo, an analysis supporting the legal basis for torture, though not specifically condoning torture itself.[21]

The Heritage Foundation is dedicated to "limited government, individual freedom, a free market, and a strong defense." It is inclined to use numerous statistics in support of its positions. Their May 27th, 2004, website articles include Joseph Leconte's "Human Rights Hypocrisy," which states that the Abu Ghraib abuses are being "overblown" and will set back the cause of offering rights to the general population. In "Hands of Horror, Hands of Hope," the story is told of seven Baghdad merchants who had their hands severed at Abu Ghraib by Saddam Hussein and are now "champions of a free Iraq."[22]

Lean a Little Left

A wide range of much more liberal magazines were brutally critical of the president's administration for its handling of the affair, as well as the war itself. In fact, some are far enough left that they tend to concur with Libertarians that there's no real difference between the parties and that presidential candidate Kerry is no different than Bush.

The American Prospect wrote in May 2004 that, "The more time goes by, the more Bush makes Clinton look like a genius of both domestic and foreign policy. Indeed, not only is the American right a house divided on Iraq but over the intensifying imperialist drift of U.S. foreign policy." Critical of U.S. unilateralism in the war, they argued that we have acted without consulting the Iraqi Governing Council, even in the design of transition to new government. They called that transition government "a sham."

"Rather than stepping up a military offensive," in response to Fallujah, "we ought to be stepping back. We need to step back from engaging every 'enemy stronghold' and setting off a spiral of conflict and hatred."

In an article called "The Devil Is in the Details," *AP* argued that the plunge into Iraq has left both the U.S. and U.K. forces unprepared. Our "pre-po," or pre-positioned stocks, sets of military equipment deployed around the world for emergencies, are depleted. "The army downloaded three of its five brigade sized sets in order to fight in Iraq." They speculated how we would respond to a real crisis thusly depleted. In sum, "Bush's blundering crusade to impose democracy is making the world less safe and less free."

The Nation, sometimes seen as the liberal counterpoint to Buckley's *National Review,* was calling for Rumsfeld's resignation as early as April 3, 2003, well before anyone had ever heard of Abu Ghraib. Even then they were making an outcry about U.S. military treatment of Al-Queda and Afghani prisoners.

On May 5, 2004, they focused on the hypocrisy of moral arguments that we have been on a humanitarian mission in Iraq, in light of the torture incidents and civilian deaths. They ridiculed "Bush and Cheney's 'torture lite'" exported from Guantanamo:

> And for a time, the government can even brag about its new purported Tough-guyness, and claim that sleep deprivation and petty cruelty to people locked up in Guantanamo Bay has been yielding "enormous gains" in the war on terror; or that "unspecified duress" convinced one Iraqi to finally reveal Saddam's spider hole. Of course, more often than not you don't learn anything from torture—your victim simply tells you what you demand to hear. . . . Deputy Secretary of Defense Paul Wolfowitz was lobbying for torturing a prominent Al-Qaedite into confessing what he's always denied: That he was secretly working for Saddam all along.

The May 31, 2004, issue pushed the advantage presented by the 9/11 commission against the White House in "Even Conservatives Are Beginning to Wonder." They discussed the conditions for a consciousness for torture, drawing psychological parallels between the My Lai massacre and Abu Ghraib, a comparison that even Secretary of State Collin Powell had made, in "Conditions of Atrocity." In "Empire without Law," *The Nation* opposed unlimited detention of suspects:

> What is happening concretely in cell blocks is also happening at the level of developments in fundamental law. . . . The Administration's across the

board hostility to the constraints of law, domestic and international, is not accidental. The constitutional structure that is the backbone to republic is stumbling block to empire.

Obviously, they supported the position that the U.S. is becoming a blatantly imperialistic power. They even noted that:

> The imperial logic was on full display in the Supreme Court. In a Brief on the Guantanamo detentions, eight former federal officials argued that "if no constitutional rights applied to offshore detainees, then the government would be free to create a parallel system of extraterritorial courts and extraterritorial prisons to punish extraterritorial crimes without legal oversight or constraint."

The Progressive, which regularly prints leftist thinkers like Howard Zinn and Dario Fo, is very concerned with human rights. So, they were critical not only of the torture of foreign persons, but of the administration's treatment of our own soldiers. In "Bush's Odd Warfare State," an ironic twist of "welfare state," they noted the economic harms to soldiers in Iraq:

> Here's one way our president proposes to "support our troops": According to his 2005 budget, the extra pay our soldiers receive for serving in combat zones—about $150 a month—will no longer count against their food stamp eligibility. . . . Military families on food stamps? It's not an urban myth. About 25, 000 families of servicemen and women are eligible and this may be an underestimate, since the most recent Defense Department report—from 1999—found that 40 percent of lower-ranking soldiers face "substantial financial difficulties."

In "The Ultimate Betrayal," Howard Zinn wrote about the forgotten number of seriously wounded men in Iraq, whose lives would be compromised forever by our lack of judgment in the war. The administration has argued that our casualties in the war are relatively small, compared "to the 10,000 Iraqi men, women and children killed, with many more seriously wounded." Yet, they argued, Republicans argued the same thing after the first Gulf War:

> The United States Government was proud that, although perhaps 100,000 Iraqis had died in the Gulf War of 1991, there were only 148 American battle casualties. What it concealed from the public is that 206,000 veterans of that war filed claims with the VA for injuries and illnesses. In the years since that war, 8,300 veterans (of that war) have died, and 160,000 claims for disability have been recognized by the VA.

As of September 2004, 6,239 have been wounded in Afghanistan and Iraq, according to a Pentagon survey, 57% so badly they were unable to return to duty.[23]

Mother Jones and **International Socialist Review** were even harder on the issue. Furthermore, they don't hold up much hope that electing John Kerry would be of any help, since he does not support total troop withdrawal, but thinks the war is mismanaged. War, in and of itself, is wrong, they argued, and nothing good can come of it. The little guy gets the raw end of the deal. So, not even torture is really a surprise.

These publications also point out that we have used brutality and torture on an ongoing basis in American prisons, something noted consistently by Human Rights Watch. Why, then, would it be shocking that we would use it abroad, they ask?[24]

Think tanks leaning left can be accessed on **Moving Ideas,** which is a project of The American Prospect discussed above.[25]

Among their allies are **Carnegie Endowment for International Peace.** Their May 27th, 2004, website reprinted an article by Marina Ottaway of the *Washington Post* criticizing the Bush transition plan in Iraq and offering "Iraq: A Better Transition Plan": "Given the continuing violence in Iraq, the idea that a government of technocrats can provide even minimal administration for six months, and also organize elections is divorced from reality."[26]

CEIP is associated with the publication **Foreign Policy** or FP. FP's website hit very hard at the American presence in Iraq. They offer an article on May 27th, 2004, by Husain Haqqani called "The American Mongols":

> The last time infidels conquered Baghdad was in 1258, when the Mongol horde defeated the caliphate that had ruled for more than five centuries. And if the ripple effects of that episode through Islam's history are any guide, the U.S. invasion and occupation of Iraq will unleash a new cycle of hatred—unless President Bush can fulfill his promises of democracy in Iraq and a Palestinian state.

In the context of Abu Ghraid, Richard Falk's "Think Again: Human Rights" stated:

> Those who argue that respect for human rights must be sacrificed to win the war on global terrorism have got it all wrong. Adherence to human rights, even for those accused or suspected of terrorist involvement would signal Washington's respect for human dignity. To act otherwise discloses a kind of secular fundamentalism that blurs the nature of the conflict.[27]

If you'd like to drive your conservative friends and relatives truly crazy, bookmark **MoveOn.org** or **"Treehuggers,"** which includes **"Fight the Right,"** "working against Right-Wing political and fundamentalist religious elements." These are not think tanks, so much as a consortium of small agencies combining to form an annotated list of liberal links.[28]

There are "eco sites" dealing with animal rights, alternative energy and environmental groups; "fem sites" dealing with reproductive rights and feminism; as well as "Lesbigay sites" dealing with gay rights, homophobia, and same sex marriages. There are also links to human rights and civil rights groups dealing with free speech, death penalty, and separation of church and state.

Other liberal think tanks focus on *domestic issues.* They include:

The Center for Law and Social Policy, or CLASP, is a national nonprofit organization founded in 1968—the year after the so-called "Summer of Love," the apex of hippy and anti-war culture—providing "research, policy analysis, technical assistance, and advocacy on issues related to economic security for low income families and children." They regard themselves as leading the national effort to establish "equal justice for all."

The Center on Budget and Policy Priorities has a similar agenda, but focused primarily on economic issues. For instance, their May 27, 2004, focus is the impact of the "deficit financed Bush tax cuts," which give only temporary relief to middle income families, but "new permanent tax cuts for higher income families, including members of Congress."[29]

Libertarians

Libertarian publications do not necessarily care to enter this discussion about Iraq. The June 2004 issue of *Reason: Free Minds and Free Markets* sports a specialized, if somewhat ominous cover for subscribers featuring *individual aerial shots of their own homes.* The suggestion is that privacy is at risk, as "they know where you are."

Issues of privacy, free markets, and free speech are common, as well as other personal liberties. Yet this passage indicates why Iraq is off the radar in their utilitarian philosophy:

> Focus on the fiscal, my fellow libertarians. The core free-market arguments have never applied to topics like foreign policy, police and courtroom procedures, the definition of marriage, abortion, the cultural effects of immigration, or the nature of addiction, as neatly as they do the everyday buying and selling of widgets (and the everyday interference with widgets by big government). There's no shame in that. Let the other political factions fight about Iraq, gays, and all those other things. If we don't weigh in loudly on more clear-cut (albeit sometimes boring) issues such as the need to simplify regulations, abolish the Commerce Department, privatize the Post Office, and taking an immense ax to the budget, we can rest assured no one else will.

One could reasonably infer that, since the war in Iraq has increased spending and the deficit, that many libertarians are concerned about the war, but primarily from an economic standpoint. The same issue of *Reason* does, however, have an article about legal defenses against the Patriotic Act. Citing the arrest of a leftist lawyer, Lynne Stewart, who represented the blind sheik Omar Abdel Rahman, a convicted terrorist, and passed messages for him to his allies. Writes Jarett Decker, an attorney for criminal and commercial law, in a critique of how the Patriot Act threatens the sixth amendment of the Constitution:

> The conduct for which Stewart was charged occurred before 9/11 and before Congress passed the Patriot Act, a statute aimed at enhancing federal powers to fight terrorism. . . . Had the timing of her actions been different, Stewart could have been charged with violating a little known provision of the Patriot Act that makes it a crime to provide "expert advise or assistance" to a terrorist group. . . . Legal representation of alleged terrorists is a crime under the Patriot Act if the lawyer can be portrayed as acting under the "the direction and control" of a foreign terrorist organization. There is no exception for "good faith" or "bona fide" legal representation.

However, there is not a single mention in the issue of the torture at Abu Ghraib.

Liberty Magazine of July 2004 made "The Conservative Case Against George Bush." They also asked the question, with ironic quotation marks, "Can We 'Liberate' Iraq."

The American Conservative, associated with Patrick Buchanan, one time candidate for the presidency, is libertarian on international issues. That is, they are non-interventionists, and they focus a lot on government hypocrisy.

Their May 10, 2004, edition was titled "The No-Win War." They had already called Bush's Administration a "Pinocchio Presidency" in their April 26 edition, complete with a cover cartoon of Rumsfeld, Cheney, Bush, and Rice all wearing long noses.

At this point, you may be very confused about libertarians. They're financially conservative, yet they sound like liberals on war and human rights.

A look at **Libertarian think tanks** might clear up some misconceptions.

The Cato Institute is difficult to place on a political spectrum, as are most libertarian advocates. On one hand, it sounds very familiar to AEI or heritage in its "philosophy of limited government, free markets, and individual liberty," but its emphasis on individual liberty, especially from taxes, tends to place it against government declared wars. Here is their self-description as it appears May 27, 2004:

> The Jeffersonian philosophy that animates Cato's work has increasingly come to be called "libertarianism" or "market liberalism." It combines an appreciation for entrepreneurship, the market process, and lower taxes with strict respect for civil liberties and skepticism about the benefits of both welfare state and foreign military adventurism.

It might be easier to place the Cato Institute, named for "Cato's Letters," a series of libertarian pamphlets that helped lay the philosophical foundation for the American Revolution—as the third point of a triangle, including liberals and conservatives, rather than on a continuum from right to left. Indeed, they seem to concur with both right and left on some points and with neither on others. Based on their stance on taxes, one could reasonably post them on the right. With regard to human rights, they may more often resemble the left.

* * * * * *

Yet again, let's remember that there are many subtle points along the broad political spectrum of Americans. It is, perhaps, a natural result of the freedoms that we enjoy. Freedom of speech, while essential to the function of our republic, allows our citizens to rave wildly. Before we get to the wildest, let's take a summary look at the sources we've looked at.

The Political Spectrum of News Sources

Left	Center	Right
The American Prospect	The Atlantic	American Spectator
Carnegie Endowment for International Peace	Boston Globe	American Enterprise Inst.
International Socialist Review	Centrist Coalition	Business Week
Mother Jones	Chicago Tribune	Fox News
Moving Ideas	Christian Science Monitor	Heritage Foundation
Moveon.org	Harpers	National Review
The Nation	Los Angeles Times	New York Post
The Progressive	New America Foundation	Wall Street Journal
Treehuggers	Newsweek	The Week
	Time	The Weekly Standard
	US News & World Report	
	Washington Post	

Libertarian

American Conservative	Cato Institute	Liberty	Reason

WWW Stands for "Wild, Wild West"

Finally, it must be said again that the Internet is still like the "wild west," a relatively unregulated territory of often unconfirmed information and exotic opinion. You will find some ***extreme fringe elements.*** Some of these sites are run by people who might qualify as ***domestic terrorists.***

Such elements are responsible for the 1995 Oklahoma City Bombing; the July 1996 bombing at Centennial Park during the Atlanta Olympics, which killed one and injured more than 100; and the summer 1999 shooting sprees by lone gunmen targeting minorities in the Chicago and Los Angeles metropolitan areas, which left several people dead. There are 10,000 to 100,000 *right wing militia* members with various degrees of radical action. Considering how few men were involved in 9/11, it's an impressive figure.

However, there are also *far leftist radicals* and conspiracy theorists. Robert Lederman at rense.com suggests that there are links between the Bush family and the German Nazi party and specifically accuses the *Manhattan Institute* for the connection:

> The man who coined GW's now infamous slogan, "Axis of Evil" was senior fellow at the Manhattan Institute before joining the Bush Administration. . . . MI also coined the slogan "Compassionate Conservative" for GW claims the Rockefeller-funded organizations' influence on his thinking as "second only to the Bible."

> MI is a right wing think tank founded in 1978 by William Casey, Bush/Reagan's CIA director. Following WWII Casey helped bring thousands of former Nazis involved in eugenics and the Holocaust to the U.S. As CIA Director he later funded Bin Laden and Co. with billions in arms, terrorist training and cash and was also a key player in arming the Contras.

> MI is funded by JP Morgan/Chase bank (owned by David Rockefeller) and by pharmaceutical companies (Pfizer and Lilly) directly connected to Rockefeller, Bush senior and many of the current Bush administration officials. Bush senior was director of Eli Lilly in the late 70s. Bush budget director Mitch Daniels worked for Eli Lilly . . . etc., etc.

Now, some of this is factually correct. A look at the Bush Cabinet reveals many connections to pharmaceutical industries, as well as oil. But the ongoing suggestions of guilt by association and circumstantial evidence lead to the fantastic conclusion that Nazi eugenics studies have been continued since WWII, in association with Bush and his pharmaceutical friends. Wow. One wonders why the Democrats aren't capitalizing on that one.

A similar website at www.sunmt.org.bushnazi.html sports an illustration of the Republican party elephant logo super-imposed on a swastika.

This kind of conspiracy theory is practiced by both extreme right and extreme left and always leads to more "heat than light," that is, more anger and suspicion than actual illumination of the facts.

Some radical links are subtle, sliding below FBI radar by parading as mainstream groups. According to *the Southern Policy Law Center,* a group focused on domestic terror or racial hate groups like the American Nazi Party and the KKK:

> The *American Media Association* claims to welcome all truth-loving, Pro-American publications and journalists. Supposedly, "no left or right political

leanings are mandatory." Yet a look at the AMA web site belies that claim. Members include the neo-Nazi German ***American Nationalist Political Action Committee,*** the anti-Semitic ***Christian Identity*** publication "America's Promise." The site provides updates on imprisoned hate crime felon Alex Curtis from white supremacist Vincent Bertollini. . . . By sharing information, they hope to increase cooperation between publications on the radical right by pooling their distribution base and raising advertising revenue. And if the members are really lucky, the AMA may be able to confer mainstream credibility on publications that have often found themselves alone in the political wilderness.

A frighteningly extensive list with 515 links to various extremists and militia groups can be found at ***The Militia Bulldog*** site which offers this proviso:

> IMPORTANT! More and more people are erroneously coming to think that all information can be found on the World Wide Web. It cannot. Although there are a number of members of the militia movement active in Usenet and on the Web, only a small amount of militia related material actually exists in cyberspace. Newsletters, shortwave broadcasts and videotapes still provide more information than can be found on the Web. Relying only on information accessed electronically will inevitably present a skewed picture of the militia movement, although particularly since 1996 the militia presence on the web has been growing.

In other words, the site encourages people to explore more direct contact with the various militant organizations, so they can avoid electronic surveillance and offer indirect forms of propaganda to indoctrinate initiates searching for a connection. Google is their search engine of preference.

It's worth knowing what's out there, simply as a matter of awareness and self-protection. During this time of heightened security and government surveillance, however, one might be careful about how much time one spends on these kinds of sites. Certainly, a mere glance should convince you that either mainstream political party is relatively sane. And, please, remember what mom used to say when somebody said something unkind to you: "Consider the source."

So, on one hand, we can chart the spin tendencies of various news sources, roughly, from left to right. Yet there is conflict within each "side" of political spectrum, and writers and speakers frequently jump ship on particular issues as a matter of reason and of conscience.

* * * * *

In conclusion, broad labels like "liberal" and "conservative" simply do not hold up in the overly simple way we sometimes think. Judgments like "tax and spend Democrat" or "war mongering Republicans" are sweeping generalizations.

This "bumper sticker reasoning" holds no more sophistication than wearing the team colors of the athletic teams that you relate to because they happen to be in your neighborhood. It's normal and fun to identify with groups, because it gives us a sense of belonging. In matters of significant social problems, however, thoughts deeper and fairer are required.

Perhaps the best thing we can do to remain as objective as possible is to look at as wide a variety of media sources as possible, as well as get a clearer sense of their prejudices and political positions.

In a very real way, what we've learned is that *sources are permeated with values* themselves. If you have a particular set of political values and want to seek support for them, being aware of the political spectrum of sources can guide you to like-minded people.

As for Iraq, at this writing in June of 2004, the new provisional government has been appointed, and some sovereignty is to be handed over to them by the last day of the month. You're in a much better position than we are to know the ultimate result and can judge the wisdom of these various sources in hindsight.

Exercises: Go to Interactive Disc to Complete

1) There is only one, exercise other than doing research for your value speech, "The Chinese Menu Exercise." Choose three publications, one from each column on pg. 171, read and compare them. See if you would place them differently than we have.

Sources

1) Brown, J.A. (1963). Techniques of Persuasion: From Propaganda to Brain-Washing. Baltimore: Penguin Books.

   Ellul, J. (1973). Propaganda: The Formation of Men's Attitudes. New York: Vintage Books.

   Jowatt, G.S., and O'Donnell, V. (1986). Propaganda and Persuasion. Beverly Hills, CA: Sage Publications.

   Pratkanis, A., and Aronsen, E. (1992). The Age of Propaganda: The Everyday Uses and Abuses of Propaganda. New York: Freeman.

   Rasberry, R. (1981). The Technique of Political Lying. Washington, DC: the University Press of America.

2) LA Times, "Surveying a Problem with Polls," LA Times, June 14, 2002.

3) LA Times, "Media Can Dish It Out but Can't Take It," June 6, 2002.

4) LA Times, "Altered Photos Break Public Trust in Media," April 7, 2003.

5) LA Times, "Fake Accent for 'Voice' of Hussein?" March 5, 2003.

6) The Week Magazine, "Journalism: Another Fraud Exposed," April 16, 2004.

7) ***Let's dispense with some stereotypes*** and sweeping generalizations that we're likely to resort to, especially in an election year, especially when we look at an issue as serious as the torture at Abu Ghraib. There is a distinct temptation to demonize an opponent by exaggerating certain negative qualities. Also, historically, some stereotypes just aren't true.

A) ***"Tax and spend democrat."*** There are those that do and those that don't. Bill Clinton, for instance, did not significantly raise taxes as President. He lowered a deficit that he inherited from George Bush, Sr., and left nearly a half a trillion dollar surplus. George W. Bush reversed that by three trillion into a deficit. Deficits, in real impact, are simply deferred taxes. It's no different than getting into trouble by overusing your credit cards and expecting your children to pay them off for you.

There have also been comments that the current Republican majority congress passed more "pork barrel" riders, adding unnecessary and irrelevant costs to bills than any congress in recent memory.

Further, it is naïve to think that we can get government services, like trash collection, police and firemen, or schools, without somehow paying for them. Costs for services come up front in taxes, or they're deferred in deficits, or the services don't exist without either massive volunteerism or a profit motive for private industry.

Have there been spending excesses by Democrats? Absolutely. Yet there have been many financially conservative democrats. Neither financial conservatism nor active overspending belongs to either political party.

B) "***'Compassionate conservative'*** is an oxymoron." There have been many Republicans possessed of a strong sense of humanity and charity. Biographies of Abraham Lincoln revealed his deep torment over human loss in the Civil War. Teddy Roosevelt founded the National Parks System out of his deep love of nature and desire that it would be preserved for all Americans for all time. It was Richard Nixon who actually instituted Democratic president Lyndon Johnson's "Great Society," a fabric of social welfare programs which attempted to actuate civil rights granted in the 60s.

The Rockefellers, including Nelson Rockefeller, briefly Vice-President under Gerald Ford, were well known for their commitment to many charities and public works. One of the finest, most sympathetic of eulogies was that given by Ronald Reagan upon the explosion of the space shuttle

"Columbia." It was said that he openly wept over the creation of those words. His words to the Soviets about the Berlin barrier between East and West Germany resounds with a sense of human liberty: "Tear down this wall." One has to wonder how he would feel today about the raising of a similar wall between Israel and Palestine.

Senator John McCain of Arizona has revealed a consistently bipartisan interest in human rights, working closely with Democratic presidential candidate John Kerry. Many Republicans now support a woman's right to choose and are deeply concerned with the well being of our civil liberties. The notion that the only hope for humane decision making on social programs is the exclusive territory of Democrats is simply absurd.

C) Also, there are typical comments about how Democrats are ***"soft on defense."*** It may be true that, in the balance between "guns and butter," or "foreign vs. domestic spending," Democrats often favor butter. However, it's also true that three Democratic presidents got us through the two world wars of the last century. A Democrat, Harry Truman, dropped the first and last atomic bombs aimed at an enemy, at Hiroshima and Nagasaki. JFK faced down the Soviet Union in the Cuban Missile Crisis.

President Clinton recently sponsored limited interventions in the Balkans and Somalia and oversaw bombing raids on Iraq. There is also evidence that he authorized the assassination of Saddam Hussein, though our intelligence forces couldn't locate him.

The only two wars of consequence fought by Republican presidents in the last half century are the two wars against Iraq, along with the handoff of the Vietnam war to President Nixon who authorized our retreat. Otherwise, only a handful of limited interventions have occurred since Teddy Roosevelt's "Rough Riders," including the first President Bush's capture of Noriega in Panama and Reagan's invasion of Grenada. While Republican presidents must certainly be credited for their work in the cold war against communism, Iraq, Panama, and Grenada have arguably not been our most formidable military opponents.

Let's also remember that both Democrats and Republicans contributed to our war policy in all of those successes and failures.

D) Libertarians and other third party candidates are fond of saying that ***"each of the major parties is no different than the other."*** Controversial documentary producer Michael Moore, a supporter of Ralph Nader's third party run, called Clinton "the finest Republican president of our time" in his book *Stupid White Men*.

There are reasons for this belief. For instance, both parties tend to steer toward the center in election years, where most voters tend to reside.

Barry Goldwater's run from the right against Lyndon Johnson led to one of the widest margins of victory in election history. I remember his campaign posters reading "In your heart, you know he's right." Many were defaced with this added phrase: "Yeah. Far right!"

Pictures of a frankly left of center Democratic presidential hopeful, Governor Michael Dukakis, in a too large helmet peeking out of a tank, backfired. He had hoped that the picture would help him aim more to the center, but he merely looked out of place, if not hypocritical.

The curious thing is that the Libertarian party actually includes people who have drifted to the right of the Republican party and others to the left of the Democratic party, along with yet others suspended somewhere in between. Focus on the position that that which governs least governs best unifies many unusual bedfellows, whom we'll discuss later.

A measure of the difference between the two parties may be defined by how polarized the present discussion happens to be. Some significant controversies certainly exist between the parties at present:

- **What do we do to solve Iraq?** Most Republicans wish to hold the course, agreeing with some portions of the 9/11 report, but not, in the President's words, "its details." While most Democrats have complaints about the way the war should be conducted, some wish to get out altogether, others follow John Kerry's analysis that it would be irresponsible to leave, but that we should gradually bring soldiers home who have served beyond their appointed term in the war. Libertarians would tend to agree with withdrawal, as they don't generally believe in foreign wars. So, while they may not agree with Kerry's analysis, they're certainly closer to Democrats on this issue. Wouldn't that indicate a difference between the two major parties?

- **Environmental issues** tend to be intensely controversial between the parties. As Republicans tend to be business oriented in their analysis, there have been concerted efforts to open National Forest land for logging, oil drilling, and other purposes. Libertarians are interested in freedom in business to the extent that they may be closer to Republicans on these issues. Again, wouldn't that suggest a difference?

- **Women's rights** with regard to their bodies remains controversial between the party majorities. Many Republicans want to reverse Roe vs. Wade. This time, their belief in total personal freedom would align Libertarians with Democrats and put them in fierce opposition to Republicans.

So, on what basis could a Libertarian, or other third party person, say there is no difference when, by the standard of their own belief system, they'd have to choose between parties on significant issues?

A reading of the actual party platforms may demonstrate that the two major parties are rather different . . . or turn you into an independent. Hopefully, it will not cause you to join the increasing number of non-voters in this country, especially since you are now probably better qualified to analyze party rhetoric than ever before.

8) http://www.pulitzer.org/2003/2003.html

9) http://www.chicagotribune.com/ and http://www.csmonitor.com/earlyed/early

10) www.washingtonpost.com

11) ***Three local papers*** with decent circulation are available near my college, *The Los Angeles Times, The Orange County Register,* and *The Daily Pilot.* Both *The Pilot* and *The Register* lean right to right of center. This provides good counterpoints for analysis, because each commits similar persuasive strategies, yet on either side of center.

Letters from the right appear in *The Times,* but are sometimes very emotional and ill reasoned. We've seen many examples throughout these chapters, making the liberal editorial policy look wise by comparison. Here's an approximated sample:

I always hear anti-abortionists call others "anti-choice." They use the term to identify people who are "pro-life." I think that's an error, to say that being pro-life means you're anti-choice. The act of becoming pro-life is a choice. And when children are created, it is our choice to give them rights and let them be born rather than murder them like other supposedly "pro-choice" people do.

It's not about Iraq, but it illustrates the point about what papers do. The *LA Times* is pro-choice, yet they print a letter with a couple of fallacies in it. There's a sweeping generalization about pro-choice people, at least. Consider Catholics who don't use birth control. There are also two fallacies of language, an equivocation of the term "pro-choice," and the emotive language associating "murder" with abortion.

At the same time, a *Daily Pilot* letter protesting a local lesbian pride parade was elevated to the status of an editorial, illustrated with pictures of some rather masculine looking women in motorcycle leathers, rather than professional women. Of course, this is a very broad sweeping generalization about lesbians. The accompanying letters in protest of an attempt to stop the parade were from an artificially polarized position to the left.

Here's the punch line. *The Times* bought out *The Daily Pilot,* and it appears daily inside the home delivered *Times.* Talk about covering your bases.

12) http://news.bbc.co.uk/

13) Various websites with directories of think tanks:

http://www.reference.com/Dir/Society/Poliics/Liberal/

http://www.reference.com/Dir/Society/Politics/Conservative/

http://www.worldpress.org/library/ngo.htm

http://www.afn.org/-afn49740/mis.html (Treehuggers)

14) http://www.brook.edu/index/about.htm

15) http://www.rand.org/

16) www.ncpa.org

17) www.urban.org

18) LA Times, May 24, 2004.

19) One wonders where Mr. Kristol studied anatomy, as he mentions "the third hand" of the problem.

20) LA Times, March 5, 2003.

21) http://www.aei.org

22) http://www.heritage.org

23) LA Times, August 8, 2004.

24) ISR (International Socialist Review), Mar-April 2004. Mother Jones, June 2004 The Progressive, April 2001.

25) http://movingideas.org

26) www.ceip.org

27) www.foreignpolicy.com

28) www.afn.org

29) http://www.cbpp.org/

X
Counter-Argument

By now, you've already got some sense of how to respond to an argument, or to counter-argue. However, let's focus on this skill as a topic in itself. Let's look at particular "pressure points" that you can press against an adversary.

Listening

There is simply no tactic that is more important than careful listening. It's been established through many studies that the average adult is a poor listener. The average efficiency is 25%. In other words, one may really absorb and retain about a quarter of what you hear. Often rates may be as low as 10%, while rates of 60% are very rare. We actually hear about half of the facts in a ten minute talk, but forget half those facts within twenty-four hours. There is significant loss in retention during the first eight hours after the talk.[1]

Think about how much bang for your educational buck you're getting, with these statistics in evidence. You also might consider studying what you just got in class before this time tomorrow, rather than waiting until just before a test. Research also indicates that an initial absorption rate of 50% drops to 35% within eight hours, then drops to 25% within a matter of weeks.

We've found, through practical experience in debate, as well as many years of teaching speech:

> *The seeds of an argument's defeat are sown within the language of the argument itself.*

In other words, you can hear the weaknesses in an argument if you listen carefully. That's easier said than achieved in practical argumentation. We've already discussed how easy it is to get overly excited during arguments. When we do that, we don't only experience more speaker anxiety, we may forget what we're trying to say. More importantly, we forget to listen to what the other person is saying, yet that's what will give us our own retorts.

Listen carefully to definitions. They define, not only the limits of discussion, but the burden of the advocate. ***Advocates must justify all the terms of the thesis*** proposition. For instance, if the thesis is:

> The comprehensive ban on human cloning is both medically and morally sound.

The speaker has created a double burden of proof. The advocate will have to defend at least two arguments, one medical, one moral. ***Listen for the weaker argument and emphasize your attack on it.*** Don't abandon your other obligations, but set yourself up for the position that the advocate cannot win, as he or she has only justified half of the proposition.

It's also important to listen to definitions to see if you are getting painted into a corner. That is, ***definitions may unfairly limit your argumentative ground.*** If you catch it, you can challenge the definition and offer a fairer one yourself. Or, you can work that definition to your own advantage, avoiding the traps implicit in the advocate's language.

You saw this kind of move in last chapter's sample debate, "Rights are more important than anti-terrorism." The opponent recognized that "better" was a burden of proof that gave him an advantage. He avoided the trap of arguing that, "no, anti-terrorism was more important." It's not as sympathetic a position as embracing rights and thinking of anti-terrorism as the means to support them. He could simply claim "equal," and force the burden of proof, "better," back on the advocate.

When we talk about ***forcing an argument,*** it means pretty much what it sounds like: you apply more pressure on some points than others. When you pressure your adversary to answer more on a particular point, you could say you were forcing the argument. Since not all arguments are of equal importance in a debate, finding and forcing the weakest points of an adversary is a standard technique, as it may force him or her into a defensive position. Again, that does not excuse you from your obligation to clash on other points. It may be an important clue for what issues you will want to pull through in rebuttal.

Understanding

This is an underestimated aspect of criticism in general, from film critique, to literary critique, and on to critique of social advocacy. One may be so anxious to oppose that one misses the main thrust of the adversary's argument, or one fails to appreciate it's complexity. We may have a "standard line" that we offer on an issue, what we've heard elsewhere and rehearsed as our own idea.

We see this in classes. One begins an argument because he has a reaction formation, an immediate and strong negative attitude against something. They put their hand in the air with vigor, before their intended adversary has finished speaking. From the point that they're trying to get my attention, they have missed what the original argument actually said. They have things to say, but they're often irrelevant. This is why we emphasize the flow sheet skills described in the last chapter. Get it down, then figure it out.

You can't understand if you don't listen, and you cannot refute until you understand.

Test your understanding by accurately paraphrasing your adversary's position. You need to express your understanding of the argument before you issue your counter-claims. It's a courtesy to your adversaries to allow them to clarify their positions.

Cross Examination

Another way to understand and clarify positions is to use questions. Parliamentary debate allows you to ask questions of your adversary mid-speech, as long as he or she will yield the floor.

What kind of questions does one ask?

The most important use of questions is **to understand and clarify** your adversary's analysis. If you don't, you may target your own arguments incorrectly.[2]

You may ask **open-ended questions,** those that invite elaboration:

> "What do you mean by X phrase?"
>
> "What is the significance of this case?"
>
> "Can you give me another example?"

It is sometimes necessary to ask speakers to paraphrase their analysis in other words, to confirm your sense of their intention. The danger here is that your adversary may go on some, wasting your questioning time with evasive answers.

You may ask **close-ended questions,** those that invite a yes or no response. The obvious advantage of close-ended questions is that you can more easily prevent abuse of your questioning time.

> "Is it A or B?"
>
> "Is it true or false that. . . ."
>
> "Am I correct in paraphrasing your first point as. . . ."

There is **an ethic** for close-ended questions, though. You should avoid the fallacy of **forcing the dichotomy,** suggesting that there are only two alternatives when others exist. In courtrooms and debates, it appears in the form of *"the fallacy of complex question"* in which a hidden presumption is assumed in a dichotomy.

"Have you stopped using drugs? Yes or no?"

It's my burden of proof to show that he used drugs, but by presuming that in the dichotomy, there's yet another fallacy potentially, that of ad hominem. The complex question is set up to diminish the credibility of the person questioned, not clarify or discover the truth.

There are **strategic uses of questions,** though. You can use questions to **attack the weakest point** in the case, to pry it loose, and put the adversary on the defensive. You can ask for additional evidence to press the burden of proof.

You can **question warrants** to set up an observation of fallacies in your own speech.

You may not make arguments in cross-x, but you can **use questions to set up your own arguments.** Remind the audience during your own speech of questions that you asked for which the answers were unsatisfactory, and launch your own counter-argument from there.

If you notice that two of your adversary's points seem in conflict, you might have an impulse to simply argue that it's a **contradiction.** A good fisherman, though, knows how to set the hook.

It would be clumsy to bluntly ask, "Doesn't A contradict B?" A clever person may simply answer, "No, and let me explain why." Rather, lead him to repeat the contradiction. Ask about one point with an open-ended question. If the adversary wanders, step in with a close-ended question, "but didn't you say A in your speech?"

Then go to the other point in conflict, and repeat the process, open-ended to close-ended. Then, you may ask, "But doesn't A contradict B?" It may take some time in questioning, but you will have attacked not one argument, but two. Also, you may have created a sense of dramatic irony between you and your audience. Since the adversary made the contradiction, he or she may be unaware of it, even as you subtly dramatize the point.

The key point is that once an advocate commits to a point of view in cross-examination, the person questioned cannot easily shift from it, and his statements function as grounds for your arguments.[3]

Let's emphasize that word "subtly." The tone of your questioning should be respectful, even conversational. Please, don't behave like some television lawyer you saw once. No drama. No histrionics. Questions aren't a time to fight, except in the time honored sense of a duel of wits. A person who comes across too aggressively may alienate the audience and cause sympathy for the adversary. Consider the Bush/Gore debates and the public reaction to Gore's audible sighing and condescending head shakes, his reaction to Bush's arguments.

Refutation

Once you've understood an argument, you can begin to refute it. Just as the advocate has the burden of proof, the opposition has a burden to refute, to challenge the advocate's arguments. To a certain degree, both sides have similar burdens. The advocate has THE burden of proof, the requirement that he or she must successfully overturn the presumption possessed by the opposition. Yet the opponent has A burden of proof, in that he must use evidence to support his positions as well. Similarly, just as the opposition has an obligation to refute, to clash with the advocate's arguments, the advocate is also obligated to refute the attacks from the opposition.[4] Thus, we'll use the more inclusive term "adversary" below, as it applies to both advocate and opposition.

A general format for refutation may go as follows:

1) You may begin with an overview about the assembly of arguments, or "case," itself. You might do this with a mind to attacking any key presumptions upon which the case depends. You can also reveal any hidden and undefended presumptions that the case depends on. The adversary may also have made some overviews that require refutation.

2) State the adversary's argument, including the number or letter he has used to identify it. You would presumably start with the first argument and work your way down the case.

3) Attack the argument in one or more of several ways, being sure to label your own argument clearly.

   A) Agree with the argument because it is either irrelevant or it helps your case.

   B) Diminish the significance of the argument for the adversary's thesis.

   C) Disagree with the argument by revealing its flaws.

   - Apply any relevant fallacies.
   - Use tests of evidence to challenge the grounds.
   - Offer contradictory evidence from your own sources.
   - Offer a counter-argument that directly opposes your adversary's.

- None of these are mutually exclusive, although the option of counter-argument may force you to defend your own position. The other options allow you to stay on the attack.

D) Summarize your position.

E) Characterize the impact of your attacks against the adversary's case.

F) Repeat with each argument.

It is also true that, given sufficient time, you should make an underview summarizing the impact of your attacks on the adversary's case.

A perfectly reasonable approach to counter-argument is ***straight refutation.*** This common strategy is to attack a case, point by point, with opposing evidence. On the opposition, this is a perfectly reasonable alternative to offering extra off case arguments of your own.[5] With nothing to defend and rebuild on your side, you can stay on the offensive all the time. However, it is a lot easier to offer this strategy effectively if you are well informed on the issues at hand.

Using Fallacies

You've had a chance to see some fallacies in action now. Let's review them by subgroups with nicknames, so that we can stay fresh and use them:

> *Fallacies of Appeal (six silly slaps):*
>   *Ad Hominem*
>   *Appeal to Ignorance—unfairly shifting the burden of proof*
>   *Appeal to the People (Bandwagon Argument)*
>   *Appeal to Pity and Fear*
>   *Appeal to Tradition*
>   *Reductio Absurdum (Appeal to Humor)*
>
> *Fallacies of Language (the three stooges):*
>   *Emotive Language*
>   *Equivocal Language*
>   *Jargonese*
>
> *Fallacies of Logic (the dirty dozen):*
>   *Causal Fallacies*
>   *Correlation vs. Causation*
>   *False Cause (propter hoc)*
>   *Oversimplification*
>   *Slippery Slope*
>   *Circular Reasoning*
>   *Hasty Generalization and Sweeping Generalization*

> *Non Sequiturs*
> *Red Herring*
> *Tranfer Fallacy of Composition*
> *Transfer Fallacy of Division*
>
> *Fallacies of Relevance (the three little maids)*
> *Avoiding the Issue*
> *Seizing on a Trivial Point*
> *Shifting Ground*

You can do a more complete review of these fallacies in chapters IV and VII.

Fallacies may occur at every level of a Toulmin argument:

Fallacies of Language may appear in the ***proposition or any claim.*** Emotive language may be quite common there. The presence of equivocation is ubiquitous. The use of "jargonese" in more technical debates may be evasive, as well.

Equivocal language is often just a matter of accidental and inexact word choice. However, it is wise to consider if an equivocation might be an intentional set-up to shift ground late in the debate. It's very important to help your adversary to define equivocal language clearly. One may use questions to achieve this purpose.

Fallacies of Appeal may appear in impassioned oratory around a claim for which no strong evidence really exists. Speakers will ***replace grounds*** with appeals and make mistakes. Appeal fallacies may also be imbedded in the warrant above weak grounds. A statement of "reason" could reveal Fallacies of Tradition, Appeal to Ignorance, or Bandwagon Argument. They could be imbedded in grounds, in overly dramatic examples, as Appeal to Pity and Fear.

Logical Fallacies should usually be imbedded ***in the warrant.*** Isolating the warrant for scrutiny may determine that, no matter how good their evidence is, the reasoning that fastens arguments together doesn't hold. Warrants may be non sequiturs, or transfer fallacies.

Hasty Generalization can occur in the sheer lack of evidence, or the abundance of personal experiences cited as grounds.

You have four ways that statements of cause can go wrong. Arguing from Cause to Effect is one of the more difficult things to achieve. So, look carefully at statements of cause and remember four fallacies for which you can look:

> Look for ***correlation vs. causation.*** If they claim causation, it will sometimes merely be a strong sign at best, or weak causation at worst. Either argument can be useful.
>
> Look for ***false cause.*** If you hear someone arguing that "A came before B, thus, A caused B," apply false cause.

Look for **oversimplification.** We've discussed how there are usually multiple causes for modern social problems. If an adversary focuses on one or two causes, you may argue *"alternative causation"* and introduce evidence of other additional causes. This tempts an adversary to leave assertion of their own position, putting them on the defensive to respond to you.

Look for **slippery slope** when opponents establish that A causes B, but then asserts a result C, D, E, etc., without establishing causal links at each extension of cause. The arguer may try to create a sense of a landslide of some kind, hence, the name of the fallacy.

Fallacies of Relevance are usually applied to **grounds.** Remember, their minimum burden of proof is to supply evidence that directly supports claims. Very often, speakers overestimate the relevance of evidence, seeing what they wish to see, rather than what the words actually say. Also, watch for simple evasion or shifting ground in the process of **cross-examination.**

When applying fallacies as counter-argument be sure that you clearly **identify the "giveaway"** in your opponent's argument—the smoking gun, so to speak—the specific wording that reveals the fallacy.

1)   Establish the argument attacked.

2)   Read the specific wording that reveals the fallacy.

3)   Identify the fallacy and describe its mental action.

4)   Emphasize the impact on the adversary's case.

Remember the stock issues involved in the debate. Certain arguments will be the lynchpin for a particular issue. You may defeat an argument at any of the three points in Toulmin's form.

Evidence Attacks

To the degree that grounds are the foundation of an argument, if you can undermine the evidence, the argument should fall.

Remember the basic goals of gathering evidence:

Find the best approximate truth of complex social matters;

Mix the Internet with library sources;

Take multiple points of view;

Use a variety of sources.

Your **breadth of research, or native knowledge,** will equate to the depth of your response. So, it makes sense to keep up with news events, whether by magazine, newspaper, Net, or TV news. Ideally, you should be looking at all four. You're too busy? Catch up on the weekend with news magazines, which summarize the week, or get the Sunday paper, also often a summary of the week's events.

The potential downside of straight refutation is that you may be tempted to yield to *a shotgun, or spread refutation strategy.* This occurs when one attempts multiple levels of attack against every single point, trying to so overwhelm an opponent with the sheer number of arguments. Apart from being inaudible to an audience, speeding is often an attempt to cover up poor quality arguments. *Prefer quality over quantity.*

You can also apply *a selective refutation strategy.* If you're afraid of missing points, remember that each argument has "pressure points." Among them are the advocate's "hidden presumptions," unsupported beliefs that are assumed but unproven in an argument. Even announced assumptions may be faulty.

If you can undermine the presumption upon which an argument is based, you may defeat the whole argument without necessarily debating each point.

Further, if you assault the reasoning in warrants, no matter how many grounds are beneath each, the argument will fall. In sum, you can select where to place your attack, or cover all the points, but dismiss some as less significant than your adversary asserts.

Tests of evidence should be applied regularly to grounds, simply as a matter of course. Don't waste time offering more opposing evidence than is required, if the evidence opposed is faulty in itself.

Here is a check list for *the "ten commandments" of evidence tests:*

> Is the grounds *consistent* with other grounds offered in the case?
> Was the evidence observed *first hand,* or is it hearsay evidence?
> Is the *method* for gathering statistics explicit?
> Are the sources *objective?*
> Are the sources *qualified?*
> Is the grounds *recent?*
> Is the grounds *relevant?*
> Is the grounds *representative* of the preponderance of evidence available?
> In the case of statistics, are the samples used representative?
> Is the grounds *sufficient* to support the claim?
> Is the grounds *verifiable?*

You can do a more complete review of evidence tests in chapter III. Then think of these catalogues—tests of evidence, as well as the fallacies—as *checklists for counter-argument.* Note that they're alphabetized to help you memorize them.

When you apply them, remember to do the basic steps. Don't just assert the test. Identify the evidence. Summarize the content attacked. Apply the evidence test. Then mention the impact of that on the argument and the case.

It might also be an enjoyable exercise, since you may be preparing to do a value debate, to look at the above tests and prioritize them in terms of which are more important. Obviously, as a hint, you're going to need more than one kind at the top, since there are different types of evidence to be tested.

Reversal of Fortune: Turns

There is also opportunity to *jiu-jitsu evidence* to your own advantage. Warrants are somewhat subjective. Different speakers may infer differently from the same evidence. If you look carefully at your adversary's grounds, you may find that they really don't support his points. In fact, you may be able to steal their grounds for your own counter-claims by applying a different warrant.

One example could be discussions of the three-strikes law in California. The law doubles sentences for second time offenders. Someone with two prior convictions for violent or serious crimes can be sentenced from twenty-five years to life for even minor offenses. Some argue that it's the most effective law ever, others that it is both ineffective and cruel and unusual punishment.[6]

> Claim: "The three strikes law has been the most effective criminal justice initiative in the history of California," said Bill Jones, co-author of the measure and former Secretary of State.
>
> Warrant A: We can tell this is so by prison statistics. One fourth of the California prison population is now from three strikes.
>
> Grounds A: "Three strikes inmates in California now number more than 42,000, one fourth of the prison population, according to the study" from the Justice Policy Institute, Washington, DC.
>
> Warrant B: It's also true that three strikes has saved money.
>
> Grounds B: "Supporters of the sentencing measure, widely viewed as the toughest of its kind in the U.S. . . . . say that putting repeat criminals in jail has saved $28 billion in costs associated with their crimes."

Now, consider a possible counter-argument:

> Counter-claim: On the contrary, the three strikes law has only been minimally effective and at too high a cost.
>
> Warrant A: *We can tell so by the same prison statistics.* We have increased the number of prisoners by a quarter, his evidence says. How is that a good thing? That may just as well show that we're arresting too many people for trivial crimes.

Ground A1: According to U.C. Berkeley law professor, Frank Zimring, "It has had a very small impact on crime." And third strike penalties "are grossly disproportionate to the crime."

Ground A2: And according to the same Justice Policy Institute study cited by my adversary, "Nearly 60% of those convicted for second or third strike offenses were serving time in prison for non-violent crimes. They included 672 third strikers serving 25 years to life for drug possession—a number that was greater than the number of third-strikers in prison for second-degree murder, assault with a deadly weapon and rape combined."

Warrant B: How has it saved money? Perhaps this is computed from the average cost of crimes in the future, but that pales against the added costs of Three Strikes that are in evidence now.

Ground B: *Again from the study quoted by my adversary,* "A decade after it was enacted, California's three strike sentencing law has had little impact on violent crime while costing taxpayers $8 billion to imprison tens of thousands of felons, most of them for non-violent offenses."

Using either a source cited by your adversary, or the particular piece of evidence used by your adversary against him, is an economical and damaging tactic.

Be careful about contradicting yourself. Obviously, you can't apply tests of evidence to grounds that you use yourself. You can certainly attack the warrants with fallacies, since you are providing different warrants yourself.

Building Opposition Arguments

In addition to refuting arguments, you can build arguments of your own, as is evidenced by the interaction above. Although your arguments in refutation can be applied directly against a particular argument, you can also build your own alternative case, points that apply to the adversary's case but raise other issues than his or her arguments. Recall that we advised you to leave some room at the bottom of your flow to make room for your own arguments.

In the context of a parliamentary debate on a value topic, you may set up arguments that support the counter-value directly. For instance, if the value in the above exchange were "lawfulness," the counter value might be "mercy." You could build positions on the usefulness of mercy. For example:

Claim I: Mercy and lawfulness are inextricably bound.

Warrant: You can't have one without the other. Lawfulness without mercy is cruel to the extent that it's counterproductive. That is, we put the relatively harmless offenders in jail, in the name of lawfulness. Yet they come out hardened criminals, likely to offend again.

Grounds A: There are a wide variety of studies suggesting that once you've gone to jail, you're likely to return. The result is an ever-worsening cycle of crime that increases in severity as the perpetrator goes.

Grounds B: Other studies say that prisons are virtual crime schools. One may go in as a petty thief and graduate to grand larceny, as a result of the people he meets in prison and their outside contacts.

Grounds C: Remember Victor Hugo's "Les Miserables." Jean Val Jean was caught stealing some golden candlesticks from a church, because he was hungry. The priest, instead of turning him in, gave him the candlesticks. Val Jean, from that time forward, was a righteous man.

Claim II: Lawfulness not tempered by mercy is a sign of a totalitarian state.

Warrant: History gives us many cases of such "lawfulness" as signs of totalitarian governments.

Grounds A: Roman emperors, like Caligula, enforced their laws against Christianity by putting Christians in the arena to be eaten by lions.

Grounds B: Middle Eastern countries traditionally cut off the hands of thieves.

Grounds C: The holocaust requires no explanation as an illustration of totalitarian ideals.

Notice that we're not citing the actual studies. We're simply recognizing the usual convention in parliamentary debate that grounds come from knowledge that is held in common by the speaker and the audience.

We can also make a point about an idea being ***counterproductive,*** when a particular act of value actually works against its own goals. Did Caligula end Christianity? No. The Roman emperors themselves became Christians during the Byzantine era. Is there an absence of thievery in the Middle East? Who knows, but looting has been a major problem during the Iraq invasion. It appears that such punishment, and worse, has little long-range effect against the impulse for thievery. Need we comment about how badly the holocaust turned out for Germany? Jews survived and were energized to organize and defend themselves in Israel and elsewhere.

Your opponent is now obligated to attack arguments as well as defend his own. He'll need, perhaps, to make a distinction that enforcing unjust laws are not really lawfulness, but then he'll have to defend "three strikes" as a just law.

We, on the other hand, need to be mindful that we've put ourselves in the same position. Instead of merely being responsible for straight refutation, we have to defend arguments as well as attack them.

Double Standards

It is a normal psychological tendency for people to perceive things in their own favor, to apologize sometimes for themselves while accusing others who behave no differently than we do.

Likewise, your adversaries may fall into the problem of "the pot calling the kettle black." In other words, they've applied a criticism to you that may equally apply to them, or they've applied a standard to one thing though not another of similar kind. We call these "double standards," and they ***can be reversed to your advantage.***

Examples would include recent issues. In "Hypocrisy Now in Fashion," it was noted that male tennis players must wear more traditional clothing, while females like Serena Williams push the threshold with clothing that is not only not traditional, but barely covers her parts.[7] Editorialist have made the point that the United States has abandoned previous international nuclear agreements, yet is pressing others to control their development of nuclear weapons.[8]

When the film "A Beautiful Mind" was made, critiques were made about the fact that a white woman, Jennifer Connelly, was cast as Mrs. Nash, who was a woman of color. This argument notes the hypocrisy of it:

> I think that people are crazy about casting, especially when it involves race. Recently people have complained about casting on the basis of political correctness, especially about Academy Award winner Jennifer Conneley. True she is not of the same race, but why was she singled out? Russell Crowe is Australian, while John Russell is not. Why reduce the art of acting to a question of race or country? Portraying people of other races and nationalities is a challenge of good performance. There was no similar "outrage" when Ben Kingsley won an Oscar for his portrayal of Mahatma Gandhi in 1982? Did anyone get angry when Irishman Liam Neeson and Englishman Ralph Fiennes were nominated for Oscars for "Schindler's List?" Did anyone propose the casting of Texan Renee' Zellweger as the British Bridget Jones? She was also nominated for an Oscar.

People have argued that Israel's tactics in suppressing Palestinians is ***counter-productive*** to the long-range goal of peace.[9] Others have thought that using force against countries harboring terrorists, rather than targeting individual terrorists, is simply breeding the next generation of terrorists.

Counter-productivity arguments in policy arguments can be very important. If we're to solve a social problem, it would be good if our solution wasn't worse than the harm that we're solving.

Also, you may be able to note that an attack from an adversary is ***not unique*** to your point of view. The bad effects you're accused of may also flow from your opponents way of thinking. Some arguments that may be issued against you can be "knives that cut two ways."

Extemporaneous Thinking

We've been primarily concentrating on text building in a written sense, with any oral delivery a later issue. Yet the most useful, even necessary skill for maximum function in employment, as well as social and civic interaction, is ***extemporaneous speaking.*** This kind of speaking is essential for effective debate.

There are basically ***four ways to deliver a speech:***

> Entirely without specific preparation, or "impromptu";
> Reading from a manuscript;
> Memorizing a text, then delivering it without a manuscript;
> Or extemporaneously, an outline, but not a fully-worded speech.

One has to pull one's thoughts together in a brief time, organize them, and present them ***"off the cuff"*** in a debate. That phrase, by the way, is a literal reference. In the old days, when men wore starched and detachable cuffs, they would literally jot a few notes on their cuff to prompt them during presentations. You'll have your flow sheet to help you.

But what have you written on it? Confronted with undifferentiated masses of thoughts and information, the mind reels at the prospect of responding so immediately. The common phenomena of speaker apprehension can be increased beyond situations in which one has a fully worded manuscript to depend upon.

We've seen certain checklists and forms throughout this text: stock issues, tests of evidence, and fallacies. Of course, Toulmin's model is a standard form. We can call these checklists and forms ***"cookie cutters."*** They help us to look at a mass of information, the cookie dough, and by applying the form of a particular cookie cutter, we can distinguish distinct uses of this mass.

There are a variety of different ways to organize texts besides the stock issues approach. They, too, can be cookie cutters to help you organize your thoughts. Look at the appendix on structures for other cookie cutters.

After a certain amount of experience with these standardized forms, one can use them to respond to argument, almost instinctively, in a natural and organized way.

So, extemporaneous speaking is not being unprepared. It's having a grasp on the above cookie cutters and applying them to open questions or issues, with some brief time of preparation. Even an impromptu speaker can use these typical patterns of speaking to shape his or her thoughts:

> What's the who, what, when, where, why, and how of this?
> What's the past, the present, and the future of this?

What are the causes and effects of this?
What is the problem, the cause, and the solution of this?
What is the least important and which the most important of these?
Or ask the stock issues of the three types of propositions.

You get a topic. Your mind is blank. Your pulse starts to race. Your mouth gets dry. Your hands get wet. You start thinking about your sense of personal insecurity instead of the issue at hand. Stop. Take a cookie cutter and apply it to the topic. You can't know everything about the topic. Nobody can. Yet you may be surprised how much you do know, if you ask yourself systematically, "What are the effects, what are the causes, etc.?"

When we teach, and we suspect this is true for other teachers, what we do in front of the room is both spontaneous and the result of long planning. We have learned many bits of lessons and examples, just as a comedian has memorized many jokes, and we pull them out of memory based on the outline that evokes them.

When you can manage extemporaneous speaking in real-world settings, you'll create a more authoritative and confident image for yourself. Even very successful businessmen join Toastmaster's Clubs to practice this very skill. In a market in which most jobs will require at least some oral communication skill, it's important. For leadership positions, it's critical.

* * * * *

A final word about ***being a team,*** if your instructor chooses to stage debates. If debating alone in a Lincoln-Douglas format, you don't have to worry about satisfying a partner's goals. In a team, however, you have to coordinate your attack, both to avoid contradicting each other and to leave each other a reasonable amount of argumentative ground.

If you listen to each other, each may pick up things that the other has missed. You will each do better if you respect your partner as you would yourself, and your experience will be more enjoyable and satisfying.

Vocabulary

Alternative Causation	Extemporaneous Speaking
Cookie Cutters	Fallacy of Complex Question
Cross-examination	Forcing an Argument
Counterproductivity	Non Unique
Open-Ended Questions	Straight Refutation
Close-Ended Questions	Turns

Exercises: Go to Interactive Disc to Complete

"The seeds of an argument's defeat are sown within the language of the argument itself." Look at the following arguments, appreciate, then counter-attack each:

1) Claim: The Red Cross is right to reject a pioneering stem cell grant.

    Warrant A: They're correct for practical reasons. It would divert their focus.

    Grounds A: According to Jerry Squires, chief scientific officer at the charity's biomedical division, "Human embryonic stem cells have the capacity to fray and disperse our focus. . . . It isn't fitting with our mission."

    Warrant B: It might also discourage contributors, due to the controversy.

    Grounds B: "I think you can assume from this decision that the political debate has a chilling effect on scientific pursuits," said Sean Tipton, spokesman for the American Society for Reproductive Medicine. "If you depend on funding from the goodwill of politicians or the good will of the public, then you stay away from controversy."

    Warrant C: To the extent that this is a non-partisan group, which depends upon its neutrality, the fact that this is so controversial might damage their effectiveness.

    Grounds C: Both Germany and the United States have put serious governmental restrictions against stem cell research (*LA Times,* Jan. 1, 2002).

2) Claim: According to Arianna Huffington, the administration's campaign against drugs is cynical and offensive.

    Warrant A: The T.V. spots, which premiered during the Super Bowl, promote the twisted reasoning that, since drug profits have found their way into the pockets of terrorists, any young American who used drugs is therefore guilty of aiding and abetting the enemy.

    Grounds A: In one particularly odious ad, a series of fresh faced young people are shown copping to a host of terrorist atrocities: "I helped kids learn how to kill . . . " "I helped to murder families in Columbia . . . " "I helped blow up buildings."

    Warrant B: It's also a highly selective campaign. It only points fingers at one specific contribution to terrorists. But diamonds are an enormous contribution to terrorism.

    Grounds B1: Huffington argues that Osama Bin Laden and Al Queda used millions of dollars in profits from the diamond industry to fund terrorism. Why don't we see a commercial with a Senator's wife, fingering her diamonds and admitting that she helped kids learn to become suicide bombers.

Fifteen out of nineteen hijackers came from Saudi Arabia, where extremists are traditionally coddled. Why are there no taxpayer funded ad showing soccer moms filling up her SUVs and saying, "Each gallon goes to the terrorist effort" ("An Unholy Alliance of Two Wars: On Terrorism and Drugs," Editorial, *LA Times,* Feb. 8, 2002.)

Grounds B2: It is also true the "Conflict Diamonds" from Africa have led to bloody revolutions, massacres, and mutilation of civilians within that continent, as well.

Sources

1) Adler, R.B., Proctor II, R.F., and Towne, N. (2005). Looking Out, Looking In. Belmont, CA: Thomson.

2) Larson, S. (1987). "Cross-examination in CEDA Debate: A Survey of Coaches." CEDA Yearbook 8, pp. 33–41.

   Miller, T.H., and Caminker, E.H. (1982). "The Art of Cross-Examination." CEDA Yearbook 3, pp. 4–15.

3) Perella, J. (1987). The Debate Method of Critical Thinking: An Introduction to Argumentation. Dubuque, Iowa: Kendall/Hunt.

4) Freeley, A.J. (1993). Argumentation and Debate: Critical Thinking for Reasoned Decision Making, 8th edition. Belmont,CA: Wadsworth.

5) Hill, B., and Leeman, R.W. (1997). The Art & Practice of Argumentation & Debate. Mountain View, CA: Mayfield.

6) LA Times, "Three Strikes Law Challenged," March 5, 2004.

7) LA Times, "Hypocrisy now in fashion," August 29, 2002.

8) LA Times, "Bush's Dangerous Nuclear Double Standard," Editorial, Sept. 13, 2003.

9) LA Times, "Sharon's Airstrike Disaster," July 27, 2002.

XI
Parliamentary Debate

There are many formats for approaching a formal debate: Oxford, Oregon and Lincoln-Douglas styles among them. We'll explore those formats briefly, but we'll focus primarily on parliamentary debate. There is a national interest in this kind of debate at speech tournaments on this level, and it's commonly practiced at many colleges today, we'll learn this format.[1] It's also, in some respects, the easiest format to master.

If you saw a formal parliamentary debate without understanding it, you might think it's a little funny. Instead of clapping, people knock on tables and say, "here, here," or "shame, shame." People stand up in the middle of their adversary's speech to ask a question of the speaker. Then the speaker may interrupt himself to take a question, or he may say, "Not at this time," if he's trying to finish a point. Audiences sometimes put their two cents in with "Hear, hear," or "shame, shame."

These behaviors are simply respects to this particular tradition of debate, which is based upon British Parliament. They knock on tables. They also stand to ask questions, and it gets quite noisy at times. Watch C-SPAN on cable and see for yourself. Parliament is broadcast intermittently on that public channel.

These **conventions** aren't really essential to your classroom experience, except that you may ask a question or two of a speaker during his turn. Otherwise, interaction is structured to allow each side in the debate equal time.

There are **six speeches** in a parliamentary debate, divided somewhat unequally among four people. That is, while there is equal time for each team, one speaker on each team will speak more. So, if one of each two-member team is a bit more confident about speaking than the other, he or she can take two of that side's three speeches. That is not to say the other speech is less important. It may be the key argument attacking or rebuilding phase of the debate. It's just a matter of time on the floor.

The two **sides are determined,** as with other types of issues, by the proposition. Unlike the previous fact text, or the policy text to follow, there are some minor **differences of terminology for the speaker roles.** The two sides are the Government and their Loyal Opposition. The government is the affirmative (advocate), and the opposition is the negative.

In tournament competition, topics are drawn and one has only fifteen minutes to prepare. For beginner purposes, though, it's fine for you have an agreed upon topic to think over and do a little research over, say, a week or two.

In speech tournament conventions, no evidence is allowed, other than that which we know from our general awareness of literature, history, and current events. When we say "prove it" in parliamentary debate, we are emphasizing the use of reason as proof. So, now is a good time for you apply the patterns of reason and their attendant fallacies with conscious attention.

We begin with *four constructive speeches,* because these are the speeches in which we build our arguments.

The *first* to speak to establish a case is the **Prime Minister.**[2] He speaks first and last for the government side. He speaks for seven minutes maximum. A timekeeper should signal the countdown of minutes to help the speakers know where they are.

His or her duties include:

1) Offering the exactly worded proposition.

2) Defining the terms of the proposition, determining argumentative ground.

3) Establishing a value standard with which to measure opposing values.

4) Proving that the value supported better meets the standard. It may take two or three arguments to demonstrate.

The **second** to speak is the **Leader of the Opposition.** He speaks for eight minutes, one more than the Prime Minister's constructive speech, but the time is equalized as the Prime Minister gets a longer rebuttal at the end of the debate. The leader's roles and obligations include:

1) Consider the definitions and either agree or disagree with them. It's possible that the definition could unfairly favor the government by undercutting the opposition's argumentative ground unfairly. Identify the argumentative ground for the opposition and the counter value they intend to defend.

2) Either accept the standard offered by the government, or establish a counter standard, an alternative that the audience may or may not find more reasonable.

3) Offer direct refutation of the Prime Minister's case.

We've spoken about the concepts of presumption, burden of proof and prima facie case. There's another obligation that we must discuss here, *the obligation to clash,* to argue directly against the case presented. Sometimes, novice debaters are so nervous about speaking "off the cuff," that they're non-responsive to their adversary and only recite what they've already prepared, no matter its fit to the case. You have to show how your points relate to the government's arguments to make it relevant, which means you have to listen carefully and record notes. We'll see more on notes later.

4) Present the opposition's case arguments.

Since you're defending a counter value of your own, you have some obligation to illustrate the merits of that value. It's possible that some of the counter value thinking you've come up with can be applied directly against the government case on a point-by-point basis. Yet you may have separate arguments for your side. This goes last, or you may not fulfill your obligation to clash.

Third, the Prime Minister's partner, the ***Member of the Government,*** speaks one time, but in a very important middle speech.

Remember the concept of presumption. The opposition has this advantage. The compromise advantage given the government is that they speak first and last. They lay out the argumentative territory, and they get the last word. To manage that, we have to reverse speaker order in rebuttal. That means two opposition speeches in row. So, the member of the government has to be sure that his side is not behind in responses going into rebuttal. The member, thus, has the following obligations:

1) Defend definitions and standard, unless of course the opposition has accepted your terms and standards. If they have, acknowledge that they've accepted the argumentative ground that you've proposed.

2) Rebuild the government case and refute the opposition's attacks.

When we say this, we don't only mean that you merely repeat your partner's original position. You have an obligation to clash, too. You ***extend the case*** with new analysis and support that answers the opposition's criticisms. The language of these moments usually has three grammatical parts:

"Our argument is. . . ."

"Their attack is. . . ."

"Our response is. . . ."

This helps a listening audience to ***keep track of the flow of arguments,*** along with a flow sheet, which we'll explain below. (Relax. You don't have to hold this all in your head, there is a note taking system we can use.)

3) Attack the opposition's case.

It's important that you rebuild your own case first, but your ***time management*** must be careful enough that you have time for this last task. If you spend too much time on your opponent's case before rebuilding your own, you'll almost certainly lose your arguments that you've neglected to rebuild. Your opposition will make the argument that it's unfair for you to wait until the last rebuttal to answer their attack, as they'll have no additional speeches left to respond.

Yet, if you don't leave time to attack our opponent's case, they can say that they must have won, since you have no response to their positions.

In either case, you'll wind up debating on your opponent's ground rather than your own in rebuttal, if you don't cover both your own and the opponent's arguments. The opposition will have drawn you out of "your fort," your argumentative territory, and the audience may very well forget your arguments during your last minute attack of theirs.

So, if you thought you were playing second fiddle to the Prime Minister, just because he has more speaking time, think again. This may be the make or break speech for your side.

Member of the Opposition speaks ***fourth*** and only once, but also in an important position. He has eight minutes. In a similar "they said, we said, they said" grammar, the member:

    1)   Defends the Leader of the Opposition's case.

That is, you respond directly to attacks against his case. You also want the audience to focus on your argumentative ground. You also must manage your time carefully here, so you can. . .

    2)   Attack the Member of the Government's Responses.

    3)   Extend and add arguments to the opposition's case.

This is your last chance to add new arguments, if an opportunity emerges. Even if you're only adding examples and analysis that go beyond your first obligation, the strategy is a sort of "sandwich your opposition." You start on your ground, and you end on your ground, sandwiching the government's case in the middle.

One thing you might do is to look particularly at the real life impacts of the value. If we actually lived out the advocate's value, how might it lead to a lesser human existence than the value you defend?

No new arguments are allowed in the last two speeches, which are called ***rebuttals.*** The leader of each side summarizes and explains to the audience why, given the value standard that has won out or been agreed upon by the two sides, their side has won. Remember, no new arguments may be issued, but new analysis and support for the arguments already presented may be necessary. Do not merely summarize if there are outstanding questions from your adversary to be answered.

The ***Leader of the Opposition has the first rebuttal,*** which lasts only four minutes to compensate for the time advantage he took earlier. It's a good time to emphasize that each speaker should have some unique analysis of their own. You shouldn't spend this time merely parroting what your partner just said.

1) Extend upon and emphasize your key arguments.

2) You should offer some clear rationale for why, given the standards discussed, your counter-value is superior.

Then, the ***Prime Minister has the last rebuttal*** during which he must:

1) Answer key opponent arguments.

2) Rebuild the government case, ending on his own ground.

3) Tell the audience why, given the standards discussed, your value is superior.

If you're doing debates in class, and you have a lot of students, you may find it necessary to modify the time limits. You can get away with a 6-7-7-7 format with rebuttal at 3 and 4 minutes. In other words, leave the format in tact, but shave equal minutes off each.

If you try Lincoln-Douglas style debates, one person against another, you could divide the speeches into a three speech format. This may be necessary if you have an odd number of people in the class (as opposed to a number of odd people, which also can occur).

Government gets 7 minutes, then the opposition gets a 12 minute block of time, including his constructive and rebuttal time in one speech, and the government gets a five minute rebuttal. You could even break this down into a 5-10-5 minute format.

It's even possible, in a non-competitive classroom setting, to forego the reversal of sides in rebuttal, and simply give each speaker a constructive and rebuttal. You may experiment with any of them with the help of your instructor.

Flow Sheets

A flow sheet is a note taking system for debate that will help listeners and speakers keep track of the "flow" of arguments from speech to speech. Take a sheet of 8x10 or legal-sized paper, hold it long side up, then fold the paper in half. Fold that half by half again, and you're left with ***four creased columns.***

You write notes in the first column on the left for the Prime Minister, being sure to leave some blank space at the bottom of the column for opposition arguments yet to come. This is important, as you want to be able to follow an argument and responses

Affirmative

Democrats Stronger Platform for 2004 election

D. Civil Rights - Vehicle for Reform

1. D platform on economy will benefit Americans
   - C1 Raising min. wage ($7/hr.)
   - C2 Tax reform to create jobs
   - C3 Middle Class is bombarded — will insure 98% will get tax cuts

2. Federal Responsibility for education
   - C1 Smaller classes, elem. Secondary
   - C2 No Child left behind
   - C3 Better teachers
   - C4 Student aid, tax credits for all students

3. Cleaner envir./future Pollution
   - C1. Strengthen enviro. act
   - C2. Restore "Polluter Pays"
   - C3. Restore leased land & respect Nat'l Parks

Negative

Republican platform will deliver

1. Economy
   - C1 Sweeping tax relief
     - W - saved americans $
   - C1 - reduces, trade agreements
     - W - reinforces SS
   - C1 - SS won't be cut taxes not raised

2. education need to meet obligations
   - C1 Children have access to free 1st rate education
   - C2 - No Child left behind
     - W - Higher education
   - C1 - 73 billion increase in Fin. Aide
   - C2 - tax credit

3. Environment Improving? Yes
   - C1 - CleanSkys report
   - C2 - Bush cleaned up Browns fields as promised.

Affirmative

Economy

1. Republicans want to keep min. wage @ $5.15/hr
   - 300,000 a year or more a year will have their tax cuts repealed.
   - 2003's 2004 tax cuts will be permanent under Rep. platform. (7trillion?)

2. Education
   - no child left behind both D & R agree on.
   - R- Want to turn it over to the federal gov.
   - most places that need the funds won't get it because they can't pass.
   * - Military: troops to teachers
   - D: after School Care, schools open till 6pm.

3. Environment
   - Clean Sky Initiative lets businesses to pollute (Browns fields (D & R's))
   - Arctic Nat'l wildlife Refuge
   * thugs Republicans want to drill here.
   - Interfere w/ Research

Negative

1. Education
   - no child left behind
   - more qualified teachers (reduced restrictions on then)

2. Economy
   - Dem. raise min. wage
   - Implies it will help economy
   - Reduced taxes 25 million Sm. business owners.
   - After 9/11 = Recession unemployment 6.5%
     this year dropped to 5.1%
   - Strongest economy (40 million in workforce)

3. Education
   - 17 mill. New grant $ to improve quality (NCLB)
   - Troops to teachers, highly qualified people & funds injured soldiers from Iraq war.

4. Environment
   - Reduced 70% of some emissions.
   - EPA: by 2020 emissions from power plants will be drastically reduced. - increased wetland

Affirmative Rebutal

1. Economy
   - America is asking for a better economy.
   - taxes not accounted for outsourcing
   ? Worst since the depression.

2. Education
   - 27 billion less than Bush has promised
   - Promised a affordable education and she being middle class doesn't see that as forseable.

3. Environment
   - 20,000 facilities to spew more smog
   - Promised 5 Billion to Nat'l parks & only delivered a fraction of this.

Negative Rebutal

Rep. better platform

1. Economy
   @ Alternative min. tax
   @ Economy is strong its in "the numbers"
   - 1.5 mil. new Jobs from last year.
   - Unemployment down in 49 States.

2. Education
   - Edu. is a state obligation & must assume & majority of the Responsibility and Obligation.
   ✶ Scapegoat?
   - Free 1st-Rate education

3. Environment
   - R. Policies geared twords results.

   (Had for over 100 Years/Fresh platform contradiction)

to it from left to right, all the way across four constructive speeches. You can then flip the paper over and use the columns on the back for rebuttal.

The language you use will have to be abbreviated. Unless you have shorthand skills, you'll get lost trying to write every word down. Lean back, listen carefully, and when you have a sense of the whole argument, jot some notes down.

To illustrate flow sheets, as well as offer a simplified sample Parliamentary debate example, let's take a look at this proposition:

The protection of human rights is more important than anti-terrorism.

Prime Minister: We support this proposition, as we fear our efforts at security from terrorism are damaging the freedoms and protections that set us aside from terrorists, and we welcome our opponents to this discussion, as well as the audience (a simple expression of courtesy which is also a convention).

1) We define human rights as those rights guaranteed by the U.S. Constitution and the Bill of Rights. Most particularly we are concerned with the right to fair trial, free speech rights, and privacy rights inferred from the Constitution by the Supreme Court. We define "anti-terrorism" as the values represented by "The Patriot Act."

But that only appears in your first column flow as: Rights = Cons. & B.Rights

Incs. trial, spch, privacy
Anti-T = Pat. Act

There are other ways to note it, but that's the idea.

2) Our value standard, then, is the U.S. Constitution and the Bill of Rights themselves. That value which best preserves the principles of those documents is the superior value. We will measure the effects of the Patriot Act against the American rights that are guaranteed in those documents, to determine if its costs have exceeded its benefits.

The notation for that could simply be: ***Pat Act vs. Con. Rights***

Costs vs. benefits to Con.

3) We find that, for multiple reasons, the value of the security provided is outweighed by the damage to human rights.

Pat Act costs 2 hi

Claim: Our first argument is that we're not very much more secure after the Patriot Act.

Warrant: We are still vulnerable to attack, since security measures asserted in name are often not, in fact, in action.

Grounds A: When my wife and I went to Europe, the jet was supposedly inspected in LAX. Once we had boarded the jet, we were asked to disembark when airline security couldn't find the inspection checklist. Then the security officers made us all get off the plane, we assumed for a thorough inspection. The security team literally walked onto the plane then off within a minute, signed a new checklist, and we got back on after the pantomime.

Grounds B: My wife and I came into Kennedy Airport in New York from Europe, and the whole passenger manifest was simply waved through customs. This was the summer after 9/11.

Grounds C: We were much more thoroughly searched in Europe, especially coming both in and out of Spain, which has always been vigilant about terror because of a Basque separatist movement. Still, they were unable to stop a train bombing that killed hundreds in Madrid on 3/11/04.

Grounds D: The U.S. Senate has held hearings to determine what our efforts against terrorism had been before 9/11. It has been suggested by the committee that both the Clinton and the Bush administration had made mistakes and had overlooked certain specific opportunities, such as chances to kill Bin Laden. They did not, it was said, because the intelligence was not considered reliable. Clinton gave an executive order for the assassination of Bin Laden, but it wasn't managed. Richard Clarke, former security advisor to four presidents in a row has said before the committee and in his book, "Against All Enemies," that the Bush team was so focused on Iraq, even before 9/11, that they underestimated his advice about imminent danger of attack. Among their recently released conclusions are that we are safer, in part because we are more aware, but far from being safe.

> **C1: not secure**
> **W: vuln. to attack**
> **GA: LAX sec. team**
> **GB: NY customs**
>   **(post 9/11)**
> **GC: searched in Spain**
>   **(still bombed)**
> **GD: 9/11 com. "safer,**
> **not safe"**

Claim: My second argument is that the rights of American citizen for fair trial have been compromised by the values of the Patriot Act.

Warrant: Racial profiling, not unlike what we did to Japanese-Americans during WWII, has lead again to prison camps. We repented of those camps in WW II. We probably should again. This violates the right of the accused to be protected from cruel and unusual punishment.

Grounds: Over three hundred Middle Easterners were detained after 9/11 without charges, without benefit of lawyer, and the Patriot Act allows secret trials. Only a small percentage of those detained have been charged, though others have been deported for overstaying student visas.

> **C2: Rights hurt**
> **W: Racial profile**
>   **Camps = WWII**
> **G: Over 300**
>   **Few charged**
>   **Stdnts. deported**

Claim. Our third argument is that free speech and free press rights have been assaulted.

Warrant: Attorney General Ashcroft has used the Patriot Act as a justification to seek various limits of expression, including criticism of the war and the reporting of details about uncharged detainees. There's even been an effort to keep photos of the war dead coming home in coffins from being published for public view.

Grounds A: It's been suggested that people who speak out against the war in Iraq are treasonous, as we're in a state of war. However, Iraq is not a congressionally declared war. It's an exploitation of the Patriot Act, passed in good faith by congress. It pretends to focus on terrorism, which is the parameter and motivation for the act, but no Iraqi link to the 9/11 terrorists has been demonstrated.

Grounds B: News agencies have continually been denied access to information about uncharged 9/11 detainees.

> **C3: Free spch + press**
> **W: Ashcroft pushes Pat Act**
> **past its limits**
> **GA: "Treason" for crit.**
> **GB: No 9/11 detainee info**

Claim: Our fourth argument is that the Patriot Act has been used to justify unwarranted intrusions into our privacy.

Warrant: Ashcroft has been trying to secure the reading lists of private citizens through libraries and bookstores, as well as sought wiretaps.

Grounds A: The FBI lied to achieve 75 unjustified wiretaps, based on suspicion alone.

Grounds B: A recent Supreme Court decision overturned attempts by the Justice Department to secure lists of book purchases from bookstores, to see if our readings reveal us to be subversives. This inhibits our ability to read, or say what we want as authors, too. So, this supports our third point, as well.

Grounds C: The Justice Department has also sought "floating wiretaps." That means that, if a suspected terrorist rented a residence from you, anyone associated with that suspect, including you, could be wiretapped, though you yourself exhibit no probable cause. Probable cause isn't even required to wiretap terrorist suspects.

> **C4: Pat Act = intrusion**
> **W: Seek read lists/taps**
> **GA: FBI 75 taps**
> **GB: Sup. Court says no on book list**
> **GC: "Floating taps"**

Side Comment: What might be next, forbidden books?

Conclusion: Security is important, and everyone wants it. Yet we should not surrender our basic Constitutional rights merely because we are afraid.

Now let's consider potential responses by the ***Leader of the Opposition*** and how his arguments would condense on the flow sheet. We'll place his responses opposite the Prime Minister's arguments, just as we would on a normal flow:

1) Thanks to the Prime Minister for his kind welcome. We support, not the exact opposite of the government position, but a more balanced position. We think that human rights are very important, and that's exactly why we should embrace a philosophy of anti-terrorism, because even some short-term restrictions are better than threatening the very basis of human rights by neglect, here and abroad, now and forever. How can undefended rights be better than rights that are protected from invaders?

We do, however, agree with the definitions offered.

PM	LO
Rights over anti-terror	**Anti-terror equal with rights since it defends rights**
Def. Rights = const./B.rights	**Def. accepted**

2) As such, we also endorse the Constitution as a standard and hold the Bill of Rights as equal in importance to anti-terrorism. What we have to show, though, is that our viewpoint better serves the Constitution, that a world without a balance between these two values is a worse world. The government must prove, then, that rights are of more, not just equally important.

PM	LO
Pat Act vs. Rights	**Agree, but their burden:**
Costs vs. Benefits	**"more over equal"**

3) In response to their case, we find multiple reasons for a balance of values. In fact, our need for rights requires the Patriot Act.

Pat Act 2 hi   **Rights need Pat Act**

Their first claim is that we're not that secure. Are we entirely happy with our security? No, there is still a threat, which justifies anti-terrorism, but . . .

Counter-claim 1: We're more secure than we were before.

Warrant: This is so because we had NO particular effort at counter-terrorism before 9/11. There was conversation and a couple of initiatives in the last two administrations, but no practical solution. Only since 9/11 have Americans taken anti-terror as an imminent American concern. So, while we are certainly still vulnerable, there are signs of improvement. Notice that . . .

Grounds A-B: His first three examples were personal ones. Can we generalize from this? Or is it a Hasty Generalization? Not that it really matters, since we've already accepted that there is an ongoing threat.

Grounds C: It's also worth mentioning that it was trains that were bombed in Spain, not planes. Bad, yes, but not as harmful as plane crashes.

Grounds D: He brings up the Congressional hearings, though, and that bears discussion. This a very important committee meant to improve our future security. The panel embraces the very attitude of the opposition. His own description of Clinton and Bush doing relatively little supports our analysis: that things are better because they were so bad before.

Grounds E: Let's extend our position by offering signs of improvement. There were no consistent search operations at airports. Now there is. Are their some slips through the cracks? Sure, but think of the persons who have been apprehended by this effort that might have gotten by and killed more people, the Shoe Bomber, for one. While the airline business was hit badly, look at the emerging confidence in flying again. Americans are traveling again. Apparently people feel a good deal more confident.

Grounds F: We also have to mention that the world of security is better for Americans without Sadam Hussein, the mass murderer who at least provided safe haven for terrorists, Al Queda as well as Syrian and Saudi Arabian, at least as a host. At least, we've done much to see that the rights of Iraqi citizens will not be cast aside by despotic leaders.

Grounds G: We are also happy about driving Bin Laden underground. Even Richard Clarke, critical of our efforts, has said that the capture of Bin Laden is probably very close.

PM	LO
C1: not secure	CC1: but better now
W: vuln. to attack	W: lack of effort before=better
GA: sec. team	GA-C: personal data
GB: NY customs	hasty G?
(post 9/11)	
GC: searched in Spain	GC: Trains, not planes
(still bombed)	
GD: cong. comm.	GD: "No effort" supports
No effort. Not Safe	analysis: "effort now"
	GE: some search (shoe b.)
	GF: Hussein
	GG: Bin Laden underground

Their second argument is that the Patriot Act has damaged fair trial rights.

Counter claim 2: Though we agree that racial profiling is a bad thing, there have been very small, justifiable violations of rights.

Warrant: We can have no rights if we allow terrorism to undermine our democratic base. We got hit by 9/11 because we didn't scrutinize persons who we suspected of terrorist connections.

Grounds A: Over 300 Middle Easterners detained, yes, but how many of these are legitimate U.S. citizens? If they violate visas, they should be held and/or deported. Also, how significant is 300, against even the number killed at 9/11, let alone the population of the country?

PM	LO
C2: Rights hurt	CC2: Profiling bad, but
	camps justified
W: Racial profiling = camps	W: No anti-terrorism =
	no rights
G: Over 300 w/no charges	G: Citizens?
stdnts. deported.	300 sig? vs. 9/11

Their third argument is that free speech and free press rights have been hurt.

CC3: The government begins to sound a little paranoid here,

W: They say there's a threat, yet discuss no actual damages. Further, rights are not absolute, the Constitution must be protected, and the government that protects it must protect itself, especially in times of war.

GA: All White Houses seek to insulate themselves from criticism: Nixon against Watergate, Reagan against Contra-gate, Clinton against Lewinsky-gate, now President Bush is holding the gates against these barbarians and needs some room to operate. The ploy is an equivocal use of the term "War Against Terrorism." You're right, there is no formal declaration of war from Congress, so no actual treason would be charged against a critic. Even John Walker Lindh, who joined Al Queda and was arrested as a prisoner of war, did not receive the full punishment of treason, death, just jail for life. So, where's the damage?

GB: The reason that the press has been denied explicit information about detainees is that they're susceptible to assassination from terrorists groups they may represent. It's for their protection.

PM	LO
C3: Hurt Free speech + press	**CC3: Paranoid**
W: Ashcroft pushes Pat Act	**W: Threat, no damage.**
GA: "Treason" for crit.	**GA: Rhetoric, no damage**
	Lindh got life
GB: No 9/11 detainee info	**GB: Silence protects**
	detainees

* * * * *

Of course, a full debate would involve two more columns, side by side, along with these, with a similar give and take, and yet two more with quick summaries of the positions in rebuttal. These are not flawless positions. Each person makes some good points and some mistakes. Consider further possibilities in the exercises.

Rebuttal

You generally cannot cover very much material in a rebuttal, because they're shorter speeches, and also because audience attention will tend to have eroded toward the end of the debate.

Thus, the major purposes of rebuttal are to focus on the key points in controversy and to "***crystallize***" **issues.** That is that we must isolate and clarify those issues that we think are critical, perhaps most especially those that we think we're winning.

It is up to the audience to decide which positions are more persuasive, but it's very important that you do more than rattle off individual points. You must go back to your standard, weigh the key arguments against that standard, and explain clearly why you have better satisfied your standard than your adversary. If you have each defended different standards, you must argue why your standard is the superior choice.

This is also the time that you want to make an issue of your opponent's burden of proof. Mention that they haven't proven what they've promised. Likewise, be able to mention the ways in which you have met your promise of proof.

Remember, the last argument you make may be the last thing they remember when they decide on the issue for themselves. Many experienced judges won't even consider arguments that do not appear in rebuttal. For a regular audience, realize that the last thing heard is often the last thing remembered.

Other Debate Formats

Oxford Style Debate was the norm for intercollegiate debate until the mid-70s. It is a form of debate which does not include cross-examination. Questions are imbedded in the constructive speeches. There are four constructive speeches and four rebuttals:[3]

First affirmative constructive Advocates the case	10 minutes
First negative constructive Attacks the case	10 minutes
Second affirmative constructive Rebuilds the case	10 minutes
Second negative constructive Argues "off case" attacks (side effects, etc.)	10 minutes
First negative rebuttal Rebuilds his attacks	5 minutes
First affirmative rebuttal Answers "off case" attacks and rebuilt 1st neg attacks	5 minutes
Second negative rebuttal Rebuilds and summarizes key arguments	5 minutes
Second affirmative rebuttal Answers second negative rebuttal	5 minutes

Notice, again, that the affirmative and negative switch speaker order at the point of rebuttals. This is to counter the negative advantage of presumption, allowing the affirmative to speak both first and last.

After that time, intercollegiate forensic competition moved toward *Oregon Debate,* or cross-examination debate. In these formats, there is a three-minute questioning by a member of the adversarial team after they have finished a constructive speech. Each person gets a cross-X as an answerer and a questioner.

It tends to lead to a more dynamic interaction of opposing viewpoints. This is why two major organizations promoting intercollegiate debate, CEDA and NDT, use variations of this format. The duties of the speakers remain much the same.

First Affirmative Constructive	8 minutes
Cross-X by Second Negative	3 minutes
First Negative Constructive	8 minutes
Cross-X by First Affirmative	3 minutes
Second Affirmative Constructive	8 minutes
Cross-X by First Negative	3 minutes
Second Negative Constructive	8 minutes
Cross-X by Second Affirmative	3 minutes
First Negative Rebuttal	4 minutes
First Affirmative Rebuttal	4 minutes
Second Negative Rebuttal	4 minutes
Second Affirmative Rebuttal	4 minutes

Notice that the person who is to speak next lets his partner do the questioning. This allows him to get his thoughts together and prepare evidence for his speech. It is possible to vary that choice, but it is usually a good idea for teamwork. Each partner should tell the other to ask certain questions to set up his arguments.

Lincoln-Douglas Debate

This is a two person debate named for President Lincoln and Douglas who opposed him. Modern presidential election debates are a variation of this format, although the questioning is usually handled by a panel, and the candidates do not actively question each other. If you do a debate in class and don't have enough for everybody to be in a four-person debate, you can fill in with this style.

Affirmative Constructive	6 minutes
Cross-X by Negative	3 minutes
Negative Constructive	7 minutes
Cross-X by Affirmative	3 minutes

Affirmative Rebuttal	4 minutes
Negative Rebuttal	6 minutes
Affirmative Rebuttal	3 minutes

The speeches are of unequal length, but if you add up each side, you'll see that the speakers get equal time on the floor. If you wanted to do a Lincoln-Douglas format for parliamentary debate, you could simply eliminate the cross-x and stick to the tradition of politely interrupting each other to ask questions.

These formats can be used for either value or policy debates. The next chapter will acquaint you with the stock issues of policy.

Vocabulary

Constructive
Costs vs. Gains Analysis
Criteria/Criterion
Flow Sheets
Government: Prime Minister and Member of the Government
Lincoln-Douglas Debate

Parliamentary Debate
Opposition: Leader of the Opposition and Member of the Opposition
Oregon Debate
Oxford Debate
Rebuttal
Value Standard

Exercises: Go to Interactive Disc to Complete

1) Take the first two speeches of the sample Parliamentary encounter at the end of the chapter, and create the next two speeches, by yourself or with another. Practice notation on a full version of a flow sheet.

2) Put together either a single value text of 4-5 pages (5-7 minutes, if spoken), or pair up into teams for a parliamentary value debate. Choose topics as a group. Decide on a time format and a schedule of debates. Take no more than a week or two to prepare. Remember, only limited research is allowed in the debate, but you should each prepare a brief on the topic, an outline of arguments for correction.

Sources

1) Coco, F., Instructor at Orange Coast College and Debate Coach (2003). Handouts Describing Parliamentary Debate Formats.

Crossman, M.R. (2003). Burden of Proof: In Introduction to Argument. Mason, Ohio: Thompson.

Zarefsky, D. (1980). Criteria for Evaluating Non-Policy Argument. CEDA Yearbook 1, pp. 9–16.

2) It may be confusing to hear that the Prime Minister is the affirmative. Didn't we say that the status quo is the negative? Doesn't the government stand for the status quo? Not in this format. Think of the role of government in terms of their capacity to lead, to propose legislation. Notice that in the sample debate, the government is proposing an alternative view to the present presumptions.

3) Freeley, A.J. (1993). Argumentation and Debate: Critical Thinking for Reasoned Decision Making. Belmont, CA: Wadsworth.

XII

Arguing Issues of Policy

Our most complex social discussions involve issues of policy, because they include both questions of fact and of value, as well as additional questions of their own. Deliberation of policy impacts all of us, as it's a method practiced daily by lawyers, leaders, and legislative bodies at every level of America. The very way that we function as a society and as a world is measured in terms of policy making. Yet policy is also, in one way, an easy format because it's very formulaic.

The action of mind is an almost mathematical formula. If a problem has A cause, then a solution to the problem consists of eliminating A (Figure 17):

If cause A—harm B, then solution C = −A

Or B harm—A cause = C solution

Figure 17

Thus, reasoning from cause is essential in policy making.

Yet most people don't reason to policy in that manner. They see a problem, then they suggest a solution that they've heard from respected authority, or which reflects their subjective beliefs. In other words, they come to policy from values rather than from careful analysis of cause.

The language of policy propositions almost always involves words like "should," "ought to," or "must" attached to an active verb, like "curtail," "increase," "improve," "implement," "eliminate," or "ban" some aspect of the subject matter.

> We should increase tax breaks for the middle class.
>
> The Federal Government ought to increase matching funds for education.
>
> Californians must improve the prevention of forest damage from bark beetles.

In other words, the language of the proposition focuses on the solution usually, rather than the problem. The solution is, in fact, the policy. Yet we must justify the change with a significant problem.

The stock issues include the same issues as fact, but goes beyond them. There are five stock issues:[1]

1) ***Topicality***

2) ***Significant Harm***

3) ***Inherency (causes of the problem)***

4) ***Workable Solution***

5) ***Side-Effects (advantages and disadvantages)***

Topicality was discussed earlier in the context of value debates, as well. You are topical as long as you stay inside the "fort" established by the proposition. If you exceed the argumentative ground of that proposition, you've taken ground that doesn't belong to the proposition. It belongs to your adversary, and he will rightfully complain. For our present purposes, it's just another way of saying something that you should already know, "***stick to the subject.***"

One might argue topicality from the negative side in situations where there's an obvious attempt to avoid the main thrust of the proposition by ***seizing on a trivial point.*** One might focus on a minor aspect within the topic that nobody really knows much about, or is insignificant, simply to avoid refutation. Yet there are risks to this approach.

At the Phi Ro Pi National Tournament in 2004, we watched parliamentary debate rounds. For the value, "The wall between church and state has grown too wide," the issue of topicality was key in one semi-final debate. The advocates took a European focus on the topic, using the conflict between Muslims and the French government's repression of their usual dress in public schools. Muslim women are not allowed to go bare-headed but are not allowed to wear head scarves to French schools.

The opposition, during its fifteen-minute preparation, focused on the notion that this was about the separation of church and state in the U.S. They argued that since there is no formal constitutional separation of church and state in France, the advocate's approach was outside the topic area. However, as the topic doesn't specify a constitutional sense of church and state, nor the United States, it was judged to be appropriate to take a more global view of the topic.

Significant Harm takes on somewhat more dramatic proportions than you might have seen in discussions of fact. In part, that's because harms are the motivating force for the change of social policy you seek. In part, that's because ill conceived policy impacts people we can identify with. Telling their stories is a part of our emotional appreciation for the issue. The pathos itself becomes rhetorical demand.

There are two terms to define for a fuller understanding, "significant" and "harm."

There are many ways that something can be ***harmful.*** The most dramatic would probably involve the ***death or physical damage*** of other human beings through violence, accident, or pestilence. If one of our most fundamental values is survival that would certainly have impact.

People can be ***psychologically*** damaged, as well as physically. Consider, for instance, the mental effects of being raped, belittled because of race or religion, or being fearful of terrorists. One psychological harm from being kidnapped or held hostage is the Stockholm Syndrome, in which one begins to identify with or even defend one's captors.

There can also be ***environmental*** harms: the disappearing ozone layer, over-fishing our waters to the point of species extinction, the polluting effects of forest fires, the dangers of oil spills. Here are some potential examples of environmental harms:

- The Navy seeks to gain exceptions to "the Magna Carta of environmental regulation," the National Environmental Policy Act of 1969.[2]

- The United States has refused to join 180 nations in signing the Kyoto Accords, a global effort to reduce greenhouse gases.[3]

- In spite of the Marine Mammal Act of 1972, 60,000 whales, dolphins, and porpoises and other marine mammals die each year worldwide as a result of a destructive fishing practice called by-catch, according to Oceana.[4]

Economic harms can evolve from property damage, budget shortfalls, Wall Street games of bulls & bears, even from homeowners caught in a hurricane, or some other natural disaster. They can evolve from trade wars, the decline of the dollar, or rising interest rates. Here are some potential economic harms.

- Auto body shop scams are both costing us money and risking our lives by use of cheaper generic parts and less qualified workers.[5]

- Oil companies like Enron have taken advantage of the American public, and stricter regulations on supply should be encouraged.[6]

- Earth Liberation Front's destruction of SUVs is a counter-productive and damaging approach to protesting for the environment. What did ELF think those fires were doing to the environment, as well as private property?[7]

Harms to human rights are a pervasive and constant issue, and when discussing this area a values analysis usually comes into play:

- Sex slavery exists in parts of Eastern Europe—Albania Turkey Bulgaria, Romania and Yugoslavia—where young women are raped, beaten and forced into prostitution.[8]

- If a pregnant unwed mother wants to have her child adopted in Florida, she must now reveal all the details of her sexual past.[9]

- Some well-meaning people have been buying the freedom of slaves in Sudan. Yet it's counter-productive. Though charities buy the freedom, the flow of cash encourages slavery.[10]

Health and Welfare harms certainly exist:

- Though most middle-class women do not work this many hours outside the home, Bush and the House are pushing eagerly at a 40-hour work week for welfare mothers. Two in every five of the nation's 11 million mothers with pre-school children don't work outside the home at all, according to the Bureau of Labor Statistics.[11]

- The prison population of California is getting older and less healthy, leading to medical and personal neglect.[12]

- Crackdowns on illegal immigrants don't reduce the flow at the border, but cause more death by exposure.[13]

These are all policy issues that have appeared in newspapers in the twenty-first century. Some may have had solutions enacted by this printing, but for those that haven't, consider how you might approach such topics.

The second word that needs definition is ***significant.*** How do you determine whether a damage is significant enough to change policy over it?

The easiest and most obvious way is to ***measure by quantity,*** by number and statistics. How many people were killed or made ill? How many illegal immigrants died of exposure? How much money was lost, etc.?

Significant harm arguments should not be generalities, but ***be specific in impact.*** If it's a physical harm, one should enumerate the symptoms of the harm, on bodies and minds. We may use statistics to "quantify" an impact, in dollars or deaths. If you say that dollars are lost, be prepared to say how many.

However, some things just aren't measurable in terms of numbers. The fact that not many people are affected by a problem does not mean it isn't a problem. We know how many people died at 9/11, but how do insurance companies measure the value of their lives to the surviving families? These we have to ***assess in terms of quality,*** as with most of our values. (The going rate for negligent death is about two million).

For instance, most Americans did not consider AIDS a big problem at first. The stereotype was that it was just a few gay men practicing unsafe sex in bathhouses. The National Institutes of Health barely had funding to study the disease. Attention was paid only once it began to affect the female and heterosexual public. By then, it was an epidemic risking all. Had we looked at the effects of the disease, in and of itself, perhaps we could have minimized this epidemic.

Even in cases in which the population stays small, or is reserved to a particular portion of the population, a harm may be qualitatively damaging. Should we not feel sympathy and offer medical support to people who have sickle cell anemia, merely because they're all black? We would make an ***appeal for them based on some basic sense of what is humane to all persons.***

There's been much conversation about the rights of 300 people of Muslim descent held without charges or benefit of counsel. The usual reasoning in such cases is parallel: If it happened to them, it can happen to you, because the right itself has been eroded.

It reminds one of a saying written from the viewpoint of common Germans after WWII: "When they took the Jews I did not care, because I was not a Jew; when they took the gays I did not care, because I was not gay; when they took the intellectuals I did not care, because I was not an intellectual; when they came for me, I looked around for help. . . but there was nobody left to help."

We also ask questions about broader impacts. How does this affect those of us not directly impacted? How do the effects of the initial harm ripple out into other ways to ***damage us collectively?*** We may, for instance, be as concerned about the surviving families of those killed at ground zero on 9/11 as we are for the victims themselves.

The country is so often impacted by economic harms, one may be as concerned for the market in general as about a particular failing sector or company. The failure of the Euro could be as destabilizing to our economy as theirs, as we are intermingled in the world of dollars. Stock panics are generated by a few powerful speculators, but they become an avalanche of panic among those near to retirement and already retired.[14]

Whether you are arguing quantitative or qualitative harms, significant harm arguments ***should be dramatic*** enough to motivate an audience to reconsider the present system's presumption. Storytelling is a critical aspect of persuasion, since we are by nature a storytelling species. So, the use of specific examples or personal testimony in a narrative voice can be persuasive.[15]

Yet it also ***important not to pass over the line from pathos to bathos,*** a melodramatic use of pathos. It may, indeed, be dramatic, but the speaker has to make a choice about whether it is so repellent that an audience may be alienated by it. They may insulate themselves from your persuasion because they find information or images too much to take.

For instance, students doing anti-abortion speeches have sometimes dwelled upon the details of surgery to the point that even those who agreed with them detached from the presentational effects. Graphic photographs on the subject caused some students to look away, register audible disgust, or even leave the room. On the one hand, the audience perception of such graphics varies from group to group. On the other hand, it may be wise to error on the side of caution and good taste.

In April of 2004, four American civilians working in Iraq to rebuild the infrastructure were not only killed, but burned and mutilated in Fallouja. Their hacked torsos were hung from a bridge while the wild crowd responsible danced beneath the corpses in celebration. Photos of that event inflamed the world. Would the above description be an appropriate use of pathos? Probably, but sensitivity to gory or pathetic detail is a matter for audience reaction. We might be less likely to show color pictures to an audience, as it's possible to so shock more sensitive audience members that it's counterproductive. Audience members may back away from the issue as a whole.

* * * * *

Let's illustrate significant harm with a Toulmin-style argument. We'll use a proposition calling for the end of by-catching among fisherman:

> **Claim:** In spite of the Marine Mammal Protection Act of 1972, which has resulted in benefits for whales and dolphins, marine mammals are still in trouble.
>
> **Warrant:** There are signs of sea mammal deaths resulting from the destructive fishing practice called by-catch.
>
> **Grounds:** By-catch is wasted catch. It results in millions of fish and marine mammals needlessly killed each year. Long lines and trawling nets drown pilot whales and common dolphins in the North Atlantic. Harbor porpoise populations suffer from shark and halibut fishing in the Gulf of Maine.
>
> Fin whales and the endangered North Atlantic right whales are on the brink of extinction because of ship strikes, as well as entanglement in lobster gear and gillnets. Various fishing gear endanger humpback whales in the Gulf of Maine and the central North Pacific.[16]

One could then go on to mention the various impacts on nature from losing these animals, as well as appeals to a primary value of conservation, simply not wasting any life in an unnecessary way.

Realize that your opponent, imaginary or otherwise, will try to press your burden of proof by arguing that your harms are not significant. He may, indeed, argue that the harms are not harms, but the natural consequence of certain kinds of business which are necessary to the survival of our species.

Inherency/Cause

A problem is inherent when it is so woven into the present system that one cannot manage positive change without removing that aspect of the system. We mentioned inherency in the fact discussion in the sense of cause, and the fundamental type of reason here will be the same.

Yet there are actually **several dimensions of inherency** to discuss.

The minimum level of inherency is to **discover a trend.** One sees signs of a change. When one finds an ongoing series of negative effects that you can quantify with statistical proof, one would normally reason that there is some cause for the trend to exist. If it is persistent and it's growing, then it's reasonable to assume that it's not going to go away on its own.

When we first saw acid rain, like AIDS, we had no idea what it was. Yet, also like AIDS, there were definite signs that something was happening. Lakes in which bass had thrived for years were suddenly barren. Their PH level was equivalent to lemon juice or battery acid. Roads that were normally repaved every five to seven years required service every three to five. Even faces on national monuments like the Lincoln Memorial had begun to erode from what we now know as acid fog. At that point, we actually began a search for solutions, and that meant looking for cause.

There are two dimensions within which one might discover cause for typical social problems, structural or attitudinal inherency. **Structural inherency** has to do with physical and systemic causes of the problem. Among the physical causes of acid rain were some very tall smokestacks that were instituted by manufacturers, ironically, to help the local pollution. Yet they were so tall that they belched toxic materials into the cloud layer, contributing to acid rain. Other factors, of course, were influential.

Systemic causes include the presence or absence of a law that contributes to the problem. One must examine **the present threshold of the law** and either eliminate bad laws or institute helpful ones.

There may be what we call an institutional barrier to solving the problem, the existence of an inhibitive agency or organization. Also, there may be a need for such an agency or organization to regulate the problem.

The existence of an unregulated nuclear energy industry would naturally call to the creation of the Atomic Energy Commission, just as pollution would demand the creation of the Environmental Protection Agency. Sometimes an organization can be a barrier, for instance, the NRA, the National Rifle Association, could be considered a barrier to gun laws.

This brings us to a third dimension of inherency, **attitudinal inherency.** Sometimes there are structural solutions in place to solve social problems, yet the attitude of the people against the system is so strong that it inhibits the system from functioning.

Consider the prohibition era of the 1930s when liquor was illegal. Not only did people respond by drinking all they wanted, there were people ready to provide illegal liquor, and gangsters were given profit motive. Resistance runs deep among American traditions.

Ever hear the phrase, "You can't legislate morality?" This point came to mind for me during an event of my youth. I was involved in Key Club, a youth service organization founded by the Kiwanis, and went to a convention in Washington. While traveling on a bus through the South in 1966, not that long after the Civil Rights Act had passed, we came to visit the state capital of Tennessee along the way. When we entered the rotunda of the legislature, I was shocked to discover their response to the Civil Rights Act.

Above the restrooms, the raised metal lettering declaring "white" men's or women's bathrooms had indeed been removed. However, the rivet holes had been left and the marble left unpolished, so that the word "white" remained in relief everywhere. The letter of the law was enforced, but in a partial and largely sarcastic way, while the real attitude of the local people remained on the walls for all to see.

We often hear some very heartfelt speeches about driving under the influence of alcohol and drugs. They usually end with the pronouncement that we need "tougher laws against drunk driving." Yet is that really so? If you actually examine the present threshold of the law, you might be surprised to find that much more can happen to DUI offenders, even on a first offense, than normally does. In other words, the inherency is not systemic, it's attitudinal, it's the propensity of courts to give warnings but to allow multiple offenses, perhaps a fatal one, before that driver is actually taken off the streets. At least, that's one arguable viewpoint.

So, when we talk about solutions, we need to be aware of the various dimensions of inherency, as that analysis is key to making workable policy, something effective, not merely symbolic.

Let's return to the "sea mammal massacre" topic and offer **a sample inherency argument:**

> **Claim:** Sea mammal deaths come from specific fishing practices not covered specifically by the Marine Mammal Protection Act.
>
> **Warrant:** The legal use of "long lines" and nets create by-catch problems.
>
> **Grounds:** According to Tim Eichenberg, marine mammal safety advocate for OCEANA, these marine mammals are hooked on long lines, entangled in nets and drowned by bottom trawling gears. By-catch also includes seabirds, endangered sea turtles, and large numbers of fish species that are later discarded.

So, there are loopholes in the law, a matter of structural inherency. There are also attitudinal problems.

> **Claim:** There are also attitudinal barriers to solution.
>
> **Warrant A:** The fishing industry has shown no particular desire to comply.
>
> **Grounds A:** By-catch results in millions of fish and marine mammals killed each year since the Marine Mammal Protection Act.

Warrant B: Even the U.S. government has shown no inclination to enforce its own laws at sea.

Grounds B: In 1994, Congress required the fisheries service to reduce the amount of incidental taking of marine mammals in commercial fishing to "insignificant levels approaching zero mortality and serious injury" by April 1, 2001. The Federal Government, however, has failed to enforce these requirements. As a result, destructive fishing practices continue to create by-catch, killing large numbers of marine mammals.[17]

Whatever the type of inherency, an opponent is likely to argue alternative causation, or challenge your sense of causation with direct refutation. One should be prepared for this by using your imaginary opponent and sufficiently broad research to anticipate such arguments.

Don't use the word "problem" interchangeably when discussing harm and inherency. Keep the issues separate and distinct. The problem is actually both issues in sum.

Having seen, then, the two issues of the problem, significant harm and inherency, let's look at the two issues associated with solution, workable solutions, and side-effects.

Workable Solutions

Remember, not everything we say in persuasive discourse is an argument. This section of your speech or paper should begin with ***a description of the policy*** itself, the solution to the harms.

Then you make ***arguments that the policy will work,*** that you can achieve ***"solvency."*** Perhaps most important to solvency is making sure that you have discovered the right causes to the problem, and that your solution is appropriate to blunting those causes.

In the best of all possible worlds, we'd like to eliminate problems. However, as we've seen in the previous section, causes may be multiple and difficult. So, it is acceptable to attempt to diminish the problem by attacking some, but not all causes, to execute a ***partial solution.*** You may be able to use statistics to suggest a percentage of a problem that comes from a particular cause. "We can diminish the problem by X%."

The most effective solutions are consciously built from a thorough analysis of inherency (Figure 18):

A Harm − B Inherency = C Solution

Figure 18

Many inexperienced policy speakers don't even have an analysis of inherency or cause, preferring to come from ideology or political party. They yield their thinking to reason by authority. However, it makes no sense to pull solutions, like magic rabbits, out of a hat without knowing what caused the harm.

However, the issue is not merely finding solutions, but determining if they're workable. That is, they should be achievable, practical, and yield "***solvency,***" the actual improvement or elimination of the harms.

It's one thing to think of a solution in principle, it's another to make one that works. To determine if the policy you propose is practical and achievable, ask yourself about "3M," not the tape company, but the ***machinery, manpower, and money*** required to make things work. (We apologize for the sexist language "manpower." We've sacrificed the more neutral phrasing "humanpower" to maintain the pneumonic device of ***the 3Ms.***)

Machinery may be literal machinery, in the sense of the technology required to solve something. We discussed the acid rain problem. Part of the solution suggested was to put "scrubbers" on the top of those tall smoke stacks to keep effluents in check.

When we first noticed water shortages, people were encouraged to use water-saving shower nozzles and toilets. Machinery may also be considered in ***the broader sense of means, or "the how,"*** developed to stop the problem, enhanced border patrol to diminish entry by illegal immigrants, for instance, or putting fingerprints on driver's licenses to make it easier to trace criminals.

Finally, machinery in the sense of ***enforcement*** may be a necessary consideration. People don't always like new systems, as in the civil rights cases of attitudinal inherency mentioned earlier. Sometimes penalties, fines, and imprisonment, must also be provided.

You also have to discuss ***manpower (humanpower) in the sense of agency.*** Who is going to administer the solution? Is it an institution or infrastructure already established and you're broadening its scope or authority? Is it one that you're going to build? What personnel is required, and are they readily available?

Are we going, for instance, to use the AEC for further development of nuclear energy, as they already have the infrastructure available? Does the agency require some special training? Are we going to have to hire and train a whole new profession, if the solution is something technical?

That may be particularly important if you have a deadline, as ***timeline*** matters with many kinds of solutions. In an environmental solution, for instance, let's say with regard to wildfires that spread through the southwest damaging millions of dollars of acreage. If the solution is to better clear dry brush and bark beetle-damaged trees, we wouldn't argue, "Oh, we should get around to it sometime." We'd probably set a timeline to help the problem before the next fire season.

Some scientists have argued that fossil fuels will be used up by about 2030. If we propose systems of alternative energy, we'd have to reasonably demonstrate that it could manifest itself effectively by approximately that time.

Let's talk money. ***Solutions require financing.*** How much is required? From where will you take it? From some other less necessary program? From increased taxes? Where in existing budgets? You can't simply fiat money into existence, so these things must be considered when discussing financing of the policy. The cost of a solution becomes a critical factor when we look at side-effects of your program. Will the cost actually be worth the benefits?

For instance, we have the technology to build non-polluting electric vehicles, but they are too expensive for the average family to own. So, there's no incentive to build many. Current experiments are moving toward hybrid cars that blend electric with more traditional fossil fuels. These can bring gas mileage up considerably. Though initial cost may seem high, it will probably drop as competition on those models picks up.

There is one final issue one needs to consider. What does one do in a case when there is attitudinal inherency? Attitudinal inherency occurs when the primary barrier to solution is public attitude, a tendency to resist a law. The civil rights struggle in the South is one example. When you have public resistance, you can use both rewards and punishments. Aspects of enforcement can be applied, but one can also consider incentives. Incentives are bonuses your plan can offer to win the public over, for instance, tax breaks to buy energy efficient cars. Cities have occasionally paid people in rougher areas a fee to turn in handguns, which are then destroyed.

* * * * *

Where do solutions come from, though?

Solutions can come from a lot of creative angles, including your own ***brainstorming.*** You can reason backwards from inherency. If you have evidence saying that something is the direct cause of a harmful phenomena, you can cross-apply some of the same, or similar evidence in your solutions.

At other times, especially with newer harms, we may have to rely on the best available ***advice from experts*** involved in the forefront of those studying the problem, in order to have a clue about where to begin.

Sometimes social solutions emerge as grass roots, ***populist movements*** that are concerned with very specific issues.

About twenty years back, during one period of inflation, meat and coffee prices rose sky high, much as our gasoline and milk prices have done recently. Housewives in the San Fernando Valley formed a grass roots movement around resistance to these growing prices. They passed coffee for tea, loaded up on peanut butter and tuna instead of meat, and it caught on. Others heard about the tactic on news, and meat and coffee prices came down as demand for them diminished.

Such grass roots movements are easier today due to the Internet. Witness the early success of presidential candidate Howard Dean's campaign among young people, based largely on Internet contacts. This tactic may have changed campaign dynamics forever.

At other times, especially with newer harms, we may have to rely on the best available *advice from experts* involved in the forefront of those studying the problem.

Apart from being creative and generating obvious solutions on your own, your credibility may be served by using *models or pilot programs* of other solutions that have served similar circumstances. One then applies parallel reason: it worked there, so it may work here with analogous problems.

- For instance, drug legalization or clean needle distribution speeches almost always discuss the Netherlands, which allowed illegal drugs to be distributed at clinics but used education to reduce the number of addicts.

- Recent changes in welfare policy, restricting recipients from more than five years of support, were first tried in San Bernadino at a county level. They saved roughly $2,000,000 by the methods entertained. So, a smaller social experiment may be magnified into a state or national solution.

- Increasing tensions between Palestinian suicide bombers and Israeli retaliations have caused Israel to move the building of a wall, much like the Berlin Wall in Germany, which used to separate the Soviet Empire from the rest of Europe.[18]

- My wife is the sales manager for a manufacturer of beauty supplies. When they look for solutions to problems of diminishing sales, they try to look at what their competition is doing that is successful. They then either borrow the idea, or trump it with something better, based on an analysis of what the competition's product doesn't achieve. They can add their own twists, since they've had a chance to examine any problems the original idea may have had. Innovations also avoid copyright problems.

* * * * *

Let's look, once more, at the sea mammal slaughter issue while *building a solution.* Remembering the two parts of solution, a description of policy and arguments that demonstrate solvency, we'll need a simple paragraph describing the policy:

> The federal government must be sued to comply with its own laws. OCEANA has filed a suit to Force Marine Fisheries to protect marine mammals from commercial fishing, as they've promised. We are joined in the suit

by the Center for Biological Diversity and the Turtle Island Restoration Network. The lawsuit asks the service to convene to prepare plans to prevent the destruction, as well as assist in recovery of the most vulnerable marine mammals impacted by by-catch, and to submit to Congress a report of delinquent progress in meeting their own zero-mortality goal.[19]

One of the weaker approaches to solution is to appoint a committee to decide what to do. One hears promises often in elections to appoint *"a blue ribbon committee"* to solve some issue. They either want to avoid being pinned down, or really aren't sure what to do. It's difficult to be convincing when you argue, on one hand, that we have a significant and imminent problem, then defer the solution to others.

In this case, however, what should be done was already decided in 1994 by Congress. Since abandonment of that decision is the inherency, it seems reasonable to sue the Marine Fisheries Service to adhere to the law.

There are times when it is appropriate to defer to committees. When we don't have a handle on causation, as with the AIDS and acid rain examples, the typical approach is *an R&D solution.* One funds R&D, research and development, searching for a solution.

When the descriptive portion of the solution is over, the *argumentation* occurs. You make solvency arguments which demonstrate the effectiveness of your solution:

> **Claim:** This solution will help to preserve marine mammals.
>
> **Warrant:** This is so, because the solution is an extension of an earlier and largely effective solution, the Marine Mammal Act of 1972. It simply did not prepare for newer fishing methods, which this solution would consider.
>
> **Grounds:** This landmark legislation reduced dolphin deaths from tuna fishing in the tropical Pacific, from about half a million per year to 4,000 per year today. Blue whales were on the brink of extinction but are beginning to recover. Gray whales were recently removed from the endangered species list.[20]

We are mindful of the fact that we have leaned on one organization, Oceana, to offer this illustration. You would need multiple sources, as seen in the speech examples in the relevant appendix.

An opponent at this point would make workability or solvency counter-arguments, suggesting reasons why the proposal won't work at several levels: agency, financing, enforcement, timeline, etc. He or she might also turn your attitudinal inherency evidence, the government's tendency not to enforce, against you. One of Murphy's Laws is, "For every solution there are two problems." Try to anticipate that as you construct your solutions.

Side Effects

After we look at a solution, we have to consider its side effects. Such side effects may *either be positive or negative.* It's possible that both effects will be present.

If they are *positive effects,* benefits beyond the solution of the problem to which you are obligated, they can be claimed as extra *advantages.* For instance, let's say you're going to offer new technology as solution in a low employment economy, like the scrubbers to help acid rain. One might argue the advantage of creating new jobs for people to manufacture and install the technology.

On the other hand, if we decided to boycott bagged lettuce to help solve water problems, we might have the opposite problem. We might be challenged by opponents because we created a *disadvantage* by destruction of the industry, leading to unemployment.

Likewise, in the case of sea mammals and by-catch, the opposition might well argue that we've inhibited a necessary industry, that helps a hungry world, with excessive costs and lesser productivity.

Here's another side effect argument about environment: We had terrible fires in the southwest due to dry brush and trees diseased by the bark beetle. Trimming the forest was among the solutions, but fears of further damage emerged among environmentalists:

> President Bush is expected Thursday to announce changes in federal rules that would speed up selective logging in national forests, embarking on a course intended to help prevent the kind of destructive fires that have plagued the Western states this summer. But environmentalists are complaining that the government is upending decades of regulations and that the White House is using fear of fires to cut down trees that are old but healthy, and fire resistant, from back-country forests.[21]

The kind of arguments examined under this issue are not necessarily presented explicitly in every presentation, but it is necessary to consider them.

Remember that the stock issues are often called *the inventional system.* That means that answering these five basic issues—topicality, significant harm, inherency, workable solution, and side effects—can help you invent arguments. If we consider in advance what the side effects of our proposals may be, we can go back to our workable solution to add preemptive positions that may prevent the opposition's most likely attacks. So, this issue may have an advisory effect, rather than an explicit one in debate.

Yet there may well be solutions that have *unavoidable side effects* that have to be explained. If it is a prominent issue in the public mind, it is impossible to avoid it.

Let's say, *for a simple example,* that you're going to advocate a policy of increased use of nuclear power.

The significant harm would be the damage from fossil fuels as energy: damage to the atmosphere from industrial burning, combustion from cars, injury to those involved in retrieving and transporting fossil fuels, and the highest insurance rates are for those who transport fossil fuels. There's still black lung disease from mining of coal, as well as the fact that we get involved in conflicts in the Middle East to protect oil resources.

Inherency is easy. It would be our reliance on fossil fuels, in combination with our failure to sustain much productive use of alternative power.

The solution would be a multi-level experiment in alternative power-solar, wind, geothermal, hydrogen-including a search for clean nuclear power. It's very possibly workable, and there have been many useful experiments that have simply lacked funding and development to be useful.

Perhaps you could even calculate the specific kinds and amounts of fossil fuel power that these methods could improve. Nuclear energy, in particular, already has an infrastructure and provides over a third of our electricity now. Perhaps the AEC could coordinate with the Commerce Department to create an agency.

The problem, of course, is with ***side effects.*** As of now, we have no dependable means of disposing nuclear wastes. Increase of usage will, therefore, increase both waste and risk of radiation. As most people would be likely to note the problem in their own minds, you can't simply ignore it. What would you do?

At that point, ***costs vs. gains analysis*** would come into play. You would weigh the damages from your significant harm against the potential negative side effects, reasoning from dilemma. Actually, the process is similar to arguing values. Here, too, you'd have to provide a standard for judgment.

With this nuclear waste issue, one might offer something like this appeal:

> It's undeniable that nuclear waste is an issue, yet we've accepted the present methods of disposal to the extent that a third of U.S. electrical power comes from nuclear power. So, my adversary's argument is not unique to our proposal. Indeed, it applies equally well to the present system that he defends.
>
> Horrific examples like Chernobyl and Three Mile Island are terrible to consider, and yet they're not the typical case. Let's consider the standard of "lives lost" as a way of comparing the harms against the side effects. Historically, consider the number of lives lost to lung cancer among non-smokers, fire victims from the transportation of incendiary fuels, or those who died in collapsed mines trying to find coal. Consider black lung disease among those miners. Consider people crushed and burned in fossil fuel driven cars. Consider the number of men and women lost in wars in Kuwait, Iran, and Afghanistan, defending our oil interest. Up to Chernobyl, which accounted for hundreds of deaths, the total number of people confirmed to be killed in

the production of nuclear energy was six. So, we're weighing hundreds of deaths against hundreds of thousands of deaths.

Finally, all frontiers of science and technology have required periods of trial and error. Our ultimate hope is to find fusion energy, a form of energy without significant waste products. Yet that will never happen if we don't fully invest ourselves in the search for alternative power.

Of course, as ever, there are refutations available:

We don't know how many deaths we'll experience from our present methods of disposal, let alone dumping that has occurred before the best available approaches. How can we count the number of cancer deaths, lung disease deaths, even genetic mutations that will affect blood lines forever? Etc.

The key point is that you have to balance your own side effects against the gains you expect to achieve. Hopefully, the analysis will fall in your favor. You can always, of course, choose another solution besides nuclear power.

It is also possible that you can avoid this issue by ***preempting*** your opponent's most likely attacks. There's an idea in persuasion called "inoculation theory." Just as you inoculate someone against small pox by giving them a small dose of it, you may preempt adversarial attacks by anticipating coming arguments. You offer them, then refute them, before they've even been offered. Again, your imaginary opponent will help you to think ahead in this way. Recall Reinhold's point in chapter IV, that presenting audiences with evidence seems to inoculate or protect them against later persuasion.

Side effects may also result from over-solving a problem, creating more damage than is necessary to end the difficulty.

A recent bill to penalize producers of raves, even the owners of buildings where raves are held, includes water bottles as a sign of a rave. They could easily overshoot the mark, stopping joggers even near raves, as well as using water bottles on the front seat of a car as probable cause for search, if you happened to park near a rave. Would penalizing people not responsible for the suspected behavior be a good idea? We could certainly claim damages on behalf of innocent citizens—joggers, for instance—arrested for carrying a water bottle.

Real-World Example

How do these issues sum up into a whole speech? Let's look at a sample at a fairly typical level of student performance at semester's end. This is another, more complete approach to the issue of over fishing the seas. It will be presented in normal prose form, instead of the more extemporaneous outlines we've used earlier, but we'll still mark claims, warrants, and grounds as C, W, G:

Introduction: Every year countless species of fish and marine life are fished to the brink of extinction. At the same time around the world, some 50 million people depend on fishing for their livelihood. Over-fishing threatens to put millions out of work, damage a source of human food, and render many species extinct.

Thesis: Our over fished oceans should be better regulated. I'll explain what I mean by better regulated when we get to my solution.

Significant Harm: My first argument is that over fishing kills species not targeted by the fishermen (C). This occurs because of the usual drift netting, as well as newer techniques (W1).

As was observed in the *San Francisco Chronicle* article, "California's Fisheries Are Collapsing," in January of 1997, "Over fishing . . . is un-doing marine ecosystems and turning rich ocean environments into a watery wasteland. Drift nets stretch for miles, trawlers scour the ocean bottom, and new mass-fishing methods range from hook-studded PVC pipe to wire mesh fish traps, which are banned in states like Florida and other countries as well (G1)."

Further, there is damage to innocent and untargeted species (W2). "Techniques used to catch massive amounts of fish," says "Too Few Fish" from an August 2001 PBS website, "also kill albatrosses, sea turtles, dolphins, and shark in large numbers. Bottom trawlers use sweep nets to drag the ocean floor often damaging coral, sponges, and rock reefs that are home to countless fish and sea life (G2)."

A second point is that over fishing damages the economy (C). In the long run, it takes away fishermen's jobs. This is so because, once an area is over fished, most local fisheries shut down (W1). "The northwest Atlantic cod stocks off Canada was once one of the world's largest fisheries supporting both U.S. and Canadian fleets, according to an article "Fishing and Jobs," dated November 2003, from the Greenpeace website. "When the cod fishery was declared commercially extinct in 1992, 20,000 people lost their jobs almost overnight. Another 20,000 people lost their jobs the same year when other fisheries were closed due to collapse (G1a)."

Again from the PBS website, "Eureka, California, over fishing caused one of the west coast's largest fishery plants to eliminate 70% of its workforce over the past 15 years (G1b)."

Finally, for the issue of significant harm, consumers are also hurt by over fishing (C). When fishery harvests run low, fishermen must charge more for their wares, and this trickles down to the consumer (W). A November

2001 article "Our Fishing Industry," from the Pacific Island Business website, says that "the orange roughy, a popular fish in the U.S., is found in the deep waters of New Zealand. The principle fisheries have recently collapsed. In the early 1990s it was found in many U.S. grocery stores and restaurants for $3.99 a pound. In 2003, it was $8.99 a pound (G1)."

The United Food and Agriculture website said in November 2003 that the rising cost of tuna has caused many canned tuna manufacturers to switch to a blend of different fishes in a can instead of all tuna. "Many of the canneries simply cannot afford to offer tuna for $.99 a can when tuna costs between $600 and $1200 per fish on the open market. The blue fin tuna can actually garner up to $20,000 a fish for a good specimin. Companies selling all tuna in a can have raised their prices 400% over the last 10 years."

Inherency: Are these harms inherent? Can we identify an ongoing cause? We can infer, first, that a cause exists, since we have an ongoing trend (C). We can identify a trend among abalone, for instance (W). The California Fish and Game website identified two studies in "White Abalone—An Extinct Possibility," 1998. One completed in 1970 in the Delta fishery generalized that abalone could be found in a density of about one per square yard. A 1995 deep water survey in the same area found 1 abalone every 12,000 square yards, an area a bit bigger than two football fields (G).

It is also likely that over fishing damages the marine ecosystem on an ongoing basis (C). Over fishing affects not only the natural balance of the food chain but damages the lower levels of the food chain, making recovery by over fished species more difficult (W). According to "Oceans Without Fish," a March 1998 article in the *San Diego Earth Times,* "Humans are not only fishing in deeper water, but also lower on the food chain. As lower levels of the food chain decline, the chances of revival at the top of the chain are diminished (G)."

Finally, our government does not handle over fishing issues effectively (C). They are inconsistent in enforcement, even reluctant to enforce (W). Proof of the scope of over fishing can be found in the 2001 report to Congress by the National Marine Fisheries Service (NMFS) on the status of the nation's fish stocks. They found that almost a third of all evaluated stocks, 93 out of 304 or 30.6%, are over fished or are on their way. Despite this, the government is considering rollbacks to over fishing regulations, and this at a time when the future of fish stocks is far from bright (G1).

Government approaches are also riddled with lack of integration and conflict of interests at the most local levels (W2). The Magnusson-Stevens

Act divides the jurisdictional waters off the coast into eight regions, each managed by separate judicial councils. According to a report titled "Taking Stock of the Regional Fishery Management Councils," dated 2003, each regional council only prepares fishery management plans for the fish stocks in their regions, subject to oversight by the NMFS in the U.S. Department of Commerce. The voting members of each council consist of state fisheries officials, who are themselves members of the fishing industry, and a single representative of the federal government. Josh Eagle, director of the Stanford Fisheries Policy Project, wrote that report (G2).

Government actually encourages over fishing at the same time it supposedly regulates it (C). The government subsidizes the industry and supports them with low interest loans (W1). A World Bank study estimates that subsidies, although declining, are still worth a total of up to $20 billion a year. Fisheries sometimes provide jobs in poor coastal regions and help countries expand their fishing industry. However, most of the time, the same subsidies encourage companies to develop high-tech fishing, thus leading to over fishing, as was noted in "Subsidies in World Fisheries: A Re-examination," World Bank Technical paper No. 406, 1998 (G1).

The industry is taking advantage of this generosity (W2). Modern fishing equipment, the kind that creates over fished conditions, is very expensive. Federal and state subsidize modern fishing factories like the Arctic-based Tyson Foods on such equipment. Tyson has received more than $65 million in low-interest loans from the federal government, to help build ten super-trawlers. A Seattle-based factory-trawler fleet has received $200 million in federal subsidies, as was recorded in *Science Magazine,* February 1998.

The Solution needs to be as multi-dimensional as the causes of the problem. First, we need to decommission the Magnusson-Stevens Act and cease subsidies for those who over fish.

The basic thrust of the solution, however, involves Individual Transferable Quotas (ITQ). The ITQ system allows each fisherman a total allowable catch (TAC) per year, instead of limiting them to a particular season. Your TAC can be sold to another under certain circumstances.

It also means banning the practice of high grading, a practice by which a fisherman throws injured catch out of his hold, only to replace it with more valuable fish.

To offer an operational definition of the idea, consider an Alaskan Halibut Fishery. In the 1980s the fishery's season had been reduced to a few days. In 1995, an ITQ program was developed. Each fisherman's documented take during the period 1984-1990 was used to determine a share formula. Each fisherman then "bought" a share of the TAC. As a whole, the fishery is doing much better economically. The fishing seasons are now much longer, about seven to eight months, according to "Fishing for Solutions: Policymakers Struggle to Curb Over Fishing in the Chesapeake Bay," by Aaron Steelman, "Resources for the Future," Summer, 2002.

This story can be added grounds to the solvency argument, that the ITQ system would help to better deter over fishing in the U.S. (C). Such systems have been implemented in some states and countries in which fishing is critical to the economy, and it has worked very well. Essentially, it privatizes the fishing industry by making each commercial fisherman an "owner" of the fishes, which makes him or her more apt to protect their property and avoid high grading (W). In South Carolina in 1987, fish called a wreckfish was found accidentally while a crew was fishing for swordfish. Three years later there were 90 boats, all fishing for wreckfish. The fishery nearly collapsed until the state stepped in and implemented ITQ. In "New Ideas Help Spawn Hope for the Future," June 1996, on the Charleston.net website, fisherman Sam Ray speaks from his forty foot boat the "Lien Machine," "I farm my spots. I don't beat them to death because the more I leave, the more I can take. So far, the ITQ program has been a success, for fishermen, consumers and the wreckfish (G1)."

Since the introduction of ITQ in Iceland in 1990, most stocks of have become stronger, in particular the valuable cod stock at the same time that other cod stocks around the world were collapsing. Problems remain in the fishery, especially regarding high grading. But on the whole, "the ITQ system performed well," as was noted in a report by Hannes H. Gissurarson, "The Icelandic Solution," June 2000 (G2).

Australia's ITQ is an excellent example of the sustainability of well-managed fisheries. ITQs were established in the South East Fishery for orange roughy in 1989 and the early stages of implementation are already showing encouraging signs. Tom Tietenberg, professor of Economics at Colby College in Maine, wrote this in an article called "ITQs in the Australian South East Fishery," on the Colby College website.

While there are no appreciable negative ***side effects,*** there are some positive ones, such as preserving the fishery preserves their jobs and profits.

Conclusions

Like introductions, conclusions help us to get a "bird's eye view" of the text as a whole, then distinguishes the elements of its substructure. ***The peroration,*** or epilogue as Aristotle also called it, is a term describing a stirring and persuasive finish to your text. It is the point at which you:

Summarize your key points and link them back to the thesis.

Relate the thesis to audience interests, showing them how the topic impacts them.

Urge and encourage them to act on behalf of the proposition.

It is important to attach audience values to such acts, so appeals may be useful.

Don't be afraid to show some passion in delivery when you feel keenly for the topic yourself.

It's also fine to use humor and wit, even with serious subject matter.

So, for our over fishing topic, what would a peroration be like? It might go something like this today, though formal perorations of the past have certainly been more "colorful":

Every year countless species of fish and marine life are fished to the brink of extinction. At the same time, some 50 million people around the world depend on fishing for their very lives, and we consumers are not only paying more for the sea foods that we enjoy—orange roughy, tuna, red snapper, and the already all but gone abalone—but those we enjoy the most may soon exist no more. Tuna isn't even really tuna anymore. And we see a clear trend of over fishing thinning the ocean at worse and worse levels.

We've discovered that the causes of these harms are many: The deep water fishing techniques are not only killing unsought species, but damaging lower levels of the food chain so that upper levels cannot recover nor restore the sea. We've also seen how the government has poorly integrated and industry influenced regional approaches to the problem, defined by the Magnusson-Stevens Act. We've also discovered that government actually subsidizes equipment for fishing companies that over fish.

We have proposed the use of ITQs, demonstrated to be effective in the United States and abroad to replace subsidies. We want the Magnusson-Stevens Act to continue to save endangered ocean species, but on a broader more systematic, national level, doing none harm where it can be avoided. This solution also provides fishermen on the line a sense of personal ownership and stewardship of the seas, and they will learn to use different techniques as a matter of enlightened self interest with regard to their future employment.

Fish are an important human food source and may become even more so as world population grows and farmlands wither away. They say that fish is "brain food." Since we've eaten so many of them, in some cases to point of extinction, we really ought to be smarter about this, for ourselves, for the employment of fishermen, and for the long, long life of the sea. It must be done now. There is no timeline left for survival. I urge you to support this policy.

You can probably see a few of our suggestions made in action above. The first paragraph summarizes the key points of harm and links them back to the thesis. There's also an appeal to our sense of taste by listing tasty endangered fish. We've touched upon a value of "do no unnecessary harm," in the context of damaging the lower portion of the food chain. And we've evoked the appeal of logos in noting that government works against itself in subsidizing over fishing and allowing fishing industry members to regulate themselves under Magnusson-Stevens. We offered appeals to ethos on behalf of the fishermen and emotional appeals in offering them "a sense of ownership and stewardship." We even managed a humorous appeal to logos in the finish, setting up a simple encouragement to act on behalf of the proposition.

Are there counter arguments to this case? Oh, my yes, as there are with almost any position. Yet it is a prima facie case which has met its burden of proof and temporarily removed presumption from the present approach to social action.

Vocabulary

Costs vs. Gains
Impact
Inventional System
Policy Stock Issues
     Topicality
     Significant Harm
          Qualitative vs. Quantitative
     Inherency/Cause
          Attitudinal Inherency
          Structural Inherency
     Workable Solution
          Agency
          Enforcement
          Funding
          Incentives
          Solvency
          Timeline
     Side Effects
Peroration (Epilogue)
R & D Solutions
Trend

Exercises: Go to Interactive Disc to Complete

At this point you should be working on an 8-10 minute policy speech, using the stock issues and format described above.

You should choose a topic immediately and have sample arguments by this time next week. More specific parameters will be provided by your instructor.

Sources

1) Corsi, J.R. (1986). The Continuing Evolution of Policy System Debate: An Assessment and a Look Ahead. Journal of the American Forensic Association 22, 158.

    Ehninger, D., and Brockriede, W. (1978). Decision by Debate. New York: Harper & Row.

    Freeley, A.J. (1993). Argumentation and Debate: Critical Thinking for Reasoned Decision Making. Belmont, CA: Wadworth.

2) LA Times, White House Must Reject Navy's Assault on the Oceans, Commentary, August 22, 2002.

3) LA Times, Nations Adopt Climate Pact Without US, July 24, 2001.

4) Eichenberg, T., consultant to Oceana, End Sea Mammal Massacre, LA Times, August 19, 2003.

5) Ibid.

6) Ibid.

7) LA Times, Earth Liberation Front Takes Destructive Path, August 26, 2003.

8) LA Times, Journey into Sex Slavery, August 17, 2001.

9) LA Times, Florida Wants All the Details from Mothers in Adoption Notices, August 21, 2002.

10) LA Times, Panel Frowns on Efforts to Buy Sudan Slaves' Freedom, May 28, 2002.

11) LA Times, The Graying of the Prisons, June 9, 2002.

12) LA Times, Even Tougher Love for Welfare Moms, June 11, 2002.

13) LA Times, Results of Crackdown at Border Called "Mixed," August 4, 2001.

14) LA Times, "A Stock Panic Shut-Off Valve," August 19, 2002.

15) Holihan, T.A., and Baske, K.T. (1994). Arguments and Arguing. New York: St. Martin's Press. Especially good on narratives as arguments.

16)   Eichenberg.

17)   Eichenberg.

18)   LA Times, Build Berlin Wall in Middle East, August 14, 2001.

19)   Eichenberg.

20)   Eichenberg.

21)   LA Times, Commentary, August 21, 2002.

XIII
Argument in Interpersonal Communication

There was a very wise professor at the University of Michigan who used to talk about "the law of the hammer." Basically, it goes, if you give a kid a hammer he'll bang everything but the nail with it. That is, there's a tendency to apply a new skill in all the wrong places. An unwise person might run about karate chopping people after a self-defense class. Likewise, an unwise person looks at normal everyday conversation as an opportunity to "win," to meet and beat others in debate.

The problem is that, ***in interpersonal relationships, winning sometimes means that everyone loses.*** Because you've alienated others that you care about, they may back away from you. Then you're left victorious . . . and alone.

In the words of successful trial lawyer Gary Spence, from his book "How to Argue and Win Every Time":

> Is it winning when we force the other to lay down his emotional and intellectual arms and surrender? Do we triumph when the other cries out, "You win! I was wrong! I am a fool and faithless, filthy knave not worthy of my space on this earth!"?

> . . . I once believed, as most do, that if arguments are to be won, the opponent must be pummeled into submission and silenced. You can imagine how the idea played at home. If, in accordance to such a definition, I won an argument, I began losing the relationship.[1]

At the beginning of this text, we made a distinction among three senses of the word argument, but we avoided the sense of personal quarrels. Now, in an effort to "debrief" you for normal interaction and, especially, your more intimate associates, let's ***consider differences between argument in the public and private senses of the word.***

The first thing to remember, in taking formal argument skills back to your personal life, is to not play lawyer with your family, your date, your spouse, or your friends. The only real way to win a conversation with someone you care about is for you to ***find a win for each of you.*** This is not to say that what we've learned here is not useful to conflict resolution, the study of fair fighting. For instance, **be aware of fallacies,** even more abundant in daily conversation, especially **in yourself:**

"You never do what I want to do." Sweeping generalization.

The same goes for "you always criticize me," or the like.

"I don't want to go out with your friends the Simpsons. We went once and I was bored." Hasty generalization.

"I'm right, and you're wrong." Forcing the dichotomy.

"You damn &8%#$!" All name calling is ad hominem.

"No, I don't want to try that new restaurant. I like the one we always go to." Fallacy of appeal to tradition.

"Well, everyone else is going." Appeal to the people.

"You make the biggest, most awful mess whenever you cook!" Emotive language. Boy, you'll find that one all over common quarrels.

"Well, so do you!" Tu quoque. You've done it, so I can do it.

Yet pick and choose your times to use such knowledge when working with others. Use it best to check yourself and your own misadventures in conversational excess.[2]

In other words, while conflict is inevitable in even the most sophisticated relationships, **the rules have now changed.**

While we can't give you a whole interpersonal course in this chapter, we can give you **some ABCs of successful relationships.**

A Is for Argument

We've already discussed how argument can be constructive, if it follows a disciplined format. This can also be the case in personal quarrels. While most people prefer not to argue, to the extent that they may pretend compliance to avoid it, conflicts can actually be good for relationships. It helps to clarify both differences and needs and can be a source of greater mutual understanding. In any case, it's impossible to avoid conflict in intimate relationships. It has even been said that no partnership of any depth is conflict free. So, if you're not having conflict, it may be that you haven't explored the relationship all that much.[3]

The difference between positive and negative results may be whether you practice dirty or **fair fighting.** Just as with formal argument, you should stay issue focused, rather than person focused. That depends on clarifying the issues between you.

A longitudinal study looking at twenty years of intimate relationships concluded that **unhappy and short-lived relationships** were marked by these behaviors:[4]

- They ignored each other's nonverbal behavior.

- They failed to listen to each other.

- They tended not to empathize with the concerns of their partner.

- They were too busy defending themselves to acknowledge their own short-comings.

Also, there are specific behaviors that accompany **happy, long surviving relationships:**

- They observed each other's nonverbal behavior. Conflict isn't always verbal. Moods, acts, and attitudes may reveal repressed concerns.

- They listened carefully to one another.

- They tried to empathize with the concerns of their partner.

- They were willing to admit their own mistakes. (That's a tough one.)

We might think of these two catalogues, respectively, as **the problem and the solution,** much as we did in policy propositions.

Add that successful couples tend to **say many more positive things than negative things** in their everyday conversation. Some research indicates that relationships that have one positive comment to every one negative comment are less satisfied. Those that have five positive comments to every one negative comment are more satisfied.

A Is for Attraction

What is it that attracts and involves us in relationships with others? There are many reasons we're attracted to others:

Attractive features cannot be denied as a persuasive influence. We mentioned research earlier suggesting that attractive people have certain advantages. Yet what's physically attractive is subjective. Factors like "chemistry" or "personality" tend to outweigh the attraction of features as people get to know each other.

Feeling safe matters, too. There's a concept of evolving attraction called **"uncertainty reduction."** We want to feel safe with others. Proximity is reassuring. Growing trust is reassuring, too.

Convenience of geography might make it easier to get to know someone. Ever try a long distance relationship? It's not impossible, but it's difficult.

Seeing someone in your neighborhood on a regular basis can also contribute to uncertainty reduction.

Disclosure, telling people who we really are and what we really want, is a way of getting to know people and building trust. I let down my guard a little and tell you something about myself. You respond in kind.

Initially, people tend to ask questions of each other. As conversation continues, participants tend to volunteer more information, sometimes within only a few minutes of conversation. They each want a sense that the other is somehow interested in their life. They reflect subject matter back and forth, to see what they have in common. Their nonverbal tends to be reflective. Researchers have noted that body posture tends to conform the longer they speak. People also tend to stand or sit closer as they go. We discover attraction in this process of disclosure, we signal that attraction with increased disclosure and compatible nonverbal behavior.

High self-monitors, people who are sufficiently aware of their own behavior that they can adjust their communication to blend with the environment, may even consciously adjust accent, speech pace or speech rhythm. Research also shows that people who manage to adjust thus are generally perceived to be better communicators. It's not much different than the concept of audience analysis discussed earlier.[5]

From the start of attraction, people tend to emphasize similarities and de-emphasize differences. We are more attentive and courteous than we might usually be. In a way, we're ***building a case*** that we are someone worth having.

A Is for Attention.

One of the most important aspects of intimate communication is that we ***be present to the person*** we're interacting with. We look at them when they talk, just as we expect them to look at us. The more urgent the topic, the more effort we should take to eliminate distractions and interruptions. We're so used to media in our lives, it seems there's always a radio, a CD, or a television in the background. Turn it off. Put down what you're doing and listen carefully. If only we gave each other the attention that we offer when someone speaks in front of a classroom.

B Is for Behavior

One challenge to interpersonal growth is an attitude that says, "I'm just the way I am in relationships, and I won't change." Adult behavior, though, is a choice. Certainly, we're influenced to behave in certain ways by our upbringing. Ultimately, though, behavior can be chosen. Failure to acknowledge one's ability to change, or to take responsibility for our less desirable behaviors, puts the burden of change and growth on our partners. ***You just altered your behavior to argue better, you can alter your behavior to relate better.***

It's also important to ***be a fair witness*** to the behavior of others, to distinguish the actual behavior of others from our subjective inferences about them. As we learn to say, "Well, he got up, shook his head and left the room," instead of, "Well, he got up real suddenly and acted all negative and turned his back on us." Just as we mentioned in pre-critical thinking, it's important to make the distinction between their action and your mental reaction.

C Is for Confirming Behavior

We can look at personal conversation and behavior as either confirming, vague, or disconfirming. Confirmation on the nonverbal level is easy to notice. Smiles. Relaxed posture. Touching. Likewise disconfirming nonverbal can be easily seen. Frowns. Gripping fists in gesture. Pointing as if in an accusation. Loud volume. In language, we listen for compliments, questions of concern, and expressions of interest and affection, rather than judgments and criticisms.

In some unhappy relationships, the habit of speaking negatively tends to be reflective. One bad word deserves another, we might think when we snip back and forth. We prefer not to get insults, even the ones that get dressed in humor, nor do we want to be told that we're less than we are, or even less than we want to be.[6]

There are three levels of confirming behaviors:

> ***Recognition:*** We look at and respond to people we know, as if we actually know and care about them. It's a sidewalk nod to stranger. It's stopping to chat with friends. It's returning letters, calls, and e-mails. Even with people we don't see much, it's being remembered on the Christmas card list, or invited to the party across the street. It's saying hello to people just to let them know that you notice their presence.

> ***Acknowledgement:*** This is an "ah-hah" for me. You don't have to simply agree or disagree with others. You can give a provisional acknowledgement of the ideas or complaints that others have.

That's not our natural tendency, though. We tend to be more reactive than thoughtful when complaints come up. We have knee jerk reactions, often defensive behaviors.

If we stop and think a minute, rather than merely react like Pavlov's dog, we may find that we can avoid polarizing the conversation. We can say, for instance, "You may have a point, let me think it over. I really do appreciate your feeling close enough to tell me." Or, "My first reaction was to get angry, but I value your opinion as a friend, so I'll give it serious consideration."

If we show friends that we care about them, they may find it easier when you say, "I thought about what you said, and I agree with some of it, but maybe not with all of it." Yet the relationship itself would have been stabilized for the extra attention you gave to the concerns of friends.

Endorsement is the most complete way to show confirming behavior. You simply swallow a little pride and support your friend's assessment. You are saying with this that you trust their opinion.

You may also endorse their behavior, for instance, "you're doing the right thing" or "I admired how you handled that." People who feel endorsed are more likely to endorse in return.

C Is for Control

Control is one of the most important issues in relationship building. The ways in which we react to control defines the nature of our relationships, as well as likely conflict styles. According to psychologist Dr. Schutz, these are three key human needs in relationships:[7]

Affection

Inclusion

Control

Another influencing dimension is the ***degree of involvement,*** or urgency, with which we feel these things.

Everyone, to one degree or another, needs some ***affection.*** Yet there are clearly low and high degrees of that need. Needs also vary over time. However, there are probably ranges of need within which a person tends to operate. So, what would a relationship between a high affection person and a low affection person be like? It's probably safe to say that their conflict style would entail a lot of begging and evasion! Of course, most of our needs are somewhere closer to the middle than these extremes. Everyone's needs fluctuate some.

Inclusion is the need to be a part of something larger than the self, your family, the groups you affiliate with on campus, the community. It's your basic need to be among people. Again, everyone has the need to one degree or another. What would a low inclusion with high inclusion person relationship be like?

The low inclusion person on a Friday night might like a take-out pizza and a DVD at home. The high inclusion person might prefer to stop at a bar and be among, if not chat with, other people. They want the low inclusion person to come along, and the pizza/DVD bit won't cut it all the time. The high inclusion person might also have a tendency to be a joiner of organizations and committees that the low inclusion person doesn't want to join.

On the surface, this might seem to be unworkable. Yet, in some respects, there are chances for mutual understanding. **Apply the thesis-antithesis-synthesis paradigm** as a pattern for analysis.

> Thesis: I want to stay in.
>
> Antithesis: But I want to go out.
>
> Synthesis: If I have a need to stay in, and you have a need to go out, maybe we can each have our way. You go out, and I'll have some quiet time to myself.
>
> Thesis: OK, but you have to stay in with me one night a weekend.
>
> Antithesis: OK, but you have to stay go out with me the other night.
>
> Synthesis: Done.

There are **two senses of control**, conversational control and control over decisions. It's possible that a dominant partner may have both, but they may also be divided. One partner may be the one to "chat up" other people, but defer to the partner on matters of decision.

There are three kinds of relationships defined by distribution of control:

The first is called a **complementary** relationship, when a high control person is with a low control person. **One wants control, the other yields control.** Opposites attract.

The downside to these relationships is that one partner may so dominate another that it inhibits one partner's growth. What happens to that partner later in life if they lose the relationship? My grandmother was 70, after the loss of her life partner, when she learned to write her first check. Also, the dominant partner may find that too much control can be exhausting. They may get tired of "having" to do everything. Another word for control is responsibility.

When birds of a feather flock together on control, we call that a **symmetrical** relationship. **Both partners want control,** so there's an ongoing negotiation, or duel for control. It can be a conflict-filled relationship. Yet it has a significant advantage. It's not boring. People who spar over control may be stimulated into more dynamic interaction and may come up with creative solutions to their disagreements.

One problem with high control people is that they may not always be fighting about what they're fighting about. I mean to say, control itself is the issue of the conflict, although there may be a symbolic subject matter that diverts us from that fact. One simply wants the other to yield, against Gerry Spence's caution.

My wife and I are both very high control people. The first year of the relationship was really about dividing up territory to determine who was in control of what. In the second year, we remodeled the house together. That study in cooperation, with the help of some special friends, taught us how to compromise. We learned to choose our battles. We let some things go in order to choose our energy for the important conflicts. We allowed each other to influence tastes and activities. High control people may have areas of control, or they may alternate control to keep the peace. For instance, my wife and I have a rule that whoever drives gets no trouble from the other. (We break that rule all the time!)

Another form of symmetrical relationship is **two low control people.** Their challenge is the opposite. Their struggle is to determine who will take responsibility, another aspect of control. They may have very static moments, in which neither wants to choose the movie, where to eat, let alone make financial decisions. Such couples may decide that both should be involved in major decision making, operating by consensus, or they can alternate decisions, as in "you plan meals for a week, then I'll plan the next."

The third type is a **parallel** relationship, in which partners share control equally. This is possibly a more recent norm in modern relationship. It may be that control is less of an issue for this group, as they seem to be at ease about sharing control. An old saying comes to mind: two heads are better than one. This does not mean that they will not have conflict, but they understand the importance of mutuality in decision making.

D Is for Defensiveness

Defensiveness in communication is one of the most difficult problems for trust and intimacy in relationships. We fight when our sense of ourselves, our face, is threatened somehow. Someone pushes our comfort zone in intimacy. Somebody challenges our values. We lose objectivity and react emotionally without critical thought or considered word choice.

Defensive behavior damages trust and tends to be reciprocal, as well as escalating. Yet studying the various types of defenses-much as we understood errors in thinking by studying fallacies-can make us more self-aware about our behavior.

Defenses divide into **three types of responses:** Aggressive reactions, responses of avoidance, and explaining problems away. In other words, it's a slightly refined version of animal fight or flight instincts.

A)   **Aggression** was characterized earlier when we distinguished it from being argumentative, a more positive approach. Aggressive defenses include personal attacks and sarcasm. It's taking a position that the best defense is a good offense.

B)   ***Avoidance*** includes several types of behaviors:

We may ***physically avoid*** people we have conflicts with. If one has money problems, for instance, and has been late with the rent before, one might avoid a roommate at the first of the month.

We may also ***repress*** critical information, pushing it down into our unconscious. The problem with this, beyond not resolving issues with people we care about, is that repressed issues may contribute to depressive behavior, a general sense of feeling low and ill-at-ease. The dominate method of dealing with depression today is the use of chemical anti-depressants, and that's perfectly appropriate in many cases. Yet 40% of those who have taken such drugs achieve no positive effect from them. It's possible that they are depressed, not due to irregular body chemistry, but because they have so many unresolved issues that they don't know where to begin to solve them.

We may be in ***denial*** about a problem. For instance, as someone slips into alcoholic behavior, the norm is that they refuse to listen to others who say there's a problem. They're just "social drinkers," or "they're the life of the party." It's often necessary for a family to make an intervention, taking the alcoholic person to a hospital for help.

It's common that we might ***displace,*** too. Displacement occurs when someone criticizes us, but we feel it's too risky to respond in any way but compliance. We then take our frustrated energy out on someone else, the family, the dog, a friend. In a way, it's a fallacy of relevancy, as we're exerting a position that really ought to be taken up with someone else. The issue never gets confronted, and loved ones are left hurt and confused.

C)   We are at our most tricky when we begin to ***explain away behavior*** for which we're criticized. We ***rationalize*** on an almost daily basis. As long as there's a reason we did what we did, it must be all right. However, it's important to note that it's often less important why we did it, than that we did it all. There are simply some behaviors that tend to be negative for relationships, like lying.

We also ***compensate.*** We do something undesirable for the relationship, but we "make up for it," so it's all right. You may have known people who lose their temper, so that they are sometimes very hurtful. Some don't apologize, nor change. Perhaps they just give compliments or gifts the next time you see them. However, to the extent that they intend to continue the behavior, the giving of gifts later becomes a justification, allowing them to act out their irrational behavior again later.

We may also ***project*** our inner conflicts onto others. If we're down on some aspect of ourselves that we're avoiding, we may notice in others those very traits we'd like not to be reminded of. And it's so much easier to dissect those problems in another than to deal with them in ourselves. If I find I have an instinctive dislike for someone, I try to use them like a mirror. What is it about them, I ask, that reminds me of myself?[8]

E Is for Emotions

Emotions are sometimes more difficult to express for men than for women.[9] This is not to say that men feel less, although it may seem this way from the woman's perspective at times. It's that men are culturally conditioned to reveal less emotion. In gym, sports, and all male settings like boy scouts, men are often taught to "be tough." If they aren't, they may be mocked by coaches or other males. This training becomes most acute in military settings, sometimes leading to acute desensitization, as we've seen in Abu Ghraib.

So, while emotions may be intense below the surface, some men act more than speak. When they're upset, they may have a tendency to go for a run, or a drive, or have a drink, which is consistent with a pattern of avoidance or repression. This is also not to say that women may also find difficulty expressing emotion. In some respects, adhering to norms of public conversation discourages such expression for both sexes.

One thing that people in relationships can do for each other is to *"midwife" each other's emotions.* There are particular ways that we can communicate with an upset other that may help them feel more free to speak to their feelings:

> We can *support* them, give them our presence and attention, just to listen if that's all that's needed. Often, that is all that's needed. We don't have to fix people who are holding back emotion. They're not broken. They're just working out a way to express something they don't quite have a handle on. You can help by being an opening, being an opportunity for their expression.

> Also, we can encourage expression by *prompting.* I once had someone do the simplest thing to help me to share a difficult emotion. Like other men, I'd say a few words, then look away, holding back. She simply kept putting her hand on my thigh, saying, "Keep talking. Don't stop." It encouraged me to continue.

Prompting may sometimes take the form of playing multiple choice. If the other has shut down emotionally, we may ask "is it X that's bothering you? Or is it Y?" This is not to play guessing games, nor to put words in their mouths, but to offer some choices, some simple closed "yes or no" questions, to kick start their own disclosure.

A friend of mine, a speech teacher of some merit, recently had a stroke. He can't always find the words, which is hard for him, so I play multiple choice with him. Since we know each other, I'm lucky enough to sense the right words for him. He says,

"Yes. Thanks." Then, he goes on. Remember, it's not to put words in their mouth, but to help them find their own. If they show irritation, stop.

We may approach others in a more reflective way, mirroring back what they're saying. In its most practical form, it's called **paraphrasing,** repeating back to the other what they said, but in your own words to show that you've processed the information. It's a way of confirming that you've understood, or to repair misconceptions if you haven't. It's also a way for the other to hear what he's saying back and adjust his words more accurately.

Questioning can be useful, **not in the sense of cross-questioning** in debate, but primarily as a matter of clarification. Sometimes people who question from their own curiosity over details may interrupt, or take the other off track.

> "So, I met this guy and . . ." "Oh, is he nice looking?"

> "Yeah, he is. Anyway, he took me to Joey's for dinner."

> "I've heard about that place. What did you have?"

> "Some fish, but the point is. . . ."

> "Oh, I just hate fish!"

The "listener" may think she's having a conversation, but at this rate the speaker may never get to the point. Wait for a natural pause before you ask questions, maybe until after you've heard the whole story. At times, though, you may lose track of the characters. Emotional people tend to be sloppy about pronoun usage: "And then he did this, and he did the other." "Which he is he?" wouldn't be an unreasonable question at that point. Ask them to use proper nouns, Mary, Joe, and Sue.

When we mention **analyzing** in interpersonal communication, it sometimes suggests some kind of amateur psychiatry. Nothing could be further from our intended meaning. The original meaning of the term is to break things down into their component parts, **much as we've done in separating out stock issues** for a given type of speech.

For instance, when you get a blood analysis, your doctor will tell you what your red and white blood cell counts are, the amount of protein in your blood, etc. This is what we mean here, helping the other to get perspective on what they've said by reporting the various categories of their expression back to them:

> "Well, I hear that you're concerned about at least two things, what you should do and how your mom will react?"

> "Yeah, that's right."

> "Let's separate things out and talk about them one at a time. Your mom can't react until you do something, so shall we talk about that first?"

When people are upset, things may come out in a confused rush. Sometimes it can help if someone sorts it out and orders it for them, perhaps simply by mentioning the components and asking the other which is most important. *You would then, as we did in value argumentation, have helped them to arrive at a sense of priority,* rather than them feel overwhelmed by a mass of undifferentiated feelings.

Consistently, when I ask students about listening responses they most favor, *advising* is very high. It seems normal, as we're in a communication era in which everybody is an expert. We watch talk shows in which audience members play psychiatrist, if not judge and jury, with the guests. Even news agencies, like CNN, ask people to give their daily reflections on world affairs by e-mail. Recently, they asked if the Kobe Bryant case should have been dismissed. How would we know? We haven't been given the details of the case!

Advising individuals is a kind of trap. It shifts problem solving from the other to you, as well as the responsibility for the issue. Advising may be satisfying to our egos, until something goes wrong with the advice and you get blamed. Advice should be given only under special circumstances. It should be asked for, and we should first try to lead people to their own decisions by answering questions with questions first.

"What should I do?"

"Well, what have you considered doing?"

Judging seems like something we would never want to do. Yet there are some situations in which it would be an appropriate response. You're an adult correcting a child's behavior. You're a boss who catches an employee violating OSHA rules for safety. A friend is contemplating some desperate or dangerous behavior. Otherwise, judging people, in the sense of telling them they're right or wrong, isn't useful to intimacy. One of the worst judgments we can make is to tell someone, "You shouldn't feel that way." It's probably well-meaning, but people have natural ownership of their own feelings. Nobody else has the right to take them away.[10]

F Is for Fun

Yes, you have to work at a relationship, but successful partners also need to play. It doesn't matter how busy you are. It doesn't matter if you're short of money. There are lots of things in most communities to do for free. Take a walk. Window shop. Go for a drive and listen to your favorite music. Just set some time aside to be together. Remind yourself of why you got together to begin with.

I'm blessed with a wife who is not only fun, but funny. Sharing humor helps to keeps us afloat in the worst times of crises, including near death experiences. We met too late to have children, so we've become our own kids. If anyone saw us playing with total abandon, they'd never guess that we were a college professor and a business manager. We once got so involved in playing a simple game of cards, we forgot to go to a very expensive concert we'd talked about all day. Why? Because we find enjoyment with each other over the simplest of things.

G Is for Generosity

There are a few words I'd like to whisper in the ear of every partner in a relationship: "Gifts for no reason. Flowers on days other than anniversaries." Notice what they like when you window shop, come back, and buy it, then save it for the right time. It doesn't have to be much. Share your sandwich. Maybe even your pizza (that's a tough one)! Show that you care.

H Is for Honesty

One of the most important dimensions of **credibility,** we've learned is honesty. We may feel that we're honest in our key relationships, but in our public conversation signs suggest that dishonesty, to some degree, is a norm. One study said that, among college students recording their statements over the course of a typical day, roughly two-thirds of the statements were not entirely true.

The reason people often give for lying, that they don't want to hurt the other person, proves not to be entirely true. Research indicates that people lie for entirely different reasons. High on the list are saving face and avoiding conflict. Some people find it hard to be "up front" about their issues with others.[11]

Lies in intimate relationships are very powerful, especially when they're perceived to be part of a pattern of lies. One study found that, among people terminating relationships, lies contributed to the break-ups two-thirds of the time.[12]

It's certainly arguable that some lies—euphemisms, false compliments, and suppressions of negative comments—are simply social grace. Yet intimate relationships seem to demand another level of honesty.

I Is for Inventory

Sometimes, when feeling unappreciated, frustrated, or overwhelmed, we may find ourselves taking other people's inventory. In other words, we make and keep lists of our partner's little offenses. It's not unlike **taking a flow sheet** of every little thing you dislike about them.

We may nurse this list until anger over it is out of proportion to the offenses themselves. We then have that last straw that breaks the camel's back, and we blow up at our partner. This leads to kitchen sink fighting (see below).

The best way to handle the small conflicts is to deal with them as they come along. One might think this is petty, but if it's important enough for you to carry around, then it's worth mentioning in a timely manner.

J Is for Jealousy

While this is a normal and understandable emotion, it can be the cause of much trouble. It may start as a simple game of flirtation. Yet the feeling itself, as well as toying with that feeling, can shred the tissue of trust that binds relationships. If one has an overwhelming sense of jealousy without cause, one should probably consider why that feeling exists. A sense of abandonment from something you've forgotten about? Insecurity about your own attractiveness? Express these feelings with your partner.

K Is for Kitchen Sink Fighting

As was mentioned under inventory, when we count up wrongs and fail to let them go, we may have a tendency to dump too much on the table during arguments. One brings up events from the past and present, all at once. It creates, not only tension, but a sense of hopelessness over how much is, all of a sudden, wrong with the relationship. Handle complaints as near to the time of the activating event as soon as possible. The other will remember and "get it" more easily, and it will help to subdue emotions in better proportion to the event.

L Is for Listening

Perhaps the most important of all interpersonal skills is listening, just as it was in debate. How can we interact if we don't know what the other is saying? Yet, as we've mentioned before, the average adult listening efficiency rate is only 25%. Sometimes this is a matter of information overload, but here are certain bad habits that make listening, even to people we care about, hard.

- Prejudging people's appearance, accent, or education level
- Prejudging the difficulty or ease of a subject matter
- Prejudging topics as inherently interesting or uninteresting
- Getting too involved in nonverbal communication, checking someone out, for instance, that we don't hear words
- Daydreaming and other distractions

On the other hand, there is also a concept called "***active listening***," a five step process:

Hearing—This is just the minimum mechanical precondition for listening. Listening and hearing are not synonyms. We hear things in our sleep, but we are not actively listening.

Attending—This is the crux of the process. Research on good versus poor listeners was conducted. From interviews with both good and bad listeners, the study derived the bad habits listed above. From physical tests on biofeedback machines, it was determined that good listeners work harder at it. Their blood pressure elevates, their heart rate accelerates, and their brain wave patterns change. There are also nonverbal signs of listening, such as sitting upright or with forward lean, eye contact, as well as head nods and brief utterances of sympathy.

Understanding—Using tools like perception checking (below) and paraphrasing to confirm message intent.

Responding—There are many possible responses. They are listed above under emotions (support, analyze, etc.). Let them know, at a minimum, that you care about what they're saying. If they're asking you for something, more attention, less criticism, react to them.

Remembering—It matters to people that you actually recall what they've told you or asked of you. If you care about the person, follow up. Write a goal for yourself. Make a note at the top of your day planner. Try to avoid having the same conflict over and over, as a matter of sheer neglect. Follow through.[13]

L Is for "Location, Location, Location"

Time and place matter in conflict. Conflict in the public may be not only destructive, but mutually embarrassing and likely to create defensiveness in the relationship (see above). While it's important to resolve conflict as soon as possible after it occurs, one or the other person may not be ready to discuss it. Calm down. Make a date to talk things through.

It's also worth noting that some environments may become associated with conflict in long-term relationships. If you have a pattern of arguing, where does it occur? The kitchen, the bedroom in the evening when you're tired, in the car? If you find there's a consistent "place of argument," change the scene. Go outside. Sit in the park. Do it differently.

M Is for Matching

. . . but differing, too. You may have heard the old saying that "birds of a feather flock together." You may also have heard that "opposites attract." Which is true for intimate communication? Actually, it's a little of each.

In some respects, the reasons we're attracted to others isn't because the other is somehow inherently attractive. ***The way we interact with them helps us to define or own identity*** and to better understand ourselves. We may be attracted to someone similar, especially in values and enjoyment of certain activities, as it helps us to reconfirm ourselves. It also may avert some quarrels, as you're more likely to agree about how to spend your time. It may be a way of reinforcing stability.

Yet we may be attracted to somebody very different, seeking a more complementary relationship. Sometimes we tire of our everyday norm and seek self-expansion through others. We attach ourselves to someone more skilled or competent in some particular way, as if to learn from them. Conversely, we may be drawn to someone just beginning what we've already done, in the sense of mentoring or stewardship. We may be drawn toward someone who is much more extroverted than we are, to provide a contrast to our own shy nature. It's a way of testing our identity to see if you might like something better.

N Is for Normal

There's no such thing. Human behavior is unique, individual, original. Do you know anyone who actually has 2.3 children, the national average? Watch your generalizations in personal relationships, as well. For instance, people say things like, "I wish I came from a normal family." Oh, yeah? Go find one. By some reports, as many as 80% of American families are dysfunctional in some way or another. Again, we're unique individuals. Families, thank heaven, are unique, too.

N Is for Nonverbal Communication

The attention we pay daily to nonverbal communication is important in both public and private life.

In public life, the sweaty upper lip and five o'clock shadow of Richard Nixon began the focus on nonverbal communication in political life. His on camera appearance against Kennedy's graceful visage probably made the difference in that presidential election. Al Gore's habit of shaking his head at Bush's responses in their presidential debates was perceived as condescension and created sympathy for Bush.

In private life, especially intimate life, it's a form of healing to touch, a form of trust to show that you're relaxed, and your facial expressions are the very language of love. As couples get to know each other's nonverbal tendencies, it actually diminishes the necessity of language in long-lived couples.

How important is nonverbal communication? By objective standards, anthropologist Birdwhistle counted the number of nonverbal communicative signals in normal personal conversations. Sixty percent were nonverbal signals and forty percent were verbal. In a more subjective self-report measure, respondents said that as much as 93% of the message impact they took away from conversations came from nonverbal communication.[14]

So, while this is a long study, it is worth the trouble to learn. There are several books on the market about nonverbal behavior, but beware of sweeping generalizations. Behavior is somewhat individual, especially within particular relationships. At the simplest level, one should simply pay attention to a partner's signals.

O Is for Openness

To be open to others is as important to human development as being open to new ideas. Indeed, the two are related. We've already discussed that people need human contact, but we can drive such contact away by being iconoclastic or suspicious of new people. We can also damage ourselves by not being open about our thoughts and feelings with those we care about. The alternative is cliché conversation, what we did at work, the weather, etc.

Part of being open with a significant other is being open to new experiences together. Couples who experience new things, classes, travel, books in common, may continually introduce new topics for conversation and personal growth.

P Is for Privacy

At the same time that people need openness, they also need time for themselves. It's been said that a relationships really consists of three people, the two people who meet (A & B below) and the relationship itself (C), which tends to take on a life of its own (Figure 19). We move into oneness and back out to our individuality, like ebb and flow of the sea.

Commonly, successful relationships have a natural ebb and flow of separateness, then togetherness, and back to separateness again. There's a period of "cocooning" for couples in the first stages of their relations, during which they hardly separate and may exclude others, family, and friends. However, to maintain a healthy relationship, each party does well, to the degree that it's possible, to keep their own interests and remember their own integrity as an individual.

This requires a sophisticated view of control within the relationship, but it's certainly possible. Remember the person you were originally attracted to and how they behaved. Don't try to make them someone else. Give them their own space to be who they are.

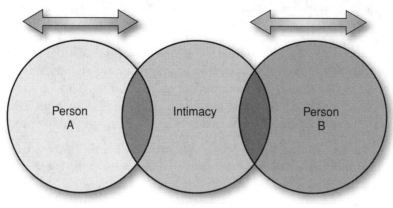

Figure 19

Q Is for Questions

All good communication requires listening, and we're not very good listeners. We're also not very good talkers sometimes. People in intimate relations may send messages obliquely, often by nonverbal means, sulking or slamming the door. We may assume or project a meaning for such acts, but we'll be wrong a good portion of the time, creating misunderstandings.

A fair amount of this is because we assume we understand the other's meaning and intent, but we do not. Rather than trust to our own subjective assumptions, asking particular kinds of questions to clarify is preferable.

Perception checking can help prevent such misunderstandings. The next time you have conflict, instead of being a mind reader, approach them with a series of questions to be clear about what they really meant.

> 1) Give an objective **description** of the behavior, or words, that you got as a message. Lay off the subjective attitudes. Don't say how you felt, say what you actually saw and heard: "Last night when we were talking, you stopped speaking and slammed the door behind you."

> 2) Offer two open, caring and non-accusatory **interpretations** of what you've described: "At first, I thought you just lost your temper over something I said. Then I wondered if I'd said something that hurt you."

Notice, the two interpretations suggests that you're open, that you haven't settled on a judgment about that person. At least one of the two interpretations takes very positive approach. It reveals that you are ready to accept responsibility for your part of the problem.

3) Then (and here's the ah-hah) you actually **ask the person:** "Was there something bothering you?" And let them explain for themselves without your projecting or criticizing defensively.

You may find that you've overreacted, that you were being paranoid about the other's intent. Maybe he hadn't slammed the door. Wind caught it and closed it harder than he'd intended. Maybe you had said something thoughtless, and the other wanted to let you know. The above format, called perception checking, can give you each an approach that you may not arrive at instinctively.[15]

Clarifying issues is as important in personal life as it was for analysis of stock issues. We learned certain stock formats for generating persuasive texts. There are other stock formats that can be integrated into personal conversation. Perception checking is one.

R Is for Reason

We want to be as reasonable as we can, but personal relations are not always reasonable, nor even based upon reason. Oh, great. Here I learned all this reason stuff, and I can't use it at home?! Sure, you can, but recognize that **relationships are often based more upon instinct and need than reason.** The usual rules of reason discussed earlier in the book, therefore, will not always apply. Someone may know at a rational level that you're their friend, but they may simply need reassurance, seemingly with no rational reason.

For instance, it would be common in conflict to try to find the cause of a certain bad effect in the relationship. In other words, couples sometimes get into blaming games. Professor of Communication Watzalawick has suggested a concept called "punctuation" which explains why blaming is futile. The impulse is to say that the other caused our negative behavior.[16]

An example would be: A loses his temper over money. He tells his wife he wouldn't do it if she didn't go out shopping so much. B says she wouldn't go out shopping so much if he wasn't losing his temper all the time and driving her out of the house. So, it's a struggle between A leads to B and B leads to A (Figure 20).

Yet neither is supportable nor useful. It's not supportable because we do not see our actions, nor those of others objectively. We see them through our own perceptions, which tend to favor our own case, especially when we argue about issues of blame. They are not useful positions, because blaming creates defensiveness and distrust.

Watzalawick suggests that we should view problems as mutually created and cyclic. We do this action and reaction together on an ongoing basis. Let's both quit, because it is an infinite regress into relational failure, as seen in the diagram above, which shows that cause and effect isn't always linear in relationships, but rather cyclic.

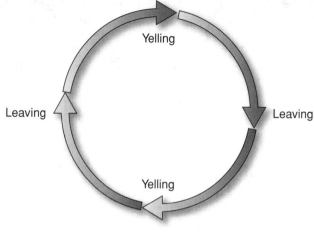

Figure 20

R Is for Rules (Not Laws)

Communication is rule-oriented behavior. We're not talking about unbreakable laws, but rules which are codes that have evolved over time as custom. You may remember mother telling you, "Don't talk when adults are talking." She was teaching you a rule about listening and waiting for your turn. Everyone seems instinctively to know that you don't talk to strangers in the close quarters of an elevator.

If you don't think there are rules, try breaking some. When somebody asks you how you are next time, stop and give them your medical status. See how they react. Since there are rules, they may stick to their role and say simply say, "That's great. See ya." So many of these situations are automatic opportunities for passing clichés.

Yet new situations require that we look for and understand the rules of the circumstance and adapt. Successful communicators are those who can best achieve this. You know the old saying about traveling abroad, "When in Rome, do as the Romans do."

R Is for "Rackets"

It's normal for everyone to have positive points and things that they should work on in relationships. There are some people, though, who run what can be called "rackets." That is, they use personal problems as a way of taking advantage of other people.

They're always looking for an ear to chew on about their difficulties, but they don't do anything to solve the problem. Why? It's an excuse for them to get lots of attention and sympathy. Someone plays helpless. Why? Because they can get a sucker to do things for them.

There are people too cowardly to confront people head on, so they use sneaky ***passive aggressive tactics*** to undermine others, talking kindly to their face and badly behind their back. They tease but not in a nice way. There are even people so insecure that they submit themselves to abusers in a pact: I'll let you hurt me, if you promise not to run away. Some "rackets" may be pathological behavior, but some are strategic choices by people who don't mind using dirty tricks. Wear headgear. Protect yourself in the clinches.

S Is for Solutions

You have to set side some mutually agreeable time to ***brainstorm*** solutions for your interpersonal problems, ***much as you did while creating propositions.*** Arguing couples tend to hunker down into rigid positions, artificially dividing people who could really be closer. We flare up in public situations, but that might not be the best time to argue. We argue on the run, but if you care about the person, it's worth some time to make conflicting communication more pleasant. Time and place matter.

Make an appointment. Set aside some time from other business to try to clarify your issues. Don't fixate on a single solution. Brainstorm a variety of ways that you might improve relationships. Try some. Make a ***follow-up*** appointment to evaluate the behavioral choices you've made.

If you've brainstormed a variety of ideas, then there's the possibility of ongoing hope and continuing action on behalf of the relationship. That didn't work? Try something different next time, and keep brainstorming so that there's always a list of possibilities for the future, always a hope of doing better.[17]

Don't lapse into language like "the relationship didn't work." The relationship is not something outside of ourselves. We're it. So, it may be more responsible to say that "we didn't work."

One of the reasons we may not be finding solutions is that we're reliving patterns from family quarrels that maybe didn't work so well, even back then. ***Make different choices.***

T Is for Timeouts

When we are upset, ***ad hominem attacks*** come into play, belittling comments, sometimes name calling. Don't do it. When we degrade our friends and partners we degrade ourselves and invite the same back. We may even belittle the ideas of our loved ones, by invalidating their right to have their own ideas and feelings.

My wife and I tell each other regularly that the other is crazy, a real nut job, but it's a private signal that it's not worth fighting about. We do it with a laugh. In fact, a certain amount of rough verbal repartee may mark trust in a relationship, especially among males.

If you continually undermine your partner, though, don't be surprised if they withdraw from you. Then you might wind up mocking yourself. Try taking a time out before you begin to say things that you don't really mean. You can never really take them back.

U Is for Ultimatums

Don't make one if you don't mean it. You want someone to stop smoking around your kids? Someone is destroying your mutual lives with destructive addictive behavior? Then at some point you may have to make an ultimatum. You want to leverage your emotional position with your partners by threatening to leave them? Don't. If you back down, you'll become the "boy who cried wolf" and lose power in the relationship. If you force it, you may lose someone you mean to keep. Find another way to express it.

V Is for Violence

An obvious thing about relationships is that they're not healthy if violence is involved. Yet people become addicted to abuse, from either side of the process. The sad fact is that people without a sense of how to argue fairly, argue most fiercely with intimates. Sadder still, approximately sixty percent of murders occur within the family or among close associates. Ninety percent involve use of alcohol or drugs. Random violence from criminals, although more widely publicized, is less common than murder among intimates.

So, consider the raised voice, the clenched fist, the pointing finger that comes close to poking. Stop before you grab someone by the shoulders and shake them. If you like to throw things or punch holes in doors, do something about it. Don't wait until there are restraining orders and a judge sentencing you to anger management classes. Enroll yourself. If you need help, get the help you need. If you're staying involuntarily in a violent environment, seek support to leave.

W Is for Winning

It has no place in personal life except for a game or a hand of cards. There is no victory for either person in a relationship that makes someone lose. This isn't a public debate. Don't abuse your new skills. Work for a win for both parties. It's a matter of enlightened self-interest. If someone wins, someone else has to get their paybacks. Try to be cooperative more than competitive.

My wife and I, for instance, had to stop playing "Monopoly." We played like the money was real. We pretty much stick to a lazy game of rummy, since we're more interested in being partners than even pretend enemies.

X Is for X-Spouses, X-Friends, Etc.

Learning to let go is hard for me. It's taken a long time to learn how to let people pass from my life without having some insecurity or resentment about it. Sometimes it's so baffling, I still wonder what went wrong with people I've known for a long time and have moved on.

One idea I've had is that some relationships are like radiation. They have a natural half-life that may last for a long time, but not forever. It seems that sometimes people learn all they can from each other, and they search for other relationships to help them learn and grow in different ways.

As they marry and grow older, they may not have the time they used to for the care and feeding of friends. I hate to let them drift away, without some kind of closure. Yet they sometimes seem to simply disappear.

Remember the good things. Try not to take it too personally. Everyone loses someone some time. They are a unique part of your life, so you can't replace them. You can grieve, however, and move on to other unique individuals who will touch your life differently, perhaps more completely.

What concerns me is that very young people who have had a disappointment over losing an intimate sometimes retrench from the risk of getting to know others. They may even say, "I'm no good at relationships." However, interpersonal communication is a skill that can be improved from learning. Each relationship may be a rehearsal for a better job later.

My wife and I didn't meet until fifty. I was surprised. She said she always had the faith that there was someone waiting for her out there somewhere. I'm really happy that she held out, and that I allowed myself to be surprised, because . . . .

Y Is for Yearning

We need communication and intimacy with others. It's a fundamental need like hunger, thirst, or shelter. One test for astronauts is an isolation study, to see how long they can take being alone in space. They simply lock would-be astronauts into a sealed chamber with no outside noise to connect them. One member of the study could only take 2 hours of being alone. Others didn't fair much better.

When people are deprived of normal communication with others, their longevity rate declines. Divorced men past 60 are many times as likely to die of various causes— heart attack, suicide, alcoholism, tuberculosis—as their married counterparts. What's hopeful is that the type of relationship doesn't matter. Friendships, church, and community involvements all contribute to longevity.

Yearning for others is natural. Yearning is good. It's the drive of your natural desire to belong and to give and receive human affection through communication.

Z Is for Zip It

Know when to quit talking. Don't talk a thing to death. I used to have a rule that I wouldn't go to bed with conflict in the air. I had many long, sad nights trying to live that principle out. Some relational problems are long-term matters of progress.

Agree to disagree when it gets pointless, go to bed, and take it up at another agreed upon time. How do you know when it's pointless? You know when you're calling names, when you're repeating the same thing over and over (assertions, maybe circular reason) and you're concentrating more on hurting each other than finding solutions.

Even if you have a great zinger, you don't need to say everything you think. Sometimes only you get to know how clever you are.

* * * * *

In sum, while it's easy to draw some parallels between formal and interpersonal argument, there are very distinct differences in the rules of each. There is a rule that applies to each, however:

Communication is reflexive. In other words, you'll tend to get back what you put out. If you argue, either privately or publicly, with an aggressive attitude, don't be surprised if all you achieve is aggression redoubled in return. In a public debate, you'll get more heat than light. In a private debate, your mutual attitudes of scorn will escalate into a more polarized conflict.

Perhaps the most important consideration is for you to look at what you're bringing to the party before you criticize anybody else's intimate behavior. Look, again, at your own **pre-critical thinking,** the attitudes and experiences that tend to make us reactive rather than considered in our thoughts and acts. When you model your best behavior, others may do the same on your behalf.

Sources

1) Spence, G. (1995). How to Argue and Win Everytime. New York, NY: St. Martin's Press.

2) Walton, D.N. (1992). Plausible Argument in Everyday Conversation. Albany, NY: State University of New York Press.

3) Adler, R.B., Proctor, R.F., and Towne, N. (2005). Looking Out, Looking In. Belmont, CA: Thomson Wadsworth.

   Cupach, W.R. and Canary, D.J. (1997). Competence in Interpersonal Communication. New York: McGraw-Hill.

4) Adler, Proctor & Towne (2005), previously cited.

Albers, J.K., Keller-Guenther, U., and Corman, S.R. (1996), That's Not Funny: Understanding Recipient's Response to Teasing. Western Journal of Speech 60, pp, 337–357.

Bradbury, T.N., and Fincham, F.D. (1990). Attributions in Marriage: Review and Critique. Psychological Bulletin 107. pp. 3–33.

Edwards, R., Bello, R., Brandau-Brown, F., and Hollems, D. (2001). The Effects of Loneliness and Verbal Aggression on Message Interpretation. Southern Communication Journal 66, pp. 139–150.

5) Aboud, F.E., and Mendehlson, M.J. (1998). Determinants of Friendship Selection and Quality: Developmental Perspectives. In W.M. Bukowski and A.F. Newcomb, eds., The Company They Keep: Friendship in Childhood and Adolescence. New York: Cambridge University Press.

Byrne, D. (1999). An Overview (and Underview) of Research and Theory Within the Attraction Paradigm. Journal of Social and Personal Relationships 14, pp. 417–431.

6) Cessna, K., and Seiberg, E. (1995). Patterns of Interactional Confirmation and Disconfirmation. In M.V. Redmond, ed., Interpersonal Communication: Readings in Theory and Research. Fort Worth: Harcourt Brace.

7) Bell, R.A., and Daly, J.A. (1995), The Affinity Seeking Function of Communication, in M.V. Redmond, ed., (Ibid.).

Frei, J.R., and Shaver, P.R. (2002). Respect in Close Relationships: Prototype, Definition, Self-Report Assessment, and Initial Correlates. Personal Relationships 9. pp.121–139.

Palmer, M.T. (1989). "Controlling Conversations: Turns, Topics and Interpersonal Control." Communication Monographs 56 (1989).

8) Festinger, L. (1954). A Theory of Cognitive Dissonance. Stanford, CA: Stanford University Press.

Stamp, G.H., Vangelisti, A.L. and Daly, J.A. (1992). The Creation of Defensiveness in Social Interaction, Communication Monographs 40, pp. 177–190.

9) Adler, Proctor and Towne (2005), previously cited. I would also recommend "Fire in the Belly" by Sam Keene, which describes the tendency of cultures with military concerns to systematically desensitize young males.

10) Clark, R.A., and Delia, J.R. (1997), Individuals' Preferences Friend's Approaches To Providing Support in Distressing Situations. Communication Reports 10, pp 115–121.

Davidowitz, M., and Myrick, R.D. (1984), Responding to the Bereaved: An Analysis Of Helping Statements. Death Education 8, pp. 1–10.

Goldsmith, D.J., and Fitch, K. (1997), The Normative Context of Advice as Social Support. Human Communication Research 23, pp. 454–476.

Notarius, C.J., and Herrick, L.R. (1988), Listener Response Strategies to a Distress Other, Journal of Social and Personal Relationships 17, pp. 97–108.

11) Turner, R.E., Edgely, C., and Olmstead, G. (1975). Information Control in Conversation: Honesty Isn't Always the Best Policy. Kansas Journal of Sociology 11, pp. 69–89.

12) McCormick, S.A., and Levine, T.R. (1990), When Lies are Uncovered: Emotional and Relational Outcomes of Lies. Communication Monographs 57, pp. 119–138.

Adler, Proctor and Towne (2004), previously cited.

13) Burgoon, J.K. (1994). Nonverbal Signals, in M.L. Knapp and G.R. Miller, Eds, Handbook of Interpersonal Communication. Newbury Park, CA: Sage.

14) Sillars, A., Shellen, W., McIntosh, A., and Pomegranate, M. (1997), Relational Characteristics of Language: Elaboration and Differentiation in Marital Conversation. Western Journal of Communication 61, pp. 403–422.

15) Watzalawick, P., Beavin, J., and Jackson, D.D. (1967). Pragmatics of Human Communication. New York: Norton.

16) Axelrod, R. (1984). The Evolution of Cooperation. New York: Basic Books.

17) Filley, A.C. (1975). Interpersonal Conflict Resolution. Glennview, Ill: Scott, Foresman.

Gordon, T. (1970). Parent Effectiveness Training. New York: Wyden.

Summation: The Approachable Argument

What should this title mean to us, now that we've completed the text? In what sense are arguments now more approachable?

At a minimum level, we've learned that there are *a few approachable techniques* that improve our skills in argument and persuasion. Think for a moment about how few things one has to remember to be at least somewhat ordered and effective:

> A single argument has only three essential parts: a qualified claim, a warrant, and some grounds.

> There are only three kinds of propositions we defend: fact, value, and policy.

> We've learned that grounds consist mostly of numbers, stories, and quotations.

> See, much of it is as simple as one, two, three.

> Warrants are more complex, since there are a mere seven patterns of reason we have to remember: parallel, generalization, definition, sign, cause, authority, and dilemma.

> There are many fallacies, but if you can just recall the one or two that are typical of each of the above patterns, you'll be doing better than the vast majority of your peers.

The truth is that *you have joined an elite few* who understand the language that runs the country and the world. Most lawyers, congress members, and presidents started with this training. Many managers and heads of corporations have this training. Even locally, we regularly receive letters that this training has increased the employment and promotion chances of even the most average students.

Not only are arguments themselves more approachable now, but understanding them can help us to make *better choices in our lives.*

While many of us receive some of our communicative inclinations at birth, communication is mostly a learned behavior. On one hand, 10% of people are born with a predisposition for shyness, and 10% are born with the predisposition to be outgoing.

Nonetheless, more than half of those surveyed report themselves as having been shy at one time or another. Why? Because people make choices in their life, for good or for ill.

Here are some of the choices in behavior that we've considered here:

> We've chosen to distinguish formal argument from everyday quarrels, as well as to conduct even everyday quarrels differently than we have. It's a choice for a more incisive, yet less aggressive form of communication.

> We've **chosen to separate our self-esteem from our arguments,** learning to view them as tools that we can hone and use. Thus, it is easier for us to keep our head in arguments, to look at other points of view on their merits, rather than as threats to our identity.

> **Do you have your arguments? Or do your arguments have you?** That is to ask, are you simply repeating the propaganda you've heard, or are you processing information by yourself and making choices on the basis of your own thinking? That is your choice.

> We've learned that **clashing points of view can be mutually illuminating,** a way that each side can improve its understanding. This is even so, we discovered, in our intimate relationships. Conflicts, well waged, can be a source of growth at both a public and a private level. So, we can choose to approach both with some hope and confidence.

> We've learned that public life of all kinds, from entertainment to politics, is imbued with a rhetoric. Most of what we hear and see has some persuasive intent. Being aware of that intent, as well as understanding something about techniques of persuasion, can help to protect us from manipulation and to **sort the wheat from the chaff among public messages.**

> We've taken a look at ourselves, not only as arguers in both a public and a private sense, but as consumers of public argument in the sometimes manipulative media. Now, instead of simply accepting the messages we receive from politicians and pundits—or ignoring them because we can't keep up, we can examine them from a new perspective of knowledge. We may even feel confidant enough to analyze and challenge them. At least, we can **participate more actively and intelligently in community issues and democratic processes.**

With new confidence and knowledge come responsibilities. True, now that we have sense of the basic structure of arguments and debates, as well as some practice with them, we may **feel confident to assert ourselves.** Excellent!

Don't hang back or repress your thoughts for want of being self-assured. Be timid no more. Stand up and speak. Or choose to be silent, not over fear, but because you think it wise.

Yet, like the karate master who walks away from a fight because he sees no need to hurt another, we should use these skills carefully. Especially with loved ones.

Use this knowledge with good will. Use it for positive change. Use it to make the right choices, at home, in the work place, and as participants in the world's greatest experiment in democracy.

Congratulations for completing this course.

Appendix: Sample Speech Outlines

These are samples of student speeches. They aren't perfect, but they're typical of above average beginning student work. They are successful in showing how each type of proposition emerges into a different kind of speech. They will also give students a sense of how to structure argumentative speeches. They can either complete a prose manuscript, or deliver extemporaneously from complete sentence outlines like these. In either format, it is useful for students to identify the Toulmin argument parts in their text. In a full prose text, that could be done by putting the notation in parenthesis at the start or end of a sentence or paragraph.

Proposition of Fact: Who Really Discovered America?

This first text fails to carefully cite the evidence she uses on this historical controversy. She was inspired to write this by an article in National Geographic, as well as some information she got from a lecture in history class. Other citations are scattered casually in the reading of the grounds. She does take up a significant controversy of history and structures her arguments well for this first assignment. To the degree that we're mostly interested in learning to build Toulmin arguments at this point, this is a useful model. It's also an interesting challenge of our cultural prejudices.

Thesis: A coalition of Celts and Phoenicians probably sailed to America well before Columbus.

Definition: "Well before" means the first millennium BC. Columbus came in 1492 AD. "Celts" were a people who occupied the British Isles to Gallatia (Gaul). "Phoenicians" were a Mediterranean people, mentioned in the Bible as Canaanites. They spread as far west as Carthage. The Phoenician alphabet is the foundation of the Latin and English alphabets.

Issue Overview: We know that the phenomenon exists because of signs of their presence on this continent, which has been carbon dated for concrete proof of time.

Claim A: Elements of Celt and Phoenician society existed in America circa 800 BC.

Warrant A: Recently discovered stone inscriptions in the continental United States are written in ancient Celtic and Phoenician languages.

Grounds A-1: "For many years, lines of scratches on lentil stones found in root cellars in New England were thought to be nothing more than shovel strikes. But in 1980, linguist Barry Fell found these scratches to be Ogam script. Ogam is ancient Celtic writing. Ogam script and Punic Script were found together on the Pontotoc stele. This stone has been dated at 800 BC." Punic is Phoenician.

Grounds A-2: "Strange markings on a stone discovered at Mystery Hill, New Hampshire in 1823, were later determined by Barry Fell to be ancient Punic script, a script which dedicated the site to the Phoenician god 'Bel.' Also, off the coast of Maine on Monhegan Island, a stone containing Ogam script translates to 'ships from Phoenicia cargo platform.'"

Claim B: The American Indian culture shows Celt and Phoenician influences dating from before the time of Christ.

Warrant B-1: Having never built stone sculptures before, American Indian culture began making sculptures that duplicated traditional Celt sculptures on the British Isles.

Grounds B1: According to the book *America BC,* "American Indians never built in stone over 40,000 years of their early culture. European and near Eastern civilizations drew from advanced cultures like Jericho (9000 BC), Sumeria (5000 BC), and Egypt (3000 BC), in developing stone monuments. Around 800 BC stone monuments did appear in the Americas. And is it a coincidence that American Indian monuments so closely resemble the structures of the Celts in the British Isles?

"One such site, found at Mystery Hill, New Hampshire, is a complex of stone-slab chambers and henge stones. The henges are oriented such that the sun sets behind specific stones on the days of the spring and fall equinox and at the summer and winter solstices. This was the custom in similar Celtic structures."

Warrant B-2: European-style bronze weapons were discovered in America dating back to 200 BC.

Grounds B-2: "Bronze spearheads, daggers, and a sword have been found in Mound Builder sites in Maine, Vermont, Massachusetts, and Connecticut. One of the essential metals for alloying copper into bronze is tin. But tin was not found in North America in any form available to ancient miners. These weapons were not made in America."

Claim C: Phoenician and Celtic influences remain in the language of American Indians.

Warrant C: A number of American Indian words are the same as or similar to those in ancient Celtic and Phoenician languages.

Ground C-1: Many Algonquin words are about the same as Celtic words. Some examples are: The word for woman in Algonquin is "banem," and in Celtic it is "ban." The word for snowflake in Algonquin is "kladen," the same as in Celtic. The word for gorge in Algonquin is "cuiche," and in Celtic it is "cuithe." The Wabanaki tribe of New England uses "abassi" for tree, the same word as tree in Phoenician.

Grounds C-2: Biographies note that Thomas Jefferson recognized the similarity between Indian languages and those of Europe and Asia. He collected over 40 vocabularies of Indians east of the Mississippi with the intent to publish them .

Issue Overview: What could possibly lead to the existence of such artifacts here? As there is no evidence of American Indians roaming abroad, it is most likely the Celts and Phoenicians found means to sail here. At least, we know that:

Claim D: Celt and Phoenecian vessels were seaworthy enough to have made the voyage.

Warrant D-1: Their early sailing vessels were comparable in stability to Viking boats, as well as those of Columbus and the Virginia Colonists, all of which crossed the Atlantic.

Grounds D-1-a: Compared to Roman vessels of 55 BC, Julius Caesar wrote in Book III of "Battle for Gaul," "The Celtic ships were large, designed to stand up to great waves and violent storms. Their hulls were made entirely of oak to endure any violent shock or impact. Their crossbeams were made of timbers a foot thick, and they used sails made of beaten hides, able to withstand the force of the violent Atlantic gales." Caesar was astonished to find the Celts so confident in their sailing ability. They carried no oarsmen and were capable of sailing into wind.

Grounds D-1-b: According to Lionel Casson in his book, "Ships & Seamanship in the Ancient World," "The capacity of the Celt vessels was greater than that of the Viking vessels used to explore Newfoundland, greater than those of Columbus, and greater than the early vessels used to settle the Virginia Colony in 1607. Some Phoenician vessels were even larger, capable of carrying 120 tons in Atlantic crossings."

Warrant D-2: Early Celt & Phoenecian sailors were skilled enough to have made an Atlantic crossing.

Grounds D-2-a: In her book *History of Beads,* Lois Sherr of Dublin tells of Phoenician glass beads found in Britain at a site dated 200 BC. "Phoenician vessels navigated open oceans well before the time of Christ. In pursuit of trade, not only did they sail the Mediterranean, but they also navigated the open Atlantic. They traded with the Celts, exchanging highly prized Phoenican glass beads for raw materials such as tin."

Grounds D-2-b: Open sea navigation was practiced in Celtic and Phoenician times. Using an early type of sextant, Phoenicians measured the elevation of the midday sun to gage their east-west position, or latitude. Their north-south position, longitude, was calculated by "dead reckoning," or time, distance, and speed calculations.

Underview: So, it was certainly possible for these cultures to have made the voyage, leading us to the reasonable conclusion that Celts and Phoenicians left signs of their culture in America themselves.

Grade school history books insisted for many years that Columbus discovered America. Then, in the 1980s, textbooks were revised after discovery of Viking presence in Newfoundland around 1000 AD. In the future, textbooks may be revised again to include evidence of Phoenician and Celtic presence in the first millennium BC.

Proposition of Value: Church and State

Overview: Religion is not something that can be forced on a child. Things like manners and skills can be taught successfully. Even some values, such as diligence or a work ethic, may be taught. Religion, however, is personal and family business. It has no place in public schools.

Thesis: The separation of church and state is important in education.

Definition: We mean by this, in particular, that organized prayer in school is potentially counterproductive to the private religious rights of children. In fact, it may have negative effects on their appreciation of the very concept of religion.

Standard: Our standard for decision is the wisdom of our founding fathers as envisioned in the Constitution of the United States of America, which instituted the separation of church and state as a protection for individual religious rights, which had been threatened in the old world. This right protects not only a wide variety of Christian sects, but atheists, as well as other religions of the world that may be practiced by our citizens.

Criterion: Our specific criterion for decision is: that which best protects the individual's right to freedom of religion is the superior value. The values in contention are the right to organized prayer in a public school vs. the right of individual students to practice their own particular religion, or not.

Claim A: Whether it be an organized activity or a moment of silence, prayer in school may have a negative effect on students.

Warrant A: Forcing religious practice on children, even religious persons tell us, may cause either indifference or resentment and resistance.

Grounds A1: Reverend William F. Schulz is a Doctor of Divinity and President of the Unitarian Universalist Association of Congregations. He's a member of the National Advisory Council of Americans United for Separation of Church & State and the National Advisory Board of Americans for Religious Liberty. He writes, in his 1991 article, "Prayer in School: Why It Does Religion No Favor," that:

> Religion that is imposed upon its recipients turns out to engender either indifference or resentment. Most American religious leaders have recognized that persuasion is far more powerful than coercion when it comes to promoting religious views. Not surprisingly, then, large numbers of religious leaders have supported the Supreme Court in its prayer decisions.

Grounds A2: Barry W. Lynn is the Executive Director of Americans United for Separation of Church and State. He says: "Religion is best left as a private matter, as the nation's founders intended. It should never be forced onto anyone, especially children."

Transition: In other words, not only is one forced to practice against his private religious rights, the practice of doing so is potentially damaging to the very concept of religion.

Claim B: Public school is simply not the place for religious education or activity.

Warrant B-1: The obvious reason is that it forces people of various religious beliefs to pay equally through taxes for the practice of a generalized, non-denominational form of Christianity, or theism. This not only uses tax money for particular religious practice, which violates the Constitution, it dilutes the essence of refined, unique, and treasured private religious practices.

Grounds B-1-a: In the words of Arthur J. Kropp and David Ramage, President and Chairman, respectively, for People for the American Way, as quoted in the Chicago Tribune:

> There is nothing more intimate and private than an individual's communion with God in prayer. To expose that sacred moment to the political invasion of state-sponsored prayers, edited, selected, or monitored by faculty or administration, is a deep offense to the spiritual lives of our children, regardless of their faith.

Grounds B-1-b: Rev. Dr. Thomas E. Dipko, Executive VP of the United Church Board for Homeland Ministries, and Valerie Russell, Executive Director of The Office for Church In Society, wrote an open letter to Congress stating:

> Truly voluntary prayer—offered out of a real spiritual need—is the most intimate and deepest expression of humanity's relationship with God. Prayer arising out of public purpose is already something less than prayer, degenerating far too easily into a matter of form and show, the kind of boastful public prayer that Jesus himself warned against.

Warrant B-2: Personal religious practices belong in the home or the privacy described above.

Grounds B-2: Rev. Charles V. Bergstrom is a co-founder of People for the American Way and was the Director of the Lutheran Office for Governmental Affairs. He wrote in his 1988 article "The Need for Separation: A Lutheran View":

> The families—not the school boards—have the overriding responsibility for children's religious education. The more we attempt to insist on common denominator religious exercises or instruction in public schools, The greater the risk we run of diluting our faith and ending up in with a vague national folk religion that confuses religious practice with patriotism.

Warrant B-3: Parents, who should have the right to decide what prayers their family members say, are offended by the imposition of school prayer.

Grounds B-3: As Barry Lynn, previously cited, noted:

> Many Americans are offended by the idea that their children may be forced to participate in religious exercises in public schools that clash with what the children are taught at home, or at the family's house of worship. These parents rightly see school prayer as a usurpation of parent authority. Other parents have no desire to have their children participate in the type of bland, watered-down prayers that are commonly offered for public consumption. To cite the word of Jesus from the sixth book of Mark, in his cautioning against gaudy public display of religion: "When you pray, enter your closet and shut the door. Pray to your father, who is in secret, and your father, who sees in secret, will reward you properly."

Claim C: Prayer in school is a disservice to those of minority faiths.

Warrant C-1: It is virtually impossible to design a prayer that can encompass the beliefs of Christians, Jews, Buddhists, Muslims, etc. What option is left? Majority wins? It would be terribly ironic for a country that was born, at least in part, as a refuge for those practicing minority faiths in Europe.

Grounds C-1: Kropp and Ramage, previously cited, acknowledge the growth of minority faiths in this country:

> In the past few decades, this nation has experienced a remarkable expansion in religious diversity. Muslim, Hindu, new strains of Protestantism, and many other faiths are part of our religious community now. To many of these new Americans it is a miracle to live in a nation where all faiths are represented and no faith is embraced by the state. These Americans are living out the dream of our nation's founders, many of whom fled religious persecution on foreign shores.

Warrant C-2: We have examples of what would happen to those of minority faiths from past history.

Grounds C-2: According to Kropp and Ramage, "When school prayer was the norm, children of minority faiths were routinely sent into the hallway while the rest of the class went through prayer exercise, a harsh exclusion of their religious heritage with the state's official blessing.

Claim D: Ultimately, there's no such thing as voluntary and organized school prayer.

Warrant D: The involvement of authority figures with power over the children negates the possibility of volunteerism by children.

Grounds D: As Bergstrom, previously cited, states:

> The Lutheran churches, like the courts, do not believe that any school organized prayer sessions can be completely voluntary. Children attending public schools are there under compulsion of law. Public school facilities are used, and the teachers—symbols of authority—supervise the exercise. These factors combine to operate with cohesive force on young and impressionable children, inducing them to take part despite freedom to be excused.

Underview: There is nothing whatsoever in this position that stands in the way of anybody's religious practice. If friends at school wish to pray over lunch, so what? That's their business. That's quite a different thing than an employee of the state telling you to pray, and pray in a particular way. America claims to have liberated Afghanistan citizens from the Taliban, which was a religion-based state. Why, then, would we foster anything remotely similar in our own nation?

The only persons who should be offended by a value that honors the religions of all as a deeply personal and familial privilege is a person who insists on determining the religious practices of others. That simply does not measure up to the standard of the U.S. Constitution. Indeed, it is the direct opposite of the criterion: that which best protects the individual's freedom of religion is best.

Proposition of Policy: Tort Reform

Overview: In 1994, a New Mexico jury awarded $2.9 million U.S. in damages to 81 year-old Stella Lieback, who suffered third-degree burns on her legs, groin and buttocks after spilling a cup of McDonald's coffee on herself. This was found on a website titled "Frivolous and Stupid Lawsuits," copyright 2002. This, among other lawsuits will be remembered, not just because they are foolish, but because they turn the issue of individual responsibility on its head, as well as gluts our overcrowded courts. Yes, she was injured. Yet it would not have mattered if it was Starbucks, or Seattle's Best, or coffee from the corner café. She spilled the coffee on herself and turned it into a three million dollar profit. What was she looking for, a cold cup of coffee?

Thesis: Frivolous lawsuits should be systematically eliminated by tort reform.

Issue Overview: There are significant harms from frivolous lawsuits.

Claim A: Frivolous lawsuits degrade our court system.

Warrant A-1: They waste time and tax dollars by occupying court time with cases that Attempt to exploit the law. Here are a few examples of such exploitation from the website mentioned above.

Grounds A-1-a: June 1998: "A 19-year-old Carl Truman of Los Angeles won $74,000 When his neighbor ran over his hand with a Honda Accord. Mr. Truman apparently didn't notice there was someone at the wheel of the car, when he was trying to steal his neighbor's hubcaps."

Grounds A-1-b: October 1999: "Jerry Williams of Little Rock, Arkansas, was awarded $14,500 and medical expenses after being bitten on the buttocks by his neighbor's beagle. The beagle was on a chain in its owner's fenced-in yard. Mr. Williams was in the yard, as well. The award was less than sought because the jury felt Mr. Williams, who was shooting the dog repeatedly with a pellet gun, might have provoked the dog."

Grounds A-1-c: January 2000: "Kathleen Robertson of Austin, Texas, was awarded $780,000 by a jury of her peers after breaking her ankle tripping over a toddler who was running amuck inside a furniture store. The owner of the store was understandably surprised by the verdict, considering the misbehaving little boy was Mrs. Robertson's own son."

Claim B: There are financial harms to individuals sued in frivolous cases.

Warrant B: This is evident from the previously cited cases, in which innocent persons and a small business paid, not only thousands, even hundreds of thousands of dollars, but court costs and the cost of their own defense as well. Even if they are not found liable, they still have to cover their own defense costs. Even good Samaritans get trapped by this problem.

Grounds B: In another case, "a neighbor helped a woman carry some burglar-proof security bars into her house. The woman dropped the bars, injuring her foot. She sued the man who helped her. Although the jury ruled against her, legal fees cost the 'Good Samaritan' $4,700."

Claim C: Businesses lose money defending themselves from frivolous law cases.

Warrant C-1: The previously mentioned costs of defense multiply dangerously for small businesses.

Grounds C-1: The Minneapolis/St. Paul Business Journal printed an article "The Cost of Frivolous Lawsuits Is No Joke" on August 11, 1997. In it they stated that: "Small business owners know firsthand that you don't have to lose a lawsuit for lawsuit abuse to affect you. Even when a clearly frivolous lawsuit is filed against a business, the time and money it takes to defend against that lawsuit could put a Main Street business out of business."

Warrant C-2: Businesses with deeper pockets tend to be held responsible, even in cases when they are not primarily responsible for an injury. There is, in fact, an inclination that they will be harmed, since they are the ones best able to pay.

Grounds C-2-a: A USA Today article from July 1998, reporting on the case of a man who negligently injured a woman at Disneyland, said that: "The jury found that the man was 85% responsible; the woman was 14% negligent; and Walt Disney was 1%

negligent. Guess who ended paying the entire judgment? The answer is Disney, of course, since it had deep pockets."

Grounds C-2-b: In an article called "Spilled Milk: Groups Call for an End to Frivolous Lawsuits," in the Shopping Center Age Magazine, July 2000, it is noted, "Whether a retailer wants to defend itself in court at a cost of $5,000 to $15, 000, for many nuisance cases. Or a retailer can choose to settle a case even when there is clearly no wrong doing, if the damages sought do not exceed expected defense fees . . . in 95 percent of the cases where liability is present, the manufacturer—not the retailer—is ultimately held responsible for the harm. But, according to the International Mass Retail Association, the retailer is subject to costly legal expenses to investigate and prepare its defense.

Warrant C-3: These cases may go on for considerable lengths of time, increasing costs and wasting court time as well as that of the businesses.

Grounds C-3: The Brown & Williamson Tobacco Corporation, in a pamphlet titled "Frivolous Lawsuits," 2000, cited the case of "a drunk driver, who was speeding, went through several detour signs and crashed. He sued the engineering company that designed the road, the contractor, four subcontractors and the State Highway Dept. Five years later, all the defendants agreed to make the case go away and settled it for $35,000. Plus, the engineering firm had to pay $200,000 in legal costs."

Transition: While one might be suspicious of Brown & Williamson's motives, as tobacco companies have paid millions in settlements over damages from tobacco, the case cited is not a tobacco case. Even if it were a tobacco case, we've known for most of a half a century that tobacco is harmful to our health. It is marked with a warning label. Yet millions continue to smoke themselves to death. No doubt, there are strong advertising inducements to smoke. Yet individuals continue to smoke, with no attempt to quit, then sue for millions when they finally get cancer. While I personally wouldn't mind if tobacco companies were sued into non-existence, it is unacceptable for us to continue to blame others and tie up a court system burdened with genuinely serious issues, over their own irresponsibility.

Warrant C-4: Yet another business cost is incurred because companies have to repackage to include unnecessary warning labels. Here are some examples of warning labels that should be a matter of common sense.

Ground C-4-a: From the *Minneapolis/St. Paul Business Journal,* mentioned previously, "The warning label on a step ladder is almost a foot long, and the warning labels on children's toys have reached the point of being ridiculous. Kid's plastic fire hats say, 'not to be used as a protective helmet,' and Batman costumes warn that 'cape does not enable user to fly.'"

Ground C-4-b: A posting from the Michigan Lawsuit Abuse Watch in 2001 notes that they held a contest for whacky warning labels: "First place went to a pair of athletic shin guards: 'Shin guards cannot protect any part of the body they do not cover.' A runner-up prize was found on a power drill: 'This product not intended for use as a dental drill.' Honorable mention went to this message on a rock set: 'Eating rocks may lead to broken teeth.'"

Transition: How does all this impact us? What are the annual sums lost to our country in such cases?

Claim D: Billions of dollars are lost annually to the U.S. economy due to frivolous law suits.

Warrant D: Here are statistics from two sources that provide a general sense of costs.

Grounds D-1: *USA Today* reported in a July 1998 article that, "One research group reports that court costs, awards, and lost time cost the economy $132 billion in 1997 alone."

Grounds D-2: And in the Minneapolis/St. Paul Business Journal, "In the United States an estimated $20 billion per year is spent on unnecessary test procedures designed only to guard doctors and hospitals against malpractice claims." This, of course, increases health insurance costs and Medicare costs, limiting access to medical care for Americans.

Issue Overview: The inherency of this problem resides both in a public motivated to make "easy money" and various errors and loopholes in the law.

Claim E: The very likelihood of winning motivates claimants to sue others.

Warrant E: Any percentage of liability on the part of the defendant may lead to large rewards for claimants.

Grounds E: According to The Minneapolis/St. Paul Business Journal, August 11, 1997, "An individual only has to be found 16% at fault to be held 100% liable for damage rewards."

Claim F: Businesses are even more likely to be held responsible than individuals.

Warrant F: The presumption has become that he with the most money should pay, regardless of negligence.

Grounds F: In the Disney example above, they were held responsible for 100% of damage rewards in a case in which they were found only 1% negligent. And we have found that rewards costs the economy billions in productivity annually.

Claim G: Reliance on juries creates opportunity for frivolous suits.

Warrant G: While judges are more savvy and more likely to dismiss frivolous cases, juries, who lack understanding of tort law reform and tend to empathize with victims, offer extravagant awards.

Grounds G: According to the Citizens Against Frivolous Lawsuits Abuse (CALA), "While most frivolous lawsuits should be thrown out, juries are not properly advised that they can find 'a just decision,' even if goes beyond instructions from the judge on the case. As a result, of their misunderstanding of the law, juries tend to exceed reasonable rewards for frivolous claims."

Claim H: Finally, defendants do not generally have access to arbitration.

Warrant H: While arbitration is used in many cases, torts do not generally include this.

Grounds H: According to a special report on ABC-TV news, August 1, 2003, "Since mediation and arbitration require mutual agreement, and frivolous lawsuit claimants have no motivation to agree to it—indeed, they have strong financial motivation not to agree—defendants in such cases seldom have these options."

Issue overview: Inherency implies certain solutions, as do the recommendations of CALA.

Solution Description: There is no question that tort reform is necessary in this country, and many businesses, including the medical profession, have urged Congress to produce a comprehensive bill. What specifically should such a bill include? CALA makes some of the following suggestions:

- All defendants should have the right to mediation and/or arbitration before a case goes to trial.

This would create a reasonable filter for cases without merit.

- We should disallow junk lawsuits, including:

  Lawsuits from people injured while they are legally intoxicated

  Lawsuits from people injured while they are committing a crime

This would prevent some of the most obvious examples of frivolity from wasting court time and protect some parties from unfair penalties in an all-or-nothing judicial system.

- Rely on judges rather than juries in most tort claims AND
- Set reasonable standards for awards of punitive damages

While judges are better aware of tort law than juries, even their better discretion is blocked when bottomless award amounts are allowed. Such awards occur, not because they are an appropriate measure of offense, but simply because somebody can pay. This motivates, not only claimants, but lawyers who derive hefty fees from such suits.

- Finally, since the attitude of the public is to use frivolous suits to profit, claimants should be charged with court costs, as well as the defendant's legal expenses, when his case is shown to be unfounded.

Claim I: There have been a couple of models that we can use for future tort reform.

Warrant I: A similar problem was occurring with litigation over securities affairs, leading to the passage of the Private Securities Litigation Reform Act of 1995 (PSLRA).

Grounds I-1: As was noted in an article in *The Wall Street Journal,* September 1, 2000:

> The PSLRA addressed the serious problem of frivolous and abusive securities strike suits. The lawyers would file literally the same boiler-plate complaint in case after case, sometimes even forgetting to change the names of the companies listed as the defendant. The point of this exercise was to extract hefty attorney's fees from companies that couldn't afford years of litigation over nuisance suits. The result was that many cases settled with token payments for shareholders and enormous fees for lawyers which did nothing for real victims of securities fraud, yet affirmatively injured the shareholders of companies that were forced to pay judicial blackmail. Now, it is harder to file such lawsuits. Instead, of making wholly unsubstantiated allegations, the complaint now has to state some facts supporting the conclusion that the defendant acted with fraudulent intent.

Transition: In other words, PSLRA sets minimum evidence standards for complaints that did not exist before.

Grounds I-2: The State of California has limited medical malpractice awards to $250,000, except in cases of wrongful death.

Underview: While this last example is a controversial proposal and has received criticism from patient advocate groups, the basic principle of limiting awards is sound.

When is it right for a single individual to get over $20 million for smoking themselves to death, which happened in Newport Beach in 2004? When is it right for a burglar to threaten you with bankruptcy because he was injured while stealing from your home?

The causes of two entirely different sets of victims require tort reform, those who pay frivolous lawsuits and those who are truly injured by others, but forced to wait in line for a court date.

INDEX